RECLAIMING LIVES

JOAN TREPPA

AWARD-WINNING AUTHOR

RECLAIMING
LIVES

Pursuing Justice for Six
Innocent Men

A lingering injustice. A city thrust back into legal upheaval. Can the actions of a
few conquer the deep-rooted beliefs of the many?

SECOND EDITION

Reclaiming Lives: Pursuing Justice for Six Innocent Men
© Copyright 2021 Joan Treppa

Printed in the United States of America
Second Edition First printing, May 2021

Second edition

ISBN: 978-1-952976-16-2
Library of Congress Control Number: 2021911072

Published by Kirk House Publishers
1250 E 115th Street
Burnsville, MN 55337
612-781-2815

To order, visit: kirkhousepublishers.com
Quantity discounts available.

*This book is dedicated to those who've suffered
in prison due to a wrongful conviction and to those who've
stepped in to selflessly help them.*

Reviews for

RECLAIMING LIVES

"This book should definitely be required in schools (high school and college) as it is incredibly insightful and a great book for discussions. I am grateful to have been allowed to read it for a class because otherwise, I do not think I would have ever come across it. This book has proven to me, yet again, that the American criminal justice system needs to be improved and held accountable for its misdeeds."
— Shannon

"Reclaiming Lives is an absolute must-read for anyone considering a career in the criminal justice system or working with the nonprofit organization the Innocence Project!"
— Erin

"This book was gripping from the very beginning. Personally, I liked the perspective of the author writing from the position of a citizen advocate, a position that is rarely talked about. Many people like to take the frontlines on these issues, and I think her perspective offers new light on the situation as a whole. If you are looking for a book about wrongful convictions that is a thrilling read while not being super heady and wordy about the criminal justice system, this book is for you!"
— Sarah

"For about a year now, I have been undecided about whether or not to go to law school. I'm currently taking a wrongful convictions class, which has inspired me to want to make a change in the justice system. I've always wondered if I would be able to make a change without going to law school. After reading this book, I see how much of an impact the author makes. I hope to be able to create change and an awareness of this social problem as well."

— Jessica

"I absolutely believe this is a must-read. I read the whole book in one sitting and immediately searched for more information on the men yet to be exonerated. The author is able to grab and keep the attention of the audience from the very beginning. Her roots may not have started in this field, but she has made an impact."

— Sarah

"This book will ignite a desire in you to crave justice and to want to stand up and do something about wrongful convictions. The book gives you compassion and a new understanding of what families and loved ones go through when their father, husband, brother, or friend is wrongfully convicted. I highly recommend this book to criminal justice practitioners and interested readers alike. You will enjoy the rawness and the passion clearly put into the making of this book."

— Kassy

"Instead of being riddled with legal jargon that can often push readers away, the author makes it clear that with just a little learning, everyday readers like you and me can become involved in helping to free the wrongfully convicted."

— C.Z.

FOREWORD

While at the James River Paper Mill on the morning of November 21, 1992, Tom Monfils disappeared from his work area and was later found dead at another location in the mill. Despite the evidence pointing to suicide, the police assumed an "angry mob" of his coworkers had murdered him. The investigation soon centered on six men who had been working at the mill that day. I know this because I am one of those six.

Few people, unless they or someone close to them has experienced what the "Monfils Six" and their families have endured, are likely to understand the anxiety and sense of helplessness that overtakes an innocent person while he cooperates with law enforcement only to have them call him a liar, a thug, and a murderer. Few can know what an innocent person suffers as he loses his job and becomes the subject of media stories and public contempt for a crime he did not commit. They will not experience or know the frustration that an innocent person experiences watching his family suffer as the investigation and trial continue.

Most people assume, as I once did, that even if the police and prosecutors do not know or admit the truth, the jury will surely find it in the end. In the "Monfils Six" case, like in other wrongful-conviction cases, this did not happen. All six of us were convicted of first-degree intentional homicide, sentenced to life in prison, and separated from our families and everything else that made our lives worthwhile. From then on, we could only hope that someday the truth would become clear and the injustice corrected. Our days would be filled with the depression, despair, and disappointment that an innocent man endures as his appeals and other legal efforts fail and he fears he will never regain his freedom and life.

Staying hopeful is difficult. Because I have been convicted, the struggle is uphill. That is something every wrongfully convicted person soon learns. What I have also learned is that an innocent person can choose to maintain his own integrity. It is one thing the system cannot take. From the very beginning, every one of us had fully cooperated with the authorities. Yet we would not lie for them. The fact is we are all honest people who have been trying for a quarter of a century now to encourage people to look at the *real facts* in this case. I will continue to speak the truth and declare my innocence, just as the other members of the "Monfils Six" have.

After I had been in prison for more than fifteen years, I received a letter from Joan Treppa, a woman I had never met but whose life was also changed by this case. She became a champion for all of us and for all wrongfully convicted people. If we regain our freedom, it will be because Joan cared and acted when she saw an injustice. I hope this book inspires others to follow her path and become advocates for the wrongfully convicted.

—Keith M. Kutska

INTRODUCTION

In December 2015, I met Dale Basten in person for the first time at the Stanley Correctional Institution in Stanley, Wisconsin. Dale was serving a life sentence for murder. At age seventy-seven, he's the oldest of six men convicted in the 1992 death of a Green Bay, Wisconsin, paper-mill worker named Tom Monfils. I knew Dale solely through the letters we'd exchanged over the past five years. All of his letters, though infrequent and brief, were kind and full of genuine warmth and sincerity.

In the prison lounge at Stanley, my husband, Mike, and I waited in anticipation for Dale to enter the room. He was required to first check in at the guard desk before joining us at our designated table #18. As we waited, we eyed an elderly man being escorted into the lounge by one of the guards. I was deeply saddened by this slow procession as they shuffled along not far from where we sat. The individual turned the corner of a nearby support column as the guard followed close behind, steadying the man's slight frame.

Seconds later and without warning, I erupted out of my seat. *"That was Dale!"* I said to Mike as I scrambled to catch another glimpse of the two men. Observing them from behind the support column, I saw that they had reached the guard desk. Dale stood motionless with his back to the desk, staring blankly into the crowded room. He appeared terribly confused and unable to identify his visitors. The guard patiently scanned the room for Dale's visitors. As soon as he glanced in our direction, I signaled for him to bring Dale to our table. I studied Dale as they approached. He looked so thin and frail. I braced myself, thinking he could fall at any moment. The guard left us to assist Dale into the seat designated for him—a maroon chair amongst three dark green ones.

The faint, noncommittal smile on Dale's face told us that he had no idea who we were, despite the regular updates from me concerning this case. "How are you doing, Dale?" I asked.

He shrugged and said, "I'm fine." He then said he'd never been in this room before. Mike and I glanced at each other, both knowing the unlikelihood of his comment. Dale had been at this prison since at least 2009, and we were quite certain his family had visited during that time. Maybe his memory wasn't the best anymore. Or maybe memories of being with his family caused more heartache than he could bear. Either way, we tread cautiously, keeping the conversation simple. We asked Dale about everyday life at the prison. His answers were short. His recollection of current activities was vague. But clarity resurfaced when we ventured into a more serious conversation about events of the distant past—like the incident at the paper mill in November 1992.

Dale told us that he had been a foreman at the mill. He said he had liked his job and that his income had provided a good life for his family. He clarified for us that he had not worked in the area of the mill where the *incident* had occurred but that he and Michael Johnson had been called there to help with one of the paper machines during the morning of Tom Monfils' disappearance. Dale obsessed over his interpretation of how Monfils' body may have reacted while inside the vat. As he described the circular motion of the vat liquid, he recreated a swirling, plunging motion with his arms.

Dale did not recall his parole hearing a month prior to this visit. There was, however, no mistaking his deep love for his two daughters, despite being unable to remember specific details about their current lives. Mike and I were mindful that Dale might be experiencing symptoms similar to those of my elderly mother late in her life—short-term memory loss, little to no recollection of current events, and an inability to retain new information, no matter how significant. After our visit, I contacted Dale's brother, Lee, who had recently noticed a rapid deterioration of Dale's physical and mental health. "He's aged ten years beyond his actual age," Lee indicated. He strongly felt that this was due to inadequate health care, a lack of human touch, and constant exposure to a high-stress situation. Dale's health was also likely affected by a major heart attack he had suffered a few years ago. Sadly, no one in Dale's family had been notified about this in a timely manner. After they did learn of his medical condition, the family was further traumatized when they were robbed of the opportunity to be with him during this critical time.

Witnessing Dale's mental state prompted me to research information about the aging prison population in the US. According to Human Rights Watch, due to the "Get tough on crime" initiative from years ago that resulted in longer prison sentences for lesser crimes, an increased number of older individuals within prisons are adding to a dangerously high volume of overcrowding. The number of men and women aged fifty-five and older (fifty-five being the youngest age the prison system defines as *elderly*) has grown dramatically, from roughly 32,600 in 1995 to 124,400 in 2010. That's an increase of 282 percent in comparison with a 42 percent increase in the total prison population during the same years. In 2000, the elderly accounted for only 3 percent of that total, and in just ten years, their numbers increased by 5 percent. Now they account for approximately 16 percent. Projections estimate this age group may increase by 4,400 percentage points according to statistics from 1981 to 2030. With this forecast, by 2030, individuals fifty-five and over will reach one-third of the total prison population.

There are major concerns over yearly medical costs for a single individual, which can easily exceed $100,000. In addition, prison staff are ill-equipped to take on the day-to-day physical care of the elderly during the duration of their incarceration. In some instances, those experiencing significant age-related health issues receive what is called "compassionate release." This is in accordance with Families Against Mandatory Minimums (FAMM), an organization that provides assistance to families and their incarcerated loved ones who are interested in applying for early release due to health issues. The FAMM site provides this clarity:

"Compassionate release is called for when terminal illness, advanced age, sickness, debilitation, or extreme family circumstances outweigh continued imprisonment." And: "Our justice system imprisons people to deter crime, punish those who commit crimes, protect the public, and rehabilitate prisoners who will one day return home. At FAMM, we believe prisoners should be released when they are too debilitated to commit further crimes, too compromised to benefit from rehabilitation, or too impaired to be aware of punishment."

However, this option presents an unavoidable dilemma. Although there are plenty of senior-care facilities across the country, the problem lies with accepting men and women who have been released from prison, which introduces safety concerns for existing residents and staff members alike.

I learned about Dale's situation in 2009 from a book called *The Monfils Conspiracy: The Conviction of Six Innocent Men* by Denis Gullickson and John Gaie—a story I found deeply disturbing about a real-life tragedy that has upset Dale's life and the lives of countless others. Reading about their difficulties angered and provoked me in a way that has never diminished since. An awakening, a revelation of a suppressed trauma from my past stirred from deep within. My outspoken self refused to accept or dismiss a situation that had developed into a horrific injustice and a prime example of the devastating effects caused by wrongful and, yes, sometimes unlawful convictions. The concept of being wrongfully convicted was foreign to me, but what captured my attention was a perceived element of bullying as the underlying theme in this case. Bullying was something my childhood had been inundated with. Bullies persistently made fun of me. They unrelentingly defamed my character. They unjustly blamed me for things I hadn't done. Years upon years of endless cruelty instigated by my peers caused deeply embedded emotional damage and lasting internal shame and self-pity. As an adult, and after a long road to establishing a semblance of self-worth, there was no mistaking those same iniquities on display in this book.

The story details the flaws of the case, which the authors claim mistakenly led a jury to convict six innocent men. The book describes circumstances well beyond what I had experienced—authorities unlawfully fabricating evidence to secure lifelong prison sentences. As I read further into the book, I realized how insignificant my past was while at the same time understanding how much it actually mattered. I could empathize with these strangers on a fundamental level because of what I had experienced, which is why I felt compelled to help defend them and their rights. My most effective tool became my personal tragedies, which motivated me to act on their behalf with a steadfast and well-defined purpose. After a while, this Good Samaritan crusade turned into an important lesson in self-discovery, in achieving a more meaningful life, and in understanding that hope is the most powerful emotion we will ever experience.

The backdrop of the story centers on events that took place in the Midwest region of the United States in the city of Green Bay, Wisconsin. The body of Tom Monfils was found inside a pulp vat at a local paper mill where he worked. A dubious investigation followed, and its outcome became a bitter pill for each of its victims to swallow. This book touches lightly on the technical and legal aspects of the case. However, the majority of the story comes from the standpoint of a social-justice advocate with no legal background, only a fierce determination to raise my voice on behalf of those silenced. My preference of being referred to as an advocate as opposed to an activist stems from feeling more comfortable assisting from behind the scenes, allowing the real heroes to shine in the foreground.

It wasn't my intention to write my own book when I first started down this path, so this book's content is based on memory, conversations with the people involved in the case, emails, blog posts, other documentation I've saved over the years, and, finally, more recent legal briefs. Although I've taken some liberty regarding dialogue and circumstances, I've done my best to recapture the essence of what was said and done in the events depicted throughout this book. Some names have been changed. Others have been intentionally left out for privacy reasons. It was necessary to exclude a few minor details due to attorney-client privilege and because legal action in this case is still pending.

Despite strong opposing views, I have ample reasons—many of which I address in this book—to believe that Dale and the other five men convicted in this case are innocent.

Truth be told, the intent of this book is not to lessen the significance of Tom Monfils' death. He will always be mourned and remembered as the first victim in this tragedy. Given the significance of more recently uncovered details that have surfaced in this case, I believe strongly that neither he nor his family has received the absolute justice they deserve. I believe that this also pertains to the secondary victims: the six men and their families.

Each time this case resurfaces, those involved on both sides relive the horrors all over again. Many people empathize with the Monfils family and favor shielding them from further trauma. But few acknowledge the real and unrelenting trauma also experienced by the six men and those who love them. In my opinion, these latest activities to achieve justice for the six men are long overdue and have always been inevitable because of the many untruths that still linger in this case. Until an honest dialogue and full disclosure of all circumstances related to this case take place, this tragedy will continue to reemerge, and the pain associated with it will never fully disappear. Truth must prevail for Tom Monfils and his family. It must also prevail for the six men and their families. I strongly believe the potential to achieve both does exist.

I do not expect those who read my book to accept the content I've provided solely on its merits. To further delve into the complexities and particulars, I urge you to read *The Monfils Conspiracy* and perform your own in-depth examination of this case and the vast amount of other wrongful-conviction cases that have placed a dark stain on the criminal justice system both in this country and globally. No doubt, your research will reveal similar problematic patterns as well as a myriad of questions about how this specific case was handled, as it has for many of us described in this book. No doubt, the number of compelling and disturbing cases similar to this that have gained widespread attention in recent years will astound and shock you.

Though it has been a humbling and daunting undertaking to write a book that I hope adequately portrays this controversial case, I am grateful for the interest it has generated. As in this particular story, because of the efforts of like-minded individuals, many innocents sitting in prison for crimes they did not commit are receiving a second chance.

Chapter 1
HOMEGROWN SECRETS

"**W**hat do you mean there are innocent people in prison?" I asked. "How is that possible?"

John replied, "Let me explain."

In a phone conversation with my sister, Clare, during the summer of 2009 prior to meeting John, she had described someone she'd met recently. "He's an author and researcher named John Gaie," she said. "We met at a place called The Lorelei. And get this—he told me I look like his mother."

Our laughter faded as Clare described her relationship with John. Both of them, longtime residents of Green Bay, had been dating a few weeks when Clare suggested bringing John to Minnesota to meet Mike and me. She was anxious for us to learn about a project that he was working on. "John is researching a true-crime story I'm familiar with," she said. "He's collaborating with two other people on a book about six men who were convicted of murder in 1995, right here in Green Bay. John says it will be published soon."

"No kidding," I said. "That's exciting. I've always been interested in true-crime stories. I'd love to hear more about this one."

Concern in Clare's voice indicated her deep distress over the circumstances and the outcome of this particular case. Her next statements shed light on the degree to which it had affected them both. "I'll let John speak for himself about his connection to the case, but I'll say this for now: Both of us have direct ties to some of the men who were convicted. John's connection compelled him to take on this project and do most of the research. In the process, he found numerous flaws with the entire investigation, many of which I never knew about. I always felt there was something terribly wrong with how it turned out, and I'm even more convinced of that now. I actually know one of the men. Rey Moore is a good friend of mine," she said. Clare touched on bits and pieces of how she'd gotten to know Rey. "When I worked with Rey's wife at the county, she introduced us. Rey and I hit it off right away, and the three of us hung out together on many occasions."

I wanted to hear so much more, but we decided to continue the conversation in person, when John could fill us in on the precise details. "When can you and John come to visit?" I asked.

"How about the weekend after next?" she said. "It'll be fun."

Chapter 2
TRAGEDY IN TITLETOWN, USA

Clare and John arrived early Friday evening, in time for dinner. Clare introduced us to a man whose grin was mischievous and sly, reminiscent of the Cheshire cat. But he was friendly and engaging, with a boisterous and infectious laugh. His slight build did not prevent him from giving bear hugs that forced the air right out of our lungs. Compliments from him seemed to flow naturally. "You're almost as beautiful as your sister," John announced.

"And you're quite the charmer," I replied.

John was retired. He reminisced about his career as a scientist and researcher who taught biochemistry for twenty-five years at Northwest Wisconsin Technical College. He shared his love of teaching and of being among innovative students. We soon learned that every conversation with John literally turned into a fifty-five-minute lecture. Talk during dinner was relaxed and full of laughter, but the mood turned somber when I changed the subject as we moved into the family room.

"Tell us about the book you are working on," I said.

John was eager to share. "I'm coauthoring the book Clare mentioned with Denis Gullickson, a local Green Bay writer who has written two other books about the Green Bay Packers." In a calm, subdued manner, John shared vast details of an intolerable and horrific story that, to him, was still unresolved seventeen years later.

His narrative started out with a seemingly mundane event that occurred on November 10, 1992, and turned catastrophic over a period of two-and-a-half years. While at work at the James River Paper Mill in

Green Bay, mill worker Keith Kutska cut a sixteen-foot piece of discarded electrical wire that he'd found in a dumpster at the mill. His intention was to take the wire home with him at the end of his shift. Typically, mill workers were permitted to remove scrap items from the mill, but they were required to also fill out a "scrap pass" so that management could keep track of and approve the removal of scrap materials. Nonetheless, Kutska felt justified in taking the wire without filling out the pass because of the item's nominal value. In fact, ignoring this formality was a common occurrence among mill workers.

A coworker, Tom Monfils, saw Kutska cut the wire. At that time, he and Kutska understood each other's differences of opinion regarding an upcoming union vote proposal. This dispute is thought to be the root cause of Monfils' possible intent to make trouble for Kutska. On the day Kutska cut the wire, Monfils made an anonymous 911 call to the Green Bay Police Department (GBPD) to report Kutska's impending theft. During the call, he expressed deep concern over remaining anonymous and described Kutska as a "violent biker type" even though, as the police later learned, Kutska had no history of violence. Monfils described the wire in question as expensive, maybe to increase the likelihood that the police would show up at the mill, presumably to arrest Kutska. Instead, the 911 dispatcher called mill security to relay Monfils' concerns. A guard stopped Kutska at the gate as he left work that day. When asked to open his work bag, he refused and hurried off. Kutska's actions prompted a disciplinary hearing at the mill on the following day. At the hearing, he denied taking the wire, in accordance with the advice of his local union president, who had told him he'd have a far better chance of keeping his job if he denied taking the scrap wire without having obtained a scrap pass. Ultimately, he was suspended from work and docked five days' pay.

At the disciplinary hearing, Kutska learned that the police had received an anonymous call from one of his coworkers on the same day that he had taken the wire. He also learned that copies of 911 recordings are obtainable by the public. While Kutska was serving his suspension, several coworkers called to ask him if he would try to identify the person who had reported him to the police. After Kutska returned to work, coworkers continued to ask him this same question. Kutska decided that he would first tell those whom he thought might have reported him that he intended to obtain a copy of the 911 call, hoping that their reactions to his intention might reveal the identity of the caller. One of those whom he told was Monfils.

Distraught over the realization that his identity could be discovered, Monfils frantically made repeated phone calls to the police department and to the Brown County attorney's office, asking them not to release the recording. Over the course of a week, Monfils received five separate reassurances from officers at the police department and officials at the Brown County attorney's office that the tape would not be released. However, because Monfils had asked to remain anonymous, none of his calls were documented in the police department's logbook. In the end, no measures were taken to safeguard Monfils' anonymity.

Despite Monfils' repeated requests regarding the tape, on November 20, Kutska drove to the police station, handed the officer on duty five dollars and a blank cassette tape, and left with a copy of the 911 call.

After listening to the recording, Kutska immediately recognized the voice as Monfils'. He then played the tape for his union president, who advised him to play it at work on the following morning for Monfils with two witnesses present. The union president explained to Kutska that if Monfils admitted to him that it was his voice on the tape, Kutska could then file a union grievance and expose Monfils as a snitch.

On November 21 at about 7:15 a.m., Kutska confronted Monfils with the recording in the #7 coop, a small employee breakroom. Also present were fellow mill workers Michael Piaskowski and Randy LePak. Monfils appeared stunned after hearing the recording. He then admitted that it was his voice on the tape and that it was he who had reported Kutska to the police. Kutska, Piaskowski, and LePak then left the room, leaving Monfils alone.

Kutska immediately called the union president to say that he had what he needed to file the grievance. Piaskowski commended Kutska for his civil manner in confronting Monfils with the tape recording. Afterward, Kutska proceeded to play the recording for other mill workers who came by after learning that he had obtained a copy of the 911 call.

During that time, Monfils returned to his workstation and performed various tasks on his assigned paper machine. He completed them by 7:40 a.m. At approximately 7:45 a.m., Monfils disappeared from his workstation. His absence was noticed by Michael Piaskowski. This concern triggered the beginning of an extensive search for Monfils. Some coworkers were concerned that Monfils might have harmed himself and searched for him along the section of the Fox River that ran behind the mill. Mill personnel called Monfils' wife, Susan, to report that her husband was missing. She went straight to the mill. When asked if her husband was capable of harming himself, she answered affirmatively. After leaving the mill, she went looking for him at local hospitals and a psychiatric facility.

On the evening of November 22, 1992, Tom Monfils' body was found at the bottom of a paper-pulp vat inside the mill. The vat held some twenty thousand gallons of water and pulp particles. It was equipped with large rotating impeller blades that were attached to the inside of the vat wall. The blades were approximately three feet from the bottom and in close proximity to where the body was found. One end of Monfils' own jump rope was tied around his neck. The other end was tied to the handle of a 49 lb. weight.

Attempts to remove the body from the vat began prematurely, before a thorough examination of the body and surrounding liquid had been completed. Further destroying important clues of what may have happened, the many failed attempts to hoist the body up and out of the vat most likely caused additional damage before it was eventually removed through an access portal near the bottom of the vat. As the body was fed through the portal, much of the liquid also escaped into the drainage system, which ultimately lessened the potential to understand how and why this death had occurred.

In addition, the GBPD neglected to cordon off the area with crime tape, allowing officers and mill workers alike to trample through the area for hours after the body had been recovered. A police officers' jacket was even left carelessly draped on the very ladder that provided access from the ground floor to the top of the vat where Monfils' body had been discovered. To onlookers, it appeared as though this death was being investigated as a possible suicide. Up to this point, there had been no mention of homicide.

The forensic pathologist assigned to the case began her autopsy examination of Monfils' body on November 23, some forty-two hours after police believed he became submerged in the vat liquid. Police homicide detectives attended the autopsy examination. By then, the body was in a state of advanced decomposition, bloated and discolored, essentially rendering it unrecognizable. Monfils had sustained many injuries, including a significant skull fracture. Solely on the basis of her autopsy and speculation regarding the movements of Monfils' body in the vat both before and after his death, the pathologist readily rejected the conclusion that Monfils' death could have been the result of a suicide. She declared it to be a homicide. It is noteworthy to point out some of what she did not do. She failed to conduct a thorough inspection of the vat, the rotation and force of the blades, and their impact on the movement of Monfils' body. She neglected to take samples of the pulp slurry to determine its thickness and the effect it had on the buoyancy of Monfils' body while inside the vat. Most significant was the failure to take into consideration the relevance of the impellor blades, including—and most importantly—the fact that they exactly matched the dimensions of Monfils' skull fracture, which she had erroneously concluded could only have been caused by a beating before Monfils' body had entered the vat. Her final report establishes that all of Monfils' premortem injuries had occurred as a result of a beating. It also states that Monfils had been beaten with one or more blunt objects and, while still alive, was placed in the vat where he drowned. If she had compared the measurements of the blades to the dimensions of the skull fracture, she would have discovered the match. She would have known that her initial theory, that all injuries had resulted from a beating prior to his body entering the vat, was incorrect.

Following the autopsy, GBPD Sergeant Randy Winkler, who was not assigned to lead the investigation initially, theorized that after Monfils disappeared from sight at around 7:45 a.m., Kutska and other mill employees had confronted him at a bubbler (drinking fountain). This idea was based upon the unsupported theory that Monfils had not admitted to Kutska that he had placed the 911 call immediately after

Kutska had played the tape recording of the call for him. Despite consistent indications from many of Monfils' coworkers who knew him that he'd committed suicide, Winkler still alleged that Kutska had incited a group of his fellow mill workers to confront Monfils and let him know that they were aware that *he* was the snitch.

Winkler further speculated that this verbal confrontation had then turned into a violent beating that had left Monfils unconscious or semi-unconscious and bleeding on the floor. Winkler next speculated that this "mob" had panicked after realizing what they had done and had resolved to hide Monfils' body in the pulp vat that was located some 150-170 feet from the bubbler. Moreover, to ensure that his body would "dissolve" and never be found, they decided to tie one end of his jump rope around his neck and the other end to the handle of a 49 lb. weight that would cause his body to sink in the vat liquid. They then carried Monfils' body with the weight attached to it to the pulp vat, where he drowned.

The initial search for the body inside of the mill included looking up into the maze of ceiling rafters for something hanging in all of the machine rooms, work areas, and storage buildings. A more extensive search led to locations outside of the mill, such as the East and Fox Rivers, the riverbanks, the railroad bridge, Monfils' car (which remained in the mill parking lot), and the Monfils family cottage. Also searched were Monfils' rental apartments, storage sheds, and garages in the Green Bay area.

To this day, Winkler publicly insists, "It appeared to be a homicide immediately." He speculates about the need to conceal this bloody attack and to quickly dispose of the body because of the men's concern over others learning of their vicious deed and the likelihood of losing their high-paying jobs as a result. Winkler rejects any evidence or arguments that point toward the conclusion that Monfils took the rope and weight and then went himself to the vat to take his own life.

Winkler's notion of the alleged altercation consistently contradicted statements made to him and to the police by Monfils' coworkers. They claimed that Monfils was an unstable individual with psychological problems who had an unusual obsession with death and dying. Monfils was known for making frequent remarks about the many drowned suicide victims he'd recovered (with heavy objects tied to their bodies) from his years as a search and rescue seaman in the coast guard. He was the subject of ongoing rumors about his failed marriage and impending divorce. One mill worker told police that Monfils was "ingenious" and "the type of person who'd kill himself and make it look like someone else had done it." Another said Monfils "fully understood the need to tie the weight to his body in order to overcome the instinctive resistance of a conscience person to drowning himself."

After examining the knots used to tie the rope around Monfils' neck and to the handle of the weight, the State Crime Lab recommended to the GBPD that it have the coast guard or navy examine the knots. This was a clear indication that the knots were likely nautical in nature and consistent with Monfils' training and service. The police, however, apparently ignored the crime lab's recommendation.

Approximately twenty-five minutes after Kutska had played the tape for him, Monfils was seen by a coworker heading toward an entrance to a coop where the weight that was used was sitting on the floor. Nearby was a storage area where Monfils' jump rope hung on a railing. This coworker assumed Monfils would enter the coop, which was occupied by other mill workers. However, Monfils never did. A logical conclusion suggests that he picked up the rope and weight and walked unseen toward an isolated area of the mill to the vat where he took his own life.

When Winkler and other detectives on the case found no one to confirm their homicide theory, their narrative shifted to the idea of a union-inspired "conspiracy of silence" to protect the murderers. Winkler resolved to employ more assertive interrogative tactics to overcome this "obstruction" and validate his homicide theory. He began threatening mill workers, subjecting them to an atmosphere of fear and intimidation. They were told they were either "a witness or a suspect," that they could be tried for obstructing justice, and that they might lose their jobs if they didn't "cooperate" with police. It was an unspoken understanding that *cooperation* meant telling the police that they had seen what the police *wanted* them to say they had seen.

Because the forensic pathologist had determined that Monfils had "bled profusely" from his head and facial injuries due to a beating, the police searched the mill for blood or trace evidence of the alleged attack. Despite a search that included the use of black lights and luminol, no such evidence—or evidence of attempts to remove or destroy it to conceal the attack—was found. They failed to locate blunt objects that matched Monfils' injuries. No trace evidence, other physical evidence, or eyewitnesses ever directly corroborated the homicide theory.

Winkler did learn that after Kutska confronted Monfils with the tape, Monfils saw the looks and the finger-pointing and heard condemnation aimed at him from coworkers. Winkler also learned that Monfils had damaged the family name at the mill where his father and other family members had established their careers.

Another interesting fact was that in early 1994, the six defendants were called in to take polygraph tests. Some of them experienced deliberate sound disruptions during those tests. One of the six, Michael Johnson, recalls hearing a sudden racket from behind, immediately after which, the administrator of the test asked him this question: "Did you have anything to do with the murder of Tom Monfils?" Johnson turned around to see Winkler pounding on the window of the room yelling, "Now we gotcha!" in an effort to skew the results. But each of the men passed his lie detector test.

Police initially targeted nine men as the main homicide suspects during the investigation. That group was later reduced to six: Keith Kutska, Dale Basten, Michael Hirn, Michael Johnson, Michael Piaskowski, and Reynold Moore. An unsubstantiated theory declaring these six men as the culprits in the alleged beating and drowning of Tom Monfils persevered. The men were openly surveilled by the police, with squad cars often spotted near their homes. Periodically, officers also rummaged through their garbage cans. The men were repeatedly asked to go to the police station for questioning. Even though all of them fully cooperated, they were still characterized by the police and the media as "murderers" and "union thugs."

On April 12, 1995, arrests were made some two-and-a-half years after Tom Monfils' body was discovered. The State formally charged the six men with first-degree intentional homicide, party to a crime. Two others were charged with misdemeanors. They all were held in the Brown County Jail. On Thursday, April 13, the Green Bay *Press-Gazette* reported: "Police wrapped up a lengthy investigation in a forty-five-minute drama in which five mill workers were led out of the mill in handcuffs. Four teams of eight officers swooped in on the mill, and other locations, to arrest eight men." Michael Piaskowski recalls being summoned to his supervisor's office, and upon entering, being thrown against the wall and handcuffed in a dramatic scene, as though he were a highly dangerous flight risk. The fact was that he and the others were in the midst of carrying out their typical daily routines.

The six defendants went on trial in late September 1995, with each of them denying any involvement in or knowledge of this alleged murder. Although each had his own defense attorney, the men were tried jointly. However, all six of the attorneys perpetuated an already dire situation. They failed to adequately defend their clients by taking into consideration the suicide defense. Instead, they conceded that Monfils had been brutally beaten and thrown into the pulp vat to conceal the beating. Instead, they each argued only that their client had not participated in the beating and murder and that their client lacked any information regarding who had done so. This incompetence left them with no alternative but to redirect blame away from their client and point a finger at others, including their codefendants—a maneuver commonly referred to as the SODDI (Some Other Dude Did It) defense. The lawyers conceded to the lead prosecutor District Attorney John Zakowski's theory that Monfils had been beaten and drowned by union thugs caught up in the moment. In addition, Zakowski set low expectations when he told the jury at the beginning of the trial, "If details are extremely important to you, you're going to be disappointed. There are gaps." The State relied mainly on the testimony of three key witnesses: Brian Kellner, David Weiner, and James Gilliam.

In November 1994, months before the trial started, mill worker Brian Kellner became a witness for the prosecution. Through intimidation, manipulation, and threats, Kellner was coerced into signing a false statement that Detective Winkler had prepared for him and demanded he sign. This statement referenced a role-playing reenactment of the alleged beating at the bubbler inside the mill. The statement alleged that Kutska had performed this reenactment while drunk at a bar located twenty miles north of Green Bay called the Fox Den Bar, in front of Kellner, his wife, Kutska's wife, and the bar owners. But according to the bar owners, no such event had occurred. However, this statement was hailed as critical by the authorities because it helped to revive an investigation that was heading nowhere.

Before trial, Kellner attempted to retract and change key aspects of his statement. But his testimony at trial closely followed the script contained in his written statement. After trial, he gave an altered version of the statement. About sixteen months later, he insisted that he had lied at trial and that Kutska had not described an actual beating but only shared his thoughts on what might have happened if the police theory was correct. Kellner said that Winkler had threatened to have him fired and to have custody of his two minor children taken away from him if he refused to sign the statement incriminating the six men. The prosecutor, in turn, dismissed Kellner's recantation as lacking credibility.

Another mill worker, David Weiner, whose workstation was located near the vat, also became a witness for the prosecution. He initially confirmed Kutska's stated whereabouts at the time of the alleged beating. He also said that he didn't see anything relevant to Monfils' disappearance and expressly denied seeing Dale Basten and Michael Johnson at any time on the morning of Monfils' disappearance. But in March 1993, Zakowski accused Weiner of lying under oath in order to provide an alibi for Kutska and that he himself might face legal consequences for doing so.

Two months after he was told this, Weiner called the police while at a wedding reception where he'd been drinking heavily and after his physician had prescribed him a number of anti-anxiety medications. He was distraught over a "repressed memory" he claimed to recall of seeing Basten and Johnson bent over as though they were carrying something heavy or cumbersome and walking in the direction of the pulp vat. Though Weiner claimed he did not actually see what they had been carrying, he certainly knew that the authorities would presume the object was Monfils' body. By the time the joint trial began in September 1995, Weiner's situation had changed drastically. He was serving a ten-year sentence for murdering his own brother in November 1993 and was looking to cut a deal—a reduced sentence in exchange for his testimony. None of this information, including evidence of deal-related communications between Zakowski and Weiner's lawyers, was ever disclosed to the defense lawyers or to the jury. Zakowski still adamantly denies a deal was ever made. However, after the trial ended, Weiner was released from prison after serving a total of 39 months of his original 120-month sentence for second-degree murder of his brother.

James Gilliam was a paid police drug informant and repeat offender, with past arrests ranging from robbery to attempted murder. On April 12, 1995, the day of the arrests in the Monfils case, Gilliam was being held in the Brown County Jail for allegedly threatening his girlfriend with a butcher knife. He later claimed to have had a conversation with Reynold Moore, saying that Moore had confided to him that he had struck Monfils during the alleged beating. After Gilliam had testified to this at trial, he cut a deal with Zakowski's office and was released. But in 2000, Gilliam was again arrested and charged with first-degree intentional homicide for the murder of his wife. He's currently serving a life sentence and is ineligible for parole.

Because of publicity concerns, the jury was comprised of individuals from Racine, Wisconsin, who were sequestered for the entire twenty-eight-day trial. It was difficult for them to keep the defendants straight. Some jurors were reportedly seen catnapping during the proceedings. After a mere eight hours of deliberation, they came back with six guilty verdicts. Ninety minutes after that, they were on a bus heading back home to their families.

As John disclosed a litany of disturbing facts about this case, familiar images formed in my mind of things I'd spent a lifetime trying to erase. It became hauntingly clear to me that these six men and their families had been subjected to the worst kind of mean-spirited bullying imaginable. They were looked upon with disgust by those in the community whose opinions were based on inadequate and misguided information, fed to them by media outlets who had gathered material from the very sources intent on making sure only one version of this tragedy existed. From the start, the authorities had branded these men as the perpetrators despite information known only to them that echoed an undeniable innocence of all six men. I believe that it was their intent from the beginning to overshadow innocence with an unlikely and, quite frankly, implausible sequence of events. The accused cooperated with police throughout the entire investigation. They were robbed of their own separate trials because of a two-pronged argument delivered by the State that no court dare refute: 1) trying the six men separately would cost taxpayers too much money; and 2) doing so would inflict additional and unnecessary emotional trauma onto the Monfils family.

All of these prejudicial disadvantages were devastating blows that came at a high cost to the men and their families when the trial ended with six guilty verdicts. To the rest of us who believe, as they once did, that the intent of our judicial system is to make sure only the guilty are convicted, this case represents a glaring wake-up call and blatant reminder of a saying reiterated for generations by scholars such as Sir William Blackstone and Benjamin Franklin: "Tis better that one hundred guilty persons should escape than one innocent person suffer."

My anger resurfaced time and again as John continued to weave this bitter tale. I finally blurted out my contempt. "You've got to be joking," I said. "What you are telling me sounds ludicrous." John agreed and, in a docile manner, sat on the edge of the couch avoiding my stare. "Where is the outrage over this obvious injustice?" I pressed. "Why is nothing being done to correct it?"

John managed a smile. "Your reaction is quite refreshing," he said, saluting my indignation. "Maybe there's a possibility that you can get involved with our mission to free the other five men."

I surmised that John's calm demeanor stemmed from being entrenched in this circumstance from its inception. I was only learning about this sordid tale for the first time. Well into his narrative, he opened up about his true motive for supporting this project. "For many years, I was married to Michael Piaskowski's sister, Francine. During that time, I got to know Mike very well. But then, Francine and I were divorced. And "Pie," as we call him, is the kind of person who feels that once you are family, you are always family—no matter what." John's voice cracked as he continued, "Mike Pie is the finest man I have ever known. I always knew that he did not commit any murder. He would never commit a vile act like that."

John said Denis had always had it in the back of his mind to write a book about this case, partly because he had worked with Pie's father, Fran Piaskowski, years ago at Sears during Denis' college days. Based on his respect for Fran, Denis is quite certain that "no son of Fran Piaskowski ever killed anyone."

The details, all of which John contended were factual, were overwhelming. The implications they represented were more than I could absorb—or stomach for that matter. But I was impressed by John's ability to refine them so that we all could grasp, at least on the surface, what had happened and begin to understand why this case was so flawed. Two bizarre aspects of the case stood out for me: 1) Zakowski's intent to convict these men without a shred of physical evidence, credible eyewitnesses, or the GBPD's ability to solicit a single non-coerced confession during the two-and-a-half-year investigation; and 2) the unfairness of subjecting the six men to a joint trial. "Why didn't they have separate trials?" I demanded. "Wasn't that a violation of their basic civil rights?"

"You are correct," John said. "I think the authorities realized that they could never have convicted all six men if they had conducted separate trials, although they dodge the question when asked about the mountain of evidence they supposedly have. The reality is, what evidence they believed they had was too flimsy to stand alone. I believe that trying them together also greatly influenced the jury into believing that all of the men played an equal role in Tom's death, and all were guilty beyond a reasonable doubt." John's assertions about this have been affirmed in more recent interviews with both Winkler and Zakowski. When asked directly if either believed that they could have achieved the six convictions without the benefit of a joint trial, both have responded with a decisive "no." But neither has elaborated on why they feel this way.

"How can people be convicted with no evidence or eyewitnesses?" I argued. "This makes no sense."

John's mention of reasonable doubt brought up an interesting facet of this case. The opening statement by the prosecution was revealing, although the jury did not seem moved by it. By stating that there are "gaps," an admission of their inability to provide a complete rendering of events in the case, they essentially told the court that there was reasonable doubt about the actual guilt of these men. Reasonable doubt is the standard used in criminal trials. When a defendant is prosecuted, the burden is on the prosecutor to prove that the defendant is guilty beyond a reasonable doubt—the highest burden of proof that the law imposes on any party in court. If the evidence creates doubt, it is then the duty of the judge and jury to find the defendant not guilty. However, the more I learned about these convictions, the more I realized that a suspect is more likely to be looked upon as guilty until proven innocent.

Like Clare had said, many of the details didn't add up. What intrigued and mystified me was that as children, we are taught to trust law enforcement and to find a police officer if we are in trouble because they are the ones who will protect us. As adults, we believe that the criminal justice system is fair. But justice is never guaranteed. Many find out about this sad reality the hard way, like when they are subjected to a wrongful conviction. John had learned this firsthand in the mid-1990s when his family was caught up in this tragedy.

As he delved further into this drama, John promoted his belief that the convictions were orchestrated on many levels in the legal community where this happened, from the police department to the lead detective, to the prosecutor, all the way up the judicial ladder. "The legal community bands together in a small town like ours," he said. He talked about the altered timeline of events regarding the victim's disappearance and witness statements that had been coerced or doctored to fit the police theory. He discussed the botched crime scene. "They didn't even cordon off the area until much later in the day. Everyone trampled the area like a herd of cattle, destroying any potential evidence," John said. "The entire investigation was flawed from day one." It was clear to me from what John was saying that these men had never had a fair chance.

John's analysis ate at me for weeks. It infuriated me to think of how it might feel to have a member of my own family unfairly taken from me and treated in this manner. It was unbearable to think this could happen to my husband, to my son, to one of my siblings, or to me. I thought of how being wrongly accused of a heinous crime and sent away for something you didn't do had to be one of the worst fates imaginable. I thought of how the circumstances could affect my life, my values, and my ability to trust—or cause internal panic because someone I love is now locked up with dangerous criminals. Think of the anger and the hopelessness of having our rights denied—our freedoms, sanctity, and everything we hold dear ripped from us. This is unfathomable and downright unacceptable.

Clare lightened the mood somewhat to tell us about her longtime friendship with Reynold Moore prior to these circumstances. "Rey and his wife invited me to their house all the time. I didn't have a car back then, so I'd ride over on my bicycle. Rey always threw it into the back of his pickup and drove me home if it got too dark before I left because he was worried about my safety. I know that Rey is not a criminal!" she said.

In 2015, when my husband, Mike, and I visited Rey in prison for the first time, I shared what Clare had said about him. His face lit up as memories of their friendship filled his thoughts. Rey was grateful for her continued support. He remembered seeing her in the courtroom during his last appeal. "I didn't know for sure who she was at the time, but she looked familiar," Rey told us.

John thought that the book would be available for purchase soon. He generously offered to give me a signed copy. For my birthday, he gifted me a hardcover version of the book signed by him, Denis, and Mike Pie.

The book was difficult for me to read, even after having discussed many of the details in depth with John. The number of people involved, the mind-numbing facts, the legal references to John Doe hearings, and the lawsuits against the men, the State, and the police department all presented a challenge for someone like me who knew nothing about our criminal justice system. I had to constantly refer back to previous chapters in order to remember the endless cast of characters and to keep track of who supposedly did what.

As I read further into the book, my anger often forced me to put the book down. I'd cringe at the absurdity of jailhouse informants looking to benefit themselves by telling a jury what they knew the prosecutor wanted it to hear, witnesses who were coerced, and another with a so-called "repressed memory." Depending on how well the State's case was progressing, the importance of the key witnesses seemed to change with the wind. Equally disturbing was the fact that two of the original attorneys were sent to prison after the trial for their own offenses, with one of them spotted in the same prison as his former client.

By the time I finished the book, my emotional capacity was spent. As each prejudicial detail leaped off of the page, many deep-rooted feelings of fear, doubt, isolation, and worthlessness reemerged. A life I'd been subjected to as a child came back with a vengeance as I read every word of this intensely appalling story. And I, like John, became personally involved.

I grew up in a large family in a small town in the Upper Peninsula of Michigan. I considered us to be poor. There were many things that caused me shame, including the outdated and ragged hand-me-down clothes I wore. The dilapidated house we lived in was a blight on the block that begged for repairs and updates. The inside was a hoarder's haven, cluttered with endless piles of junk that had collected over the years. Lining the walls and covering nearly every surface were boxes of discarded clothing that my mother had saved for making rag rugs that never got made, piles of old receipts, old newspapers, and miscellaneous possessions that she could never part with. I had seen how beautifully organized my friends' homes were, and I lived in constant fear of the utter embarrassment of them finding out about the mess in which I lived. They'd surely be shocked but then proceed to make fun of me and tell others about it. I became introverted and withdrawn, pushing away the few friends I had. This isolation attracted bullies whom I could not defend myself against. Taking advantage of my reticence, they taunted me at every available opportunity with their sarcastic remarks, spiteful pretenses, and finger-pointing. Most classmates distanced themselves from me. Only when they found themselves in need of one more player with no one left to ask was I approached to engage in sports activities. I wanted to scream, to combat the cruelty, to make it stop. But I feared the consequences of being seen as an antagonist. So I endured the abuse. I suffered alone with no one to defend me.

The most catastrophic aspect of this case was that until the bitter end, the six men—all law-abiding citizens—believed in a legal system that was fair and that would ultimately support their innocence. They depended on lawyers who would fight for them. Instead, they were victimized. Their freedom was taken, and their lives were turned upside down. The final blow was being separated from their loved ones and being condemned to serving life sentences for something they had no knowledge of.

I also learned about how the lives of their families were upended as a result of these convictions. I started to refer to the family members as the "collateral damage" of wrongful convictions because of the massive price they've paid. When a person goes to prison, especially for a crime they did not commit, the entire family experiences the same kind of hell. The day-to-day emotional scarring, financial woes, and exposure to ongoing contempt from an unsympathetic community that was lied to pose a heavy burden. These families lost their ability to trust. Even friends turned their backs on them and became distant, readily accepting the lies. Money became a concern when their men, the primary wage earners, were absent and funds from savings accounts were depleted. Some families were forced to sell their homes and combine living arrangements just to survive. They grappled with additional traumas resulting from failed appeals and adjusting to life without a husband, father, or brother.

John shared an unanticipated piece of information during that weekend that stunned us but added a glimmer of hope for the men still in prison.

"Our family got lucky," John began. In 2001, five-and-a-half years after the six men were convicted, a major development occurred. A writ of habeas corpus was filed on Mike Pie's behalf. This is an order to bring someone who has been criminally convicted in a state court to a federal court. Senior Federal US District Judge Myron Gordon (1918–2009) from the Eastern District of Wisconsin ruled that the evidence against Piaskowski was insufficient to sustain his conviction. In his statement, Judge Gordon noted that the only evidence against Piaskowski was that he reported Monfils missing minutes after Monfils disappeared and that he was with five other defendants before and after the alleged beating but was not cited as having participated in the alleged incident. He was eventually cleared of all charges and released from prison. A total of five federal judges essentially graded the jury as "unreasonable" and "irrational" and charged it with "failing its duty" when it found Piaskowski guilty. In his ruling overturning Piaskowski's conviction, Judge Gordon described the case against him as "conjecture camouflaged as evidence" and said that "a guilty verdict required the jury to pile speculation on top of inferences that were drawn from other inferences . . . such a verdict is not rational."

John talked about the difficulties the jury faced. "When we contacted the jurors in 2007 while writing the book, most of them wouldn't speak to us," he said. "However, one of them did." John repeated a statement made by this juror that was completely outrageous and quite revealing. "It was too much to process and too easy to just make the same decision for [all] of the defendants."

Mike Pie was released on bond on April 3, 2001, while the State appealed Judge Gordon's ruling. On July 10, 2001, the Seventh Circuit Court of Appeals upheld Judge Gordon's decision and added, "The jury's conclusion that Piaskowski participated in the beating and/or conspired with the other defendants to kill Monfils is speculation." Mike Pie could never be retried for this crime again, and the case was dismissed.

"Essentially, Mike Pie was exonerated," John said. "That's the term used by organizations such as the Innocence Project to describe a person being cleared of a conviction based on new evidence or proof of innocence. It was a great day when we learned that news."

"Mike Pie was a big help with details for the book," John explained. "He was able to fill in the blanks that we were not privy to. He was at the mill that day. He knew exactly what happened. He gave us valuable feedback about how the mill was run, and technical aspects of how paper machines operate, et cetera. In his basement were file drawers filled to capacity with documentation he had saved over the years about the case. He became our eyes and ears for what happened inside the mill in the days before and after Monfils' disappearance. This book took eight years to complete. It became our labor of love. Mike Pie, Denis, and I put every ounce of energy we had into it for no other reason than to help the other five men because, unfortunately, Mike Pie is still the only one of the six to be exonerated."

I managed to finish the book by Thanksgiving. By then, Clare had heard plenty from me regarding my outrage and disbelief over this tragedy. Mike and I were planning to spend an extended holiday weekend in Titletown, USA—a term used by locals to indicate Green Bay's high ranking in overall sport-team championships despite its modest population. After learning about this case, it became a place that represented, more than anything, a grave injustice. Clare mentioned that John and the others had a book signing scheduled there during that same weekend. "I'll take you over to meet Denis and Mike Pie," she said. "They are great guys, and I think you and Mike should meet them."

Chapter 3
SIGNING UP FOR A CAUSE

On the Saturday after Thanksgiving, Clare, Mike, and I went over to The Reader's Loft bookstore in Green Bay. The guys—John, Denis, and Mike Pie—were set up at a table near the entrance. John acknowledged us briefly as we walked in. All three were engaged in conversation with patrons who were attending, so Clare and I stood nearby and waited. My husband had wandered off by this time. He was in a bookstore. Enough said.

There appeared to be genuine interest in this story judging from the conversations we heard amongst the crowd. Most people seemed to either know one or more of the convicted men or the authors. Although concerted sadness hung in the air, a hopeful energy lingered as if to alert us to the potential of this book to positively influence the public and to ultimately help the men in prison.

"This book lays out the absolute facts in this case," I heard Denis say.

"I combed through three laundry baskets full of information to recreate the more accurate timeline," said John to a customer as she paid for her copy.

Many community members had come to support the purpose behind book sales, which was to raise funds to hire legal counsel for the men in prison. I learned afterward that others who came had accused the authors of profiting from this tragedy. But I sensed a distinct dedication between these three men and a devotion to their self-imposed mission. Over eight years of their lives, they had produced an astounding compilation of factual details that opened my eyes to a profane side of a flawed case and of our overall judicial system. The amount of dedication the guys had poured into producing this book was not about profit margins.

There was plenty of buzz on the local news. Opinions varied. Some said the book depicted a true account of what happened. One critic with vested interests in this case stated it was "a complete and utter waste of time." Many felt it contained no new revelations about the case. I was angered by the negativity that seemed to dictate public opinion. I felt that those comments were repulsive, unfounded, and demoralizing to the importance of this latest research. But even as the rhetoric flowed, I was pleased about the resurgence of this controversy. I hoped it could bring broader attention to the case.

John walked over to greet us. "You look respectable in a suit and tie," I said. He laughed as he apologized for the delay. He then escorted us over to meet Denis. The contrast between Denis' white hair, bright blue eyes, and dark suitcoat was striking. He towered over Clare and me as we all shook hands.

"Welcome, Joan. Hello, Clare," he said. He looked at me and said, "John has told me all about you and your spirited opinions of this case. It is indeed a grave cataclysm. I appreciate your interest and for stopping by today."

My admiration for Denis was immediate, as voracious compassion radiated from him. His tenacity and commitment to publicizing this injustice appeared genuine. I was encouraged by his outspoken and unyielding nature in sending a forceful message to the authorities that this controversy was not going away anytime soon. As Clare and I stepped aside to allow other people to speak with Denis, he quickly stated, "Make sure you talk to Mike Pie. He's the one who truly understands the scope of this tragedy."

John introduced me to Mike Pie, the exoneree—a man whose nightmare of living a life behind bars had ended. He was fully exonerated, meaning that he had regained the same freedoms as every American. He could vote and purchase firearms. His status as a felon had also been expunged from his record. But aside from all of this, his most urgent accomplishment since his release had been to expose the truth about this case and to seek the same justice for the other five men.

Clare stood talking to John, which gave me an opportunity to speak with Mike Pie alone. Like John, he gave big bear hugs. "This must run in the family and will take some getting used to," I thought.

Mike Pie was easy to talk to. His manner of dress, jeans and a button-down shirt, matched his relaxed and carefree attitude. "I'm going to live my life how I see fit from now on," he said. His unabashed and unapologetic tone was warranted given the horrific experience he had endured. But he was friendly and animated as he spoke nonstop, using hand gestures to convey an array of emotions. I was grateful for his assertive nature, as I struggled to add to a conversation with someone who had been in prison for a crime he didn't commit.

In this setting, with the emphasis being placed on a devastating and personal tragedy, I was afraid to say something offensive, silly, or ignorant. "Do I ask what prison was like? Do I offer my sympathies for his grief?" I wondered. He was open about his experience, but I didn't want to insult him, nor did I want my remarks to sound hollow. So I allowed him to dictate the direction of our conversation.

Mike Pie made an impactful statement to me right away. "I was fortunate enough to have been freed, but the other five men are still in prison, and it's my duty to help them however I can." I was moved by this declaration and the tears that appeared as he spoke. The honesty he displayed in discussing his incarceration and the suicidal tendencies many like him experience from being locked up seemed to be second nature to him. But the realities were frightening and heartbreaking to me.

Mike Pie harbored no malice when he stated how he had lost everything—his family, home, and a good-paying union job with a pension. He now worked for little pay and lived in modest surroundings. As he pointed these things out, I never got the sense that he was complaining. He accepted what happened and that he could not change the past. He was grateful for his freedom, and as with most exonerees I've since met, he refused to relive the anger he once felt.

As the crowd dissipated, we gathered to talk about the positive effect this book could have moving forward. I was certain of my interest in getting involved, and this book event gave me an idea of how to help. "If you want, I can take books home to try to sell them in Minneapolis. It might help it to gain broader exposure," I said. "But whether or not I'm any good at selling them is another matter altogether." The guys were thrilled.

As we prepared to leave, John said, "Bring the money for the sold books on your next visit."

"You are trusting and very sure I will succeed," I said.

John chuckled. "You have your sister Clare's determination. Plus, I know where you live."

That evening, my mind wandered back to my conversation with Mike Pie. His unruffled attitude and determination had left a profound impression on me. His was the defining face of this injustice. The clarity in his words begged for the vindication of the others, and his dignified attitude toward those who had bullied him was astounding. "There's no love lost for those who did this to me, but I still see goodness in them," he had said. I admired his ability to forgive despite the abuse he'd suffered. There was a lot to be learned from this man and his deeply rooted beliefs, which caused me to reevaluate how I felt about those who had hurt me. I felt a definite connection between us.

Being involved in this cause meant standing up to bullies, which absolutely unnerved me. But it was a necessary step if I was ever going to fully work through the burdens of my past. I was grateful for the extraordinary circumstances that had led me to this place in time. Maybe my assistance could make a difference. In spite of the dismal circumstances, the prospect of becoming a part of this movement was exhilarating.

Chapter 4
EARNING A TITLE

After Thanksgiving, an array of thoughts invaded my mind—continued disbelief and the outright mistrust of our criminal justice system, sadness for the victims in this case, and admiration for those who stood in their defense. These thoughts increasingly fueled my determination as I tried to reckon with the horror of what had happened.

At the same time, I could not shake off feelings of self-doubt as I contemplated the box of fifteen books that John and Denis had sent home with me. I was unsure about my ability to sell them—about who would be interested or even have the time to read the 487 pages of highly detailed facts and data. I questioned who would believe the story, and I could not ignore my own conscience asking me, "What did you get yourself into this time?" Reactions from potential buyers about my inclination to label this death as a possible suicide nagged at me. This was a bold hypothesis considering that there were overbearing arguments in the book that leaned toward an alternative mill worker who may have murdered the victim. And people typically avoid the uncomfortable subject of suicide. They like to rationalize it away by saying that nobody in their right mind would take his own life in this specific manner. And while this is absolutely true, they neglect to consider that anyone with thoughts of suicide is never in a rational state of mind. The fact remained: numerous fellow mill workers who worked with and knew Monfils felt he was capable of ending his own life. Their arguments certainly seemed plausible.

I also found the title of the book troublesome. John had explained the use of the word *conspiracy* as a direct play on the prosecution's claims of a "union conspiracy to commit murder." No matter—it conjured images of paranoia, the wearing of tinfoil hats, and living in remote shacks in the wilderness. I also worried that others might dismiss this book as a defamation of our entire judicial system. However, in an age when police brutality, prosecutorial misconduct, and record-breaking numbers of exonerations fill news headlines, this criticism no longer sounds far-fetched. I eventually dismissed these concerns and focused on my commitment to civic duty. "This is not up for debate," I thought. "I will sell these books. I will find a way to help out. I said I would, so I shall. I will help to find justice for these men."

My husband listened patiently to my self-doubt. "While we were in Green Bay talking to the guys, it sure seemed like a no-brainer," I said to him one day. "But now I'm not so sure I can sell any of these books, let alone all of them."

Mike then talked me through my dilemma and offered a reasonable solution, as he always does, proving he understands me better than I do myself. He's intuitive about my moods, and he inspires me to forge ahead despite my periodic bouts of self-doubt. There was a time when he voiced his concern about my involvement in this mission because of the uphill battle it presented. He understood my tendency to become overly optimistic before I properly evaluate a situation. He also knew how disappointed I could be when I fail. But rather than dissuade me, he offered a warning laced with encouragement. "Changing the outcome of this situation may be harder than you think, but I know you'll find a way," he said.

An idea inspired by his thirty-five-year career in engineering kicked in. "Start small with friends and people at work," Mike said. "Build up from there." This advice motivated me to sell all fifteen books in one month. I acquired more books. They sold. It seems I had a knack for engaging people and persuading them with genuine compassion and unpretentious enthusiasm. I continued to pour similar energy into every sale, and in less than six months, I sold over one hundred books. Moral support increased. People cared and were reading the entire book. Conversations started at work, at company parties, and with friends. I even overheard my husband praising my efforts at various gatherings, which meant that his enthusiasm had intensified. He eventually helped out at fundraisers and traveled with me to the prisons to meet the five incarcerated men, all of whom graced him with gratitude for his sponsorship of my mission.

This surge in readership was acknowledged on a trip to John's house to pick up more books. John presented me with a box of business cards complete with my name and the title of midwest marketing director. I was delighted and surprised. "This recognition is a bit overstated for selling a few books," I quipped.

"You've earned it, and it's the least we can do since we're not paying you," John teased.

Chapter 5
FAMILY CONNECTIONS

U ntil the spring of 2015, I worked part-time as a packing assistant for Gentle Transitions, a Minnesota company founded in
1990 by Mercedes Gunderson. Mercedes had learned through
personal experience about the monumental challenges of having to
move one's parents out of the family home and into assisted living. Because of her ingenuity, an agency to help make that transition easier for
others was born. My employment lasted close to ten years, until my focus centered on this new calling. During my time at Gentle Transitions,
my bosses, Bill and Diane, and many coworkers were exceptionally supportive of my mission. They bought books, made monetary donations,
and participated in related events. Sometimes, they'd get caught up in
unexpected situations.

One of our larger jobs required the help of every employee, which
at that time was close to sixty, to transport an entire building of clients
from an old assisted-living facility to a brand new one. The individual
apartments were small, with each client occupying a space consisting
of a single room and bath. These were intense moves because of the
number of clients we worked with in a restrictive timeframe. Jobs of
this type were completed in as little as two to three days. Each of us was
assigned multiple clients, and on this particular day, my list included
packing up an apartment occupied by an older gentleman whom I will
never forget.

The man's room was filled with a large collection of memorabilia from the NFL's Green Bay Packers. Green and gold blankets, jerseys, and various trinkets were on his bed, on the furniture, on shelves, and hanging from door handles and walls. His obsession gave me the impression that he had more of a connection with Wisconsin than Minnesota. If that was true, maybe he knew of and remembered this case—unless, of course, he had relocated to Minnesota before it had happened. He was not in the room that day, but Tammy, my move manager, assured me that he'd be there the following day.

As predicted, the client was there with his daughter on the second day. I asked the daughter where they were from. "Green Bay," she said.

Her dad heard us talking and began reminiscing about his souvenirs. He then mentioned that he had a nephew who worked at a business in Green Bay that produced promotional videos for the Green Bay Packers. I immediately stopped what I was doing. "Are you talking about Mark Plopper?" I asked.

The client, looking quite surprised, nodded yes. "Do you know him?" he asked.

"I do," I said. "And you must also know who Mike Piaskowski is because they are related through marriage. I met Mark on one of my trips to Green Bay for an event. He likes wearing hats and dark sunglasses, and he belongs to a rock band with a cool name: Conscious Pilot. I'm also familiar with his place of employment called Made Ya Look."

In his response, the client used the same nickname John had used to refer to Mike Piaskowski. "Mark is my nephew, and he's married to Pie's sister, Christine," he replied. "We visit Pie whenever we go to Green Bay."

"It sure is a small world," I said. They expressed fondness for Mike Pie and gratitude for his release. Trying not to forget my packing duties, I worked furiously as I told them about my connection with Mark, Mike Pie, and the book.

"We heard about the book, but we don't have a copy," the client's daughter said. I shared how I had received mine.

The client left to have lunch with his daughter. I finished up in the old apartment and went over to unpack his belongings in the new space.

Nearly every surface was again covered with his treasures, save for one. The only thing missing was a copy of *The Monfils Conspiracy*. I retrieved one from my bag and placed it on the empty table next to the client's favorite chair. The black and red cover was a stark contrast to the sea of green and gold. I thought about the client's delight in finding it and of the hope it represented for the remaining five men.

On another occasion, I arrived at a job site early. As I waited inside for my coworkers to arrive, I scanned the list of resident names and apartment numbers on the wall in front of me. One name caught my eye—causing my heart to race. The name *Monfils* was on the list, and this person's apartment was in close proximity to the one we were scheduled to pack up. I wondered if there was a connection to the Monfils family in Green Bay. I'd have to mention this to Melissa, my move manager, and see if she'd allow me to ask the client about this. My anticipation grew as I explained the situation to my fellow coworkers while we neared the client's apartment.

The client and her son, who was also there to assist with the move, were gracious and cheerful. Before our tasks were assigned, I discreetly asked them if they knew the person next door. "Yes, I do," the woman offered. "I believe she is widowed. Why do you ask?"

Everyone there was curious. I promised to explain as soon as I returned. I ran to retrieve a book from my bag. I always had copies with me . . . just in case. Everyone gasped when they saw the same name on the cover. I shared the initial story and included details such as the involvement of the Wisconsin Innocence Project (WIP), the book having been coauthored by a scientist and researcher, and the potential connection between the victim and the client's neighbor.

Moments of silence passed before Melissa spoke up. "Well, I have to buy a book because my daughter just applied for a job at the Innocence Project here in Minnesota," she said.

The client's son shared his fascination as well. "I'm interested in reading what this scientist has written," he said. "I'm also a scientist by trade."

The client chimed in, "Well, I'm curious to know if the woman next door is related," she said. She grabbed her son's arm and said, "Let's go and ask!" They rushed next door. I stayed behind. By then, I was feeling anxious because of how adversarial this topic was for the Monfils family in Green Bay. I feared possible hostility from this woman.

I brushed aside those worries to focus on my assigned task. For a short while, the crumpling of paper and the whining of tape holders rippling across box seams were all that could be heard.

Soon, however, the client and her son rushed back into the apartment. With an unmistakable urgency in his voice, the son declared, "The neighbor *is* related to the victim, and she wants to talk to you," he said.

"She's very curious about the book, so go and wait for her in the hall, and bring one along," said his mother. Stunned, I glanced at Melissa, who excitedly gave me a thumbs-up.

Located in an alcove near the woman's apartment was a table and chair. I sat, sliding the book out of sight behind the table's centerpiece. "Let's not rush things," I thought. Tension in the air increased as the seconds ticked by.

The door to the elderly woman's apartment slowly opened. As she approached, I was captivated by the look of stern bewilderment on her face. "Are you Joan?" she asked.

I stood. "Yes, I am."

"I'm Lillian," she said as she offered her hand. As we shook, I hoped that she did not detect my nervousness. "My husband was Tom Monfils' uncle," she said. "But he is deceased now."

"I'm very sorry," I replied.

She went on to explain their situation. "We moved to Minnesota before the incident happened at the mill. There were *issues* between my husband and the rest of his family, which is why we left Wisconsin. We did not concern ourselves with the events following Tom's death, and I have not been back to Green Bay since my husband died," she said.

I felt sad for her apparent disconnect with the rest of the family and the loneliness she must have felt following her husband's absence. This revelation caused me shame. My concern for the five imprisoned men and their families had clouded my concern for the Monfils family. Lillian herself was not to blame for how I felt, as she directed no anger or ill will toward me. Instead, I heard genuine sincerity in her quest to learn more about what had happened. Her eagerness to reach beyond boundaries and to understand the opposing side of this tragedy was admirable. It was something I had failed to consider.

"I'd like to read the book," she said. "Do you have a copy I could buy?" I retrieved the book from the table and gave it to her. I insisted she accept it as a gift. "I can pay for it," she said, her tone sounding defiant, as though I had insulted her. Feeling rather foolish, I apologized once again. She left and returned with a twenty-dollar bill.

"My card is inside if you'd like to contact me when you are finished reading it," I said. "I'd be interested in hearing your thoughts." She promised to contact me, and I was delighted to receive this brief message soon thereafter in an email:

Date: Fri, 8 Jan 2010

> *We met when —— was moving out. I have finished* The Monfils Conspiracy *and have passed it on to my daughter. There is no doubt these men should be released. Please let me know where it all stands now and what is being accomplished. — L. Monfils*

Chapter 6
CHANCE MEETING

For an entire year, I successfully sold books, though interest was modest at best. Friends and coworkers remained consistent in their support. They'd ask for updates. They became much-appreciated cheerleaders during periods of doubt as to whether I or any of my fellow crusaders could make any headway. Most troubling was our inability to find anyone with a legal perspective to actually get involved. This was weighing heavily on my mind one afternoon during the summer of 2010 as I walked to the row of mailboxes at the end of our driveway. I grabbed the contents from ours and skimmed through what appeared to be junk mail.

As I headed back toward the house, I heard a vehicle pull up to where I'd been standing. I recognized the sound of the vehicle as belonging to my neighbor Ken's SUV. There was chatter coming from inside the cab, so I waved but kept on walking. This acknowledgment solicited a boisterous retort from a familiar voice. "Hey, Treppa!" I rolled my eyes in amusement. Ken's new friend Johnny was with him. I had met Johnny briefly prior to that day. He reminded me of Colm Meaney, the actor from the *Star Trek* series, with his round face and small, squinty eyes. Johnny did not have an impenetrable personality, but he was enigmatic and liked to show off his flamboyant side. Both he and Ken started harassing me, albeit in a fun sort of way, so I turned to face them, countering their attack with a quip or two of my own as I approached the vehicle.

Many of my conversations during the past year had focused on one thing—creating awareness through book sales. Today was no different. After some light banter, I redirected the conversation to focus on my mission. As I talked, a contemplative look appeared on Johnny's face. He sat there listening intently for some time before speaking. "You don't know what I did for thirty years, do you?" he asked.

"No," I said. "Why don't you tell me?"

He summarized his vast career in law enforcement, from being a police officer to heading up security at a racetrack to conducting high-profile investigations. His career was impressive . . . if it was to be believed. According to him, he knew a lot of famous lawyers and other notable figures in the legal field. Although his narrative sounded a bit embellished, I was mesmerized by every word. I, in turn, assumed that he might think *I* was the one overstating things. He indicated otherwise with his analysis of the good cop–bad cop dynamic. "I pride myself on being one of the good guys," he said. "But I know there are bad ones out there because I've worked with several."

The heat of the midday sun intensified. My mind raced and my heart skipped a beat as this exchange continued and his shift to a more serious demeanor rose to an almost uncomfortable level. Feeling somewhat unqualified to discuss legal matters on the same level as this supposed expert, I respectfully excused myself, but not before recapturing the playful teasing and emphasizing that I had better things to do than entertain the likes of them! The truth was that I needed to process our conversation. Ken pulled away and parked in his driveway. Before I entered the side door of my house, I turned one last time to see him and Johnny disappear around the back of Ken's house.

As I resumed my routine, a nagging feeling consumed my thoughts, compelling me to bring a book over to Johnny. Unable to dismiss this feeling, I grabbed one and hastened across the street. I knocked on Ken's back door. Seconds later, Johnny appeared. "What can I do you for?" he said in a tone as genuine as before.

"Because of your background, I'd like you to read this," I said. "I want to know what you think."

"How much?" he asked.

"I'm not charging you. Just take it," I replied.

He looked at the back cover, then retrieved the money from his wallet. "Here, take this," he said. "Give a book to someone who cannot afford it. I can afford it."

I didn't argue. I took the money and thanked him. "Call me. My card's inside," I said. I immediately hurried down the steps as tears threatened to reveal my gratitude at what my intuition was now telling me—that I had found a partner.

Chapter 7
A QUEST FOR ANSWERS

A semicircle driveway winds around the front of our house, allowing visitors to drive right up to the front door. Large floor-to-ceiling windows make up the entire west wall of the dining room and run parallel to the driveway, making it easy to spot any activity.

About a week after the encounter with Ken and Johnny, I heard a vehicle pull up. "Must be a mail delivery," I thought. I peeked around the doorway of the kitchen. From my vantage point, I could see the back end of a red pickup. I heard a door slam shut. The doorbell then chimed multiple times. I finally spied the culprit who by then had begun banging on the large windows. It took a moment to realize it was Johnny. I thought he'd gone crazy. His eyes bulged from their sockets when he spotted me. He motioned furiously for me to open the door. I wondered what was up. Although he was frantic about something, I ascertained it was safe to let him in.

As he entered, Johnny held up the Monfils book. He was beside himself and appeared rather disgusted. "I went through this book three times," he scoffed. "I read it the first time. I then studied it a second time. I went through it for a third time with a fine-tooth comb. Now I want answers!" I was speechless. He continued before I could utter a word. "I've worked more homicide cases than I can count, and there's something very suspicious about this one! Where's the evidence that the investigator supposedly found? I couldn't find any! And where the hell are the witnesses to the bubbler confrontation?" he demanded. By then, his voice was high-pitched and agitated. I thought he might pop one of the veins now visible in his neck. He drew imaginary diagrams on my wall. "I'm trying to decipher where these guys were standing while this tape was being played and where they were supposed to be during the so-called confrontation," he said. "Time is connected to distance, which is connected to the probability of these men having time to commit this act! There are too many critical details missing from this book."

My voice sounded weak, given the volume of his tirade, as I did my best to share my limited knowledge of the technical aspects. The layout of the mill, the location of the men, and the restructured timeline were beyond my aptitude. "The authors who wrote the book are better equipped to answer your questions," I said. "I can ask them to make a special trip here if you'd like to discuss the broader details with them. I'm sure they'd be willing to meet and give you more definitive answers."

My words seemed to fall on deaf ears as Johnny resumed his outburst. "I need to do some research," he said. "You and I are going to have to investigate. We are going to have to go to Green Bay." And as though the idea had originated with him, he said, "Set up a meeting. I want to meet those authors. Oh, and make sure you invite the guy who was exonerated." Before he left, he looked directly at me and uttered with authoritative urgency, "Set it up soon. And keep me informed of when they are coming. We need to get going on this."

Out the door he went, waving as he sped off. I stood in silence, my mouth agape and head spinning. But excitement also stirred inside me as I marveled at what had happened. "Wow," I thought. "Wait till the guys hear about this!"

Chapter 8
FORMING A FELLOWSHIP

Denis, John, and Mike Pie were thrilled when I told them about Johnny. They bombarded me with questions like, "What did you say this guy does?" "You met him where?" "He wants to have a meeting . . . with us?" As expected, they were so eager to meet Johnny that they quickly adjusted their schedules to spend an entire weekend here in Minnesota.

It felt like forever, but the weekend finally arrived. On Friday morning, I was a busy bee in the kitchen. "You're awful chipper this morning," Mike said.

I whisked over, threw my arms around him, and laughed, citing an earlier conversation between us. "I know you think I should tone down the excitement, but I can't help it," I said. "I think good things will happen this weekend. I can feel it. Besides, they have to—for the sake of the mission that has been stagnant for the past year. We need a jump start before this fizzles altogether. This meeting with Johnny may be our lucky break."

Deep down, I was certain great things were coming our way. It felt like a premonition—a prediction on steroids. I relished those moments as they were rare at that early stage. This connection was too necessary to risk losing. Having someone like Johnny in the picture could boost our efforts greatly. And as my dear husband looked out for his vigorously animated wife, she searched for something greater than her. Something greater than life itself. Something meaningful to fill an empty void from the past.

Standing in the room where Johnny and I had held our first "pow-wow," as per Johnny's words, I reflected on the events of the past year. I had lost count of how many books we all had sold or given away in desperate attempts to provoke interest. Copies to politicians, lawyers, and news outlets like *48 Hours* had produced no results. The disappointments surpassed the victories by a wide margin. Now there was ample reason to be hopeful.

Johnny and I were one and the same. "Go for the gusto" was a mantra we both shared. As I got to know him, I felt an unstoppable force between us. We were effective partners thanks to our diverse talents. Johnny could lead us straight to an interested and able attorney, and I could be the persuasive and inspiring one to seal the deal. After seeing Johnny's reaction on the day he first showed up, I could see that this injustice had gotten under his skin like it had mine. My hunch told me that there was no way on earth he'd be satisfied until he was fully engaged and reinvestigating this case. That's what I was going to help him with. We were going to break this case wide open and expose the corruption, the trickery, and the deceit of the people who had perpetrated this injustice. The crusaders—the ordinary citizens intent on vindicating the innocent, the wrongly accused, and the bullied—would remain under the radar and in the shadows to save the day! And no one would be the wiser, until it was too late.

I was jolted back to reality when the phone rang. The guys would be on the road from Wisconsin soon. The drive from Green Bay to our house in Blaine, Minnesota, took about five hours if you stopped for lunch, so they estimated an arrival time of late afternoon. Before resuming my chores, I allowed myself a few more moments of reflection. "The potential for this alliance is infinite, and there will be no stopping us," I thought. "We will open doors." It all sounded so romantic. How naïve of me to think it could be that easy.

That afternoon, Johnny was the first to arrive. He reiterated his impressions of this case. "Inserting myself into this wrongful-conviction stuff is a new avenue for me," he said. "My entire career has focused on making sure the bad guys are locked up. There's irony in the direction I'm heading. But from what I gather, these men are not the bad guys. It troubles me that they were convicted with no tangible proof of guilt. I keep asking myself, where's the element of reasonable doubt?" He was resolute. "I am convinced—*convinced*—that the authorities not only allowed this to happen but made it happen," he said. "These men were not given a fair shake when they were deprived of their own separate trials. If details were overlooked, ignored, and even altered, it left the jury to decide the fate of these men with insufficient and perjured information. That is not how our system is supposed to work. As an investigator, I was never personally involved in illegal dealings, but that doesn't mean I was never pressured into doing so."

This last statement was something that Johnny had alluded to earlier. It said volumes about our legal system and why Johnny was so agitated. He knew that corruption was not unheard of, and he seemed to believe that it was rampant in this case. I also suspected that he was troubled because he had not been there to stop it from happening. Given Johnny's background, his disdain for how this case had been handled was refreshing and a relief. Since I first learned about it, I had believed that the case was rife with corruption. Having someone with his experience and expertise agree with me was self-affirming and gratifying. I was proud to be bridging this connection between him and the guys, and I felt it was reasonable to think Johnny could help us.

Denis, John, and Mike Pie pulled up in John's black SUV. As they piled out, they looked road-weary but cheerful. Each time I saw them, I was reminded of how this mission wore on them emotionally and physically but also of how they refused to let it suppress their enthusiasm. We all agreed with Denis' tenacious analysis, "Let's see where this takes us."

Johnny introduced himself when they walked in. His attention soon zeroed in on the hat Mike Pie was wearing, which revealed he had served in the US Army. Johnny was an army veteran too, which gave them plenty to talk about. They soon realized that they had served in a similar area in Vietnam. "Assisting veterans is what I do," Johnny said that day. For a brief time, Johnny had assisted my neighbor, Ken, with veteran's concerns. It is why I ran into him at my mailbox, and it was why I had the opportunity to ask for his help. There was no mistaking the bond already forming between Johnny and Mike Pie or the opportunity that this instance presented—Johnny's ability to aid this veteran in his personal mission.

The guys grabbed their belongings and settled in while I set out refreshments. We soon relaxed in each other's company, engaging in small talk. I rolled my eyes more than once at their mischievous wise-cracks and trivial jokes. For the first time in years, I appreciated having grown up with brothers. It was a relief when the dialogue finally turned serious.

John reminisced about wading through piles of documentation, police reports, and witness testimony to put together a more accurate timeline. "It's vastly different than the timeline put forth by the police," said John. "Theirs was fabricated to fit their theory of when the murder occurred. When you look at how much actual time it would take to confront Monfils with the tape, to beat him up, to drag his body off to the vat, to dump it in, and then to clean themselves up along with the entire bubbler area before going back to work . . . well, it was simply impossible to have done all of that in the time they said—and without anyone seeing something. Besides, there was no consideration given to the paper break that occurred during that same timeframe," he said. "Zakowski was hell-bent on trickery. He figured that as long as there was reasonable doubt about their innocence, he could convict them. It's a trick many prosecutors use."

There was talk of the investigation. Mike Pie described his thoughts of the day he was arrested. "They blew it all out of proportion," he said. "They sensationalized it. It was over-the-top and only for show."

Denis talked about how quickly the jury had rushed to judgment. "Eight hours of deliberations hardly seems acceptable to interpret the evidence and then decide the fate of six mill workers," he said.

The slant of the sun infiltrating the west-facing windows signaled the approaching dinner hour. "Guys, Mike will be home soon," I said. "Johnny, why don't you pick up your wife, Linda, and come back here for dinner. I'd like for us to continue our conversation." I proceeded to warm the meal I'd prepared earlier.

Linda's bubbly personality filled the air shortly after Mike walked in. Her cheerful presence and robust laughter never failed to lighten the mood and, oddly enough, conjure Johnny's sentimental side. So, when we gathered at the dinner table, Johnny motioned for us to raise our glasses. "I pledge my allegiance to this new partnership with you fine people and to lend my assistance in any way I can," he said. "The oath I took many years ago is my solemn word to work diligently and effectively alongside you in this quest for justice." He sure could lay it on thick sometimes, but the mood was ripe, and given our immediate dilemma, his assurances were readily embraced.

That evening Johnny said, "I want to be clear about one thing. I absolutely loathe those in the legal community who defame their oath of office. It annoys me that persons whom I will leave unnamed would crave attention to the point of complete disrespect to citizens and to civic duty. This case represents the worst of any I have ever investigated. Illegally obtaining any conviction is criminal in and of itself, and it has no place in our judicial system."

That night, I lay in bed, too excited to sleep but mindful not to disturb my slumbering husband. It felt good to be promoting something meaningful and important. As I relived the activities of the evening, I thought about each of our guests and their unique perspectives toward this injustice.

In the bedroom next to ours was Mike Pie, an exoneree who had been deemed a murderer and union thug. To me, he was a trusted friend who had seen firsthand the horrors of war in Vietnam, only to return home to experience the injustice of being falsely accused and imprisoned. He had every right to be angry because even though he had been exonerated, he was forever tied to these circumstances. During his time in prison, his conduct had been exemplary. Ever since his release, he had remained steadfast as a kind and forgiving soul intent on correcting an inexcusable injustice.

Mike Pie could have looked the other way and left this nightmare far behind, but he chose to devote himself to the cause until the other five men were free. These were not the actions of a criminal. In fact, as a result of being exonerated, Mike Pie could literally have said anything he wanted to about the case. He could claim he did it without consequence because he can no longer legally be retried for this crime. However, his only intent has been to put forth nothing but the truth.

In the front bedroom was an author with three books under his belt. Denis' determination and selflessness in promoting this one were commendable. He involved himself as emcee in any and all events, no matter how busy his life became. This mission coincided and sometimes took precedence over his current activities of teaching journalism, acting as family-coordinator at the Oneida Nation High School, and bailing hay for his horses. We'd get an earful about how busy he was, but his belief in the innocence of these men had compelled him to prioritize the task of writing the Monfils book, a feat requiring eight years of diligence. His involvement was unwavering, and my house became his second home as we collaborated further. "That's my bedroom whenever I stay here, right?" he would ask. "The bed is really comfortable. Helps me sleep like a baby."

Tucked away upstairs was John, a staunch supporter of all six men. But John's love for Mike Pie stretched beyond the unfairness of this situation, and he'd become emotional each time he reiterated the integrity of his former brother-in-law. John's ability to recall and recite intricate details on demand amazed me. "Zakowski said in his opening remarks that if you want adequate details, you're going to be disappointed. Then, in his closing remarks, he said something never addressed during the entire trial when he told the jury that Mike Piaskowski was the one who got the rope and the weight that was used. It's preposterous! You can't introduce something that was not addressed during the trial," said John. "But none of the defense attorneys spoke up because it is considered rude to interrupt during closing arguments." His knowledge was limitless and his enthusiasm contagious. "With Johnny on board, there is nothing we cannot accomplish," he had said. And his charm was ever-present. "With you supplying us with such wonderful meals and a cozy setting, how can we fail?" He never missed an opportunity to break a solemn mood by reciting some silly joke. But when he needed to be, he could be as serious and as sharp as a hawk eyeing its prey.

I observed Johnny closely that evening. He pursed his lips and sat in his chair with a slight shrug here and sudden shift there, saying nothing as details poured out of the three men. I felt it was an inability to find the appropriate words to convey his utter disgust for the deception exacted on these innocents, a deception that he believed should have been circumvented. I understood his thoughts because he had shared them on many occasions while exhibiting the same body language. Watching him react to a myriad of malfeasance reminded me of something Ken had warned me against when Johnny and I had begun to collaborate. "Don't ever lie to Johnny or let him find out that you did because there will be hell to pay. He hates liars."

Throughout our activities, Johnny was hell-bent on discovering the truths that would bring justice to these men and restore the kind of integrity he expected within our judicial system. He swore he'd make damned sure that the authorities who had imprisoned these men would not get away with it. Listening to him gave me the sense that he'd succeed.

Saturday morning's aroma of brewed coffee summoned an early riser. John appeared in the kitchen. As I poured coffee, he shared his observations on the previous evening. "That was an invigorating conversation with Johnny," he said. "He sure seems to know what he is talking about. You did good when you found him. He'll be a great asset. He's even fun to be around." Hearing this from John and receiving similar praises from Denis and Mike Pie never failed to boost my spirits and self-confidence. I felt I was making a significant contribution to this mission. This meant more to me than they would ever know.

Thirty-plus years ago, when my husband, Mike, met me, he met a woman who felt ordinary and insecure. I was on public assistance with a nine-year-old son. I didn't know how to cook or manage money, and I was afraid of attempting anything other than menial, low-paying jobs. I never felt smart, even after earning an associate degree from college. I was a stereotypical small-town girl who had grown up poor, voiceless, struggling to matter, and in need of constant affirmation. Mike was the best thing that happened to my son and me. Thanks to his insight regarding my potential and his extraordinary patience, we had become an emotionally strong family. I felt better equipped to take risks, to use my talents to get a good job, to manage the household finances, to cook scrumptious meals, and, eventually, to manage a successful small business. But in order to feel truly complete, there was more I needed to accomplish. The Monfils case became a cause that filled a void created by bullying. I was learning to put respect for myself before the fear of what others might think while putting the concerns of others before my own. Being treated as an equal by these scholars was therapeutic and helped me to further escape my own perceived limits.

Johnny and Linda showed up midmorning. Everyone gathered in the dining room with coffee mugs full and spirits high in anticipation of our second round of talks. This day was spent discussing the contents of a list of one hundred case-related items Johnny felt needed to be further investigated.

"There are criteria that must be met in any investigation," Johnny explained. "I see this case as unresolved because of the lack of evidence. I'm all about the evidence because I'm an investigator. I go to a crime scene and let the evidence speak to me. That is how I determine what occurred—by collecting and then studying the evidence. This idea seems to have been disregarded in the original investigation. The authorities were not looking for evidence of what happened. They were looking for anything to pin a murder on these guys, to close the case, and to cover up their mistake of releasing the tape. Having said that, I want to know more about what evidence there is. I want to find out how it was collected and packaged and where it was and is stored. When items are sent to a lab for analysis, they must be handled in a certain way. But according to what you've told me, there's no actual evidence reflective of a murder. That's why I'm here. I need to find this out for myself, and the only way to do that is to get involved."

Johnny fueled this mission. He became our guiding light. He understood the challenges we were up against, and he was way ahead of us as he went over the list of factors he had deemed most important. "I've already started an online search for specific documentation related to the case that is accessible to the public," he said. "From there, I need to visit the police department, obtain and read the trial transcripts, interview witnesses who were at the mill that day, and find out what role the fire department played. This information is vital and is what we will need to give to an attorney once we find one."

During the meeting, we addressed basic strategies to create more awareness in Minneapolis. "This topic is still a sore spot in Green Bay," Denis said. "We need to focus our efforts here in the Twin Cities, away from the barrage of rhetoric in Green Bay. This book is our main avenue for spreading the word, so distribution is essential."

"The people I've sold books to so far are tremendously supportive," I said. "We should keep the momentum going." Everyone agreed, and we decided to schedule a series of book events in Minneapolis in the near future. "The holiday season is about five months away. Now is the time to plan and grab the attention of early holiday shoppers," I said. "Johnny and I will see what we can do to find appropriate venues."

We parted ways that weekend with a sense of accomplishment. And as Johnny and I worked on possible book events, he privately absorbed infinite details about the case.

Chapter 9
RALLYING THE TROOPS

The next few months were intense with activity. Because of the numerous trips all of us took back and forth along Interstate 94 and Highway 29, we started referring to Highway 29—the stretch of secondary highway between Interstate 94 and Green Bay—as "Freedom Highway." The title commemorated that stretch as the location of the Stanley Correctional Institution where Dale Basten and Michael Johnson were housed at the time.

In addition to securing venues for book signings and organizing a book club meeting at a large church in Minneapolis, there was talk among us of an outdoor event that would be held in the heart of Downtown Green Bay at the courthouse where the trial had taken place. Due to the notorious nature of this case and the amount of misinformation still being circulated, it made sense to flood the community with facts. We felt that a public rally was an effective way to broadcast more accurate information and at the same time appeal to and embolden those in the community who had supported the innocence of these men in more subtle ways in the past. One major priority was to find a way to conduct ourselves appropriately to counterbalance any and all negative perceptions. Our intent to convey these specific convictions as faulty or intentional was not going to bode well in a community steeped in years of rhetoric from law enforcement and the county attorney's office, and we considered the possibility that our efforts could invoke aggressive opposition. My personal attitude was "bring it on." This could invite media coverage, which was the primary intent.

I asked Johnny for guidance. He was all about action. "You and I, we're cut from the same cloth," Johnny assured me. But I was unsure if these actions were too antagonistic. He disagreed and said, "Go for it. Let your presence be known but keep things low-key and peaceful. Don't break any laws or give them a reason to arrest you."

I asked John Gaie to share his thoughts. According to him, an event similar to this had already been discussed among family members but was never acted upon. "We should do this," I urged. I shared Johnny's feedback with John.

John agreed and said, "Let me talk to the others." John was great for gauging the reactions of the families. Both he and Denis held the most influence because of their obvious commitment to this cause. John did not disappoint when he offered to set up a conference call that included John, Denis, Mike Pie, and Joan Van Houten.

Joan is the stepdaughter of Michael Johnson and a staunch defender of his innocence. Unsuccessful in her efforts to hire an attorney after the trial to further assist their family, Joan became discouraged. Her family was shunned as they dealt with unique struggles. Joan's mother, Kim, is from Korea, where she gave birth to Joan. The language barrier Kim experienced back then had made it difficult for her to understand what was happening to her husband. His conviction had also forced her to seek employment, making her the sole breadwinner of the family. And as with the other families, the circumstances led to extreme hopelessness.

John said of Joan, "Her ability to bounce back is amazing. She's a great resource for ideas and a good representative for the families." I hoped her involvement in this event could help her to heal and to beckon action among the other family members.

This was my first encounter with a family member of the convicted mill workers. I was nervous and wary that my assertiveness might be seen as arrogant or inconsiderate. But during the call, I learned how like-minded Joan and I were. She was and is candid but respectful. Her anger emerges but is never misdirected. "It's time to stop talking," Joan had said. "I'm tired of doing nothing when we have nothing to lose. We've already lost so much and too many years since our men were sent to prison." She expressed deep gratitude for all we had done, and she was ready to take this leap with us.

"Let's challenge the apathy in this community," I said.

Joan predicted a moderate crowd at best. "This situation is still very painful and very real for us," she explained. "As much as we want justice, this will be a hard first step for many, but it's one I'm willing to take."

I stressed the urgency to act quickly and to hold the rally on October 28, 2010. This was the exact date of the 1995 trial when the six guilty verdicts were delivered. "Let's not wait another year," I said. "The time is now." The end of our discussion brought a unanimous vote to commence our first "Walk for Truth and Justice."

Joan's inclination to vindicate her stepfather and to expedite his return home influenced her decision to endorse this event. It also motivated her to form a select group in Green Bay known as Family and Friends of Six Innocent Men (FAF). The group met regularly to plan the rally and discuss ways to fundraise. It was a good way for them to stay connected. This group defined whether events succeeded or failed because of how it encouraged involvement.

Chapter 10
UNEXPECTED RECOGNITION

In the late summer of 2010, I was on my way to Green Bay to attend a meeting at John's house to plan the rally. While driving, my thoughts were focused on our latest efforts—or lack thereof—as they often were while traveling on Freedom Highway. I wondered what the future held for this mission in lieu of our shortcomings. Aside from book signings, book sales, and simply spreading the word, the bottom line was that legal help was still beyond our grasp. I felt desperate. Johnny was on edge from getting the same response over and over from every attorney he encountered—that it was much too difficult and too costly for a small law firm to fund the overturning of one conviction, let alone five.

When I joined this fight, I had been naïve about many things. I saw a flawed case. I was outraged. I assumed that any reasonable person would be too. Fifteen years had passed, but the same level of apathy persisted. Nothing had changed despite the authors' efforts to shift public opinion. The loudest critics were hateful and uninterested in considering the facts presented in the book. It was hurtful to hear them criticize our efforts and dismiss us as lunatics. I struggled with my faith in humanity and the ability to convince them how misguided they had been and still were.

During these upsets, Clare kept my spirits up. "Joan, you *are* making a difference by giving the families hope." But I didn't feel it. It felt more like providing a platform for the cynics. It was hard for me to swallow the flood of negative comments. I could only imagine the impact this turmoil might be having on these already humiliated families. I knew I could handle the pressure, but what about them? I imagined it made their blood boil to hear insults aimed at their men. Comments like "rot in hell" or "they are exactly where they belong" dominated social media sites in response to more recent news stories. Labels such as "con artist," "liberal fanatic," and "wacko" were eventually aimed at me. I was told to stay home and mind my own business. I felt like I had traveled back in time to my old grade school, only these attacks were especially mean-spirited. The ignorance angered me, but this time, it wasn't going to get the best of me. What they thought of me was their business. I was not about to back into a corner and cower. Instead, my determination allowed me to push back even harder in a constructive way. This time, the bullies would get no satisfaction from belittling me.

An influx of unsavory opinions from the past regurgitated at every turn, and was fueled by predictable reactions from those within the Brown County District Attorney's Office, who persistently cited the book as complete fiction. Law enforcement officials collectively adhered to the same notion, confirming John's evaluation of the bond within the Green Bay criminal justice community. I was appalled at the continual barrage of misleading and untrue fallacies in their narrative. It was time for the families to have their say and to be heard. This rally was the perfect platform to make that happen, to stand with them, and to support their objectives. I would be living proof that these victims were not alone and that their side of the story had merit. It was one thing to dismiss the opinions of the families. Of course, they'd plead the innocence of their loved ones. But it was another matter altogether to have someone completely unrelated to them or the situation who staunchly supported them.

After arriving at Clare's house and sharing my usual rant, she cheered me on. I then drove to John's, committed to making this rally count. He greeted me in the usual manner with that big grin of his and a glass of wine. For some reason, he was in an especially cheerful mood. He excused himself with a wink and went into his office. He returned with a sheet of paper. Handing it to me, he said, "Have you seen this?

Denis just wrote it about an amazing woman that we're affiliated with."
I wondered whom he was talking about until I started to read it.

> *Tue, 20 July 2010*
> **One Woman's Story—Can You Help as She Has?**
> *Written by Denis Gullickson*
>
> *Thanks to the response of a number of you to last week's information release, we wanted to bring you the story of Joan Treppa, who was referenced in a couple of places in that release. Joan is an example to all of us of the kind of power one impassioned person can make on behalf of a cause—in this case, the cause of justice and freedom for five innocent men who remain incarcerated in Wisconsin prisons . . .*

The letter listed accomplishments I had sponsored. More importantly, it confirmed Clare's assertions about the real concerns of the family members. They were not preoccupied with opinions from the general public or even about immediate solutions. They felt empowered and significant. The general message was evident—that how they felt was partly due to my efforts. I was deeply touched by what I deemed a premature gesture because of how far we still were from resolving this conflict. But the generosity, the hope, and the firm belief in the prevalence of true justice radiated from this collective appreciation. It was all that mattered to me from then on.

While writing this book, a good friend, Jennifer Thompson, shared an affirmation she had heard from her father's lips right before he died. He had said, "Jennifer, the last thing to go is hope." To me, this speaks to the immeasurable resilience I've witnessed in these Wisconsin folks.

Chapter 11
VALUABLE INSIGHT

Johnny and I managed to set up a somewhat promising book signing on August 21, 2010, at a large and well-patronized shopping mall in Roseville, Minnesota, called Rosedale Mall. We were given a decent spot, and mall management supplied tables, chairs, and the manpower to set them up. All we had to do was show up and inspire. The event was listed on the mall website. Prior to that day, we had passed out 4x6 announcement cards in nearby coffee shops, bookstores, and other public places to ensure the success of this event.

John, Denis, and Mike Pie attended. Mike and Linda sat among the modest audience made up of our closest friends and family members. To outsiders, it looked like we had a decent turnout. The mall was bustling with shoppers, but there was one problem—we had forgotten to order a sound system.

The place was loud, and the acoustics were terrible. When I made the introductions, my voice didn't carry well, and no one beyond our immediate area could hear me. The guys prompted me to continue. Shoppers passed by in large numbers but kept walking with hardly a glance in our direction. If they did look, it was more out of curiosity than genuine interest. I saw empathy on the faces of those who sat there watching a presentation that felt excruciatingly uncomfortable to me.

In contrast, those in attendance heard an animated and amplified intensity from the guys as they spoke. No matter the circumstance, they gave all they had. They were skilled and well-versed in stating their case for innocence. Their enthusiasm for telling this important story did not weaken, even in front of this meager audience. To them, each platform available to us was vital. Their passion washed over the crowd like a tidal wave, with their voices rising to a deafening crescendo over the white noise, reaching those standing on the balcony above. This was what they did, and it was extraordinary to witness.

This heart-wrenching presentation should have compelled pass-ersby to stop dead in their tracks. Two of them did. Still, I felt deeply discouraged about us being largely ignored. I had the opportunity to give a speech of my own, but I could not muster that same enthusiasm to give one. The guys later explained their philosophy toward these so-called failures. "This is a small glitch in the overall scheme of things and an opportunity to improve on technique and delivery," said Denis. "But next time," he added, "let's pay closer attention to details, such as re-membering to bring the sound system, shall we?"

After the presentation, a schoolteacher approached a table where books were laid out for purchase. She looked at the cost and then at each of the guys. "I'm very touched by what I heard today," she said. "This is such a tragedy. Thank you for being here. I may be interested in purchasing books for a class I'm teaching, but I'm not sure I can af-ford them. I'll have to check my budget allowance and contact you later." Unfortunately, we did not hear from her.

Another person also spoke with the guys. "I'm dismayed about what you told us, and I feel bad for the people whose lives were de-stroyed," he said. "I didn't know something like this could happen. I'd like to buy a book and keep up with your progress." As he walked away, he said, "I'll be sure to share this with my friends."

Both of these individuals had come, stayed awhile, and walked away with a new perspective, as did I that day. Theirs was in reference to a tragedy. Mine was another lesson in humility—the fact that others may not care about things dear to our hearts, even when we believe they should. It only takes one or two individuals to make something happen, and we will never know the extent of the impact our presentation had on either of them. But after thinking about the event and my specific role, how had I not seen this? Both of them had exhibited empathy and, in hindsight, were representative of a growing number of supporters we encountered over time. This experience caused me to realize how valuable each event is and that awareness is a culmination of many events and experiences. Even when only one book sells, knowledge can still travel far—as it may have done in that crowded mall on that busy Saturday afternoon.

Chapter 12
PEN PALS

A year into this mission, I started to write to the men in prison. Johnny and I both felt that it was time to introduce ourselves. They'd most likely heard about us, and we felt compelled to contact them directly. It was December, so the obvious way to break the ice was to send a Christmas card to each one. This sounded practical enough, until I found myself standing in the card shop trying to decide on an appropriate greeting. Exactly how does one send holiday wishes to someone in prison for a crime they did not commit? How are they supposed to have a Merry Christmas? What if our festive cards came across as insensitive or hollow? Nothing about this journey was ever easy. I eventually decided on cards with adequate inscriptions and included handwritten notes explaining our objectives and who we were.

I clarified our mission to aid in their eventual release. I wrote about how we could not be so easily explained away like family members with vested interests. I closed with a precarious statement—a promise to stay involved for however long it took. I added a disclaimer about possible failure but countered it with lots of enthusiasm. As I put pen to paper, thoughts of how we might accomplish this miracle eluded me, but it seemed counterproductive and premature to share such thoughts at that early stage. The overall message was simple and positive—we're here, we care, and we will not abandon you. In the weeks following, reply letters arrived. We were apprehensive about what they might contain. Not knowing what to expect, we anticipated negative rants and cynicism. This was not what we found.

The first response came from Dale Basten. He sent a card that read "Thinking of You." His brief written message revealed gratitude for our thoughtfulness but indirectly contained a mountain of loneliness. He said, "Thank you, ma'am, for the mail. It's the right time of year to get it." Dale had taped an old photo of himself to the inside of the card. The caption explained that it had been taken shortly after he had started working at the mill in 1961. It was the face of a handsome young man. I recalled reading about Dale's family life in the Monfils book. When he was convicted, Dale had been a proud husband and family man with a devoted wife and two young daughters. This photo represented a dreadful reminder of a happier time before the troubles began, valuable time wasting away with him behind bars, and an ideal existence shattered into a million pieces. Future letters from Dale were full of kind aspirations for my longevity and a place for me in heaven. Dale's letter was the first, but many more would arrive from all of the men in the years to come.

All of the letters that arrived had similar messages. They were powerful testaments to an injustice that had caused sorrow, pain, and the loneliness of being separated from loved ones. As letters traveled back and forth, Johnny, Mike, and I absorbed information about the men and about prison life. For the men, they became a lifeline to the outside world and a newsletter of sorts about ongoing activities. They also became a sounding board for the men to share their personal thoughts. Even when little was happening or when *I* felt depressed, writing to them became my way of staying focused and positive. I filled the pages with encouragement, asking them to never give up or succumb to the belief that nothing could change. Many times, those words benefited me also. As inadequate as some of my messages may have sounded to me, the men expressed how reassuring they were to them. The letters conveyed a renewed belief in themselves, in humanity, and in the concept of eventual freedom. It was a relief to me when I could write about legal activities that eventually came about, giving real substance to my optimism.

As our correspondence continued, an emotional connection to the men was established. They slowly became part of our extended family. My life was less about me and more about their struggles. The things I had faced seemed insignificant compared to what they had endured. I couldn't imagine being separated from everything and everyone I loved because society was punishing me for something I hadn't done. The isolation they were experiencing was always on my mind, and I started to make comparisons between my life and theirs. Enjoying picnics, parties, dining out, or seeing a movie were things I took for granted but were things they could only dream about. I could choose to spend time with family during holidays, weddings, or funerals, but they could not. Helping a loved one get through an illness, a pregnancy, or even a simple homework assignment were things they missed. In essence, I was present. They were absent. Privileges for them were minimal or a thing of the past. I felt guilty about their inability to experience the freedoms I had. So I held on to the one thing that served as our direct connection and kept me focused on my commitment to them—the anguish of being bullied.

I sent blog posts that I had begun to write along with photos of our events—anything permitting them to visualize the outside world that was so foreign to them now. More recent letters to them were filled with a flurry of activities and the vast amount of interest that was being generated through our efforts. I did my best to see my entire existence through their eyes, simply to gain an appreciation of what they had suffered. In a mere moment in time, their lives were altered, and for some reason, it had happened to them instead of me. Still, they focused on the positive and expressed their gratitude that their existence mattered and that many strangers cared.

Chapter 13
UNSUNG VICTIMS

About a month prior to our first Walk for Truth and Justice in 2010, Johnny and I traveled to Green Bay to meet with family members and close friends of the men. I wanted a better understanding of who these people were. I also wanted to know how they felt about the publicity that would likely develop because of our event. On our drive there, we talked about what their reactions to us might be. "Why would they trust us?" said Johnny. "They don't know us from a hill of beans." Though I agreed with him, we were both wrong. We could never have foreseen the atmosphere we encountered soon after we arrived.

Denis worked at the Oneida Nation High School and was able to set up the meeting in their lunchroom. We arrived early at its location just off of Highway 172, east of the Green Bay city limits. As we carried in a large box, we were met by a handful of people, including John, Mike, and Denis. We placed it on a side table for later when it would be time to reveal its contents. Before long, the room was filled with a considerable amount of people. Johnny and I found ourselves overwhelmed with curious stares and greetings. While we had expected resistance and mistrust, we were instead met with uncensored emotion coming from adult children and grandchildren who struggled with having a loved one still in prison, wives who continued to defend their husbands' innocence, and sisters missing their brothers. It was heartbreaking but comforting to see the camaraderie of goodwill and support among them. Gratitude toward us was evident through affectionate hugs, smiles, handshakes, and tears. Our presence mattered to them. It was humbling to witness a silent minority of those who had experienced more abandonment and betrayal than anyone ever should.

Although they shared a common plight, we learned of their reluctance to socialize with each other on a regular basis, of those who could not bear to be reminded of the struggles they had collectively endured, and of the heartache that was still unbearably raw. Many who wanted to avoid the risk of getting their hopes up were absent. Those who came saw value in attending but understood the uphill battle yet to be fought. We offered no guarantee that things would change, but we hoped they regarded our participation as a reason to believe in possibilities.

We met Joan Van Houten in person. She hugged us both as though we were the best of friends. With tears in her eyes, she introduced us to her daughter, Tiffany. Tif was good-natured and appeared mature beyond her years, as was evident by the defiance in her eyes. One could assume a young age of twenty-two would make it difficult to understand the situation. Not with Tif. She was far from typical for her age. She had no illusions about the dismal realities of an unjust system. And she was not alone.

We spoke with Keith Kutska's daughter-in-law, Brenda Kutska, and her three children, Kelsey, Katie, and Matthew. Brenda was bubbly and talkative. "Their dad, Clayton, is at work, so he couldn't be here," she said. "This is Matthew. He's the youngest, and he was not born yet when the case happened. Our twin daughters, Kelsey and Katie, were babies when their grandfather, Keith, was convicted."

The girls, timid and shy, were overcome with emotion as Brenda talked about them not knowing their grandfather outside of prison. I recalled the photo in the Monfils book of Keith holding both of them as babies. Brenda revealed troubling details. "Clayton and I were twenty-two years old, and this should've been the happiest time in our lives. We were newly married and starting our family when the trial was looming before us. Keith's wife received nasty phone calls and letters while other people wanted to befriend her to find out information about the case. It was very hard," she said.

Everyone we met appreciated our concern. Laughter and tears surfaced again and again as they openly shared their experiences and misfortunes. Their faces conveyed deep loss and a desperate lack of hope. But they had managed to survive without harboring extreme negative reactions to things that they had no control over. Even though they experienced grief every single day of their existence, they did their best to live normal lives. They loved, respected, and cherished these men above all else. It was heartbreaking and shameful that no one had come to their aid before now.

Denis instructed everyone to take a seat. Half of the rows were soon occupied. Johnny and I waited as Denis gave a detailed summary of the many activities we had pursued in Minneapolis. All eyes then turned to us when it was our turn to speak.

Denis introduced me first. The apprehension I felt then was partly because I'd never considered myself much of a speaker. This was compounded by the more daunting thought of addressing a roomful of people who'd heard it all before—promises, reassurances, and predictions made by shysters who had taken every last dime and given them nothing in return. However clumsily my presentation may have come across, I did my best to at least sound genuine. The main focus of my message was our commitment to increasing the chances of finding legal help for the men by broadening the geographical area of awareness. "We cannot predict what will happen, but I feel we have a better shot if we continue to spread the word in Minneapolis," I said. "I'm truly sorry for what has happened to all of you. I had no idea these things happen to such good people. It's not right, nor is it fair, and for those reasons alone, we want to help." I talked about the support we had already summoned in Minneapolis. I then pointed to the box we had brought in earlier, which held a multitude of candles Johnny and I had collected from friends for the upcoming Walk. "These candles represent real support in Minneapolis. They will light a new path for us that will become brighter as we move forward," I said. I focused on my reasoning for the Walk. I referred to it as a new chapter in this fight for freedom and a reawakening for those who'd like to see us fail. "This is far from over," I said. "This is only the beginning of what we can do to bring this case back into the forefront." I asked for more of their patience that day and expressed my gratitude for their attendance. And I said a silent prayer that our efforts could produce the results that they urgently deserved.

Johnny spoke next. He was more adept at addressing a crowd and appeared relaxed as he talked about the legal aspects of the case. I was proud of his reassurances to them of his strong commitment to get to the truth and to eventually find legal assistance. "In every case, there's some detail that surfaces that can change the whole direction of an investigation," he said. "I know it's there. It just hasn't come to light yet. But it will."

He also impressed upon them the difficulties involved in pursuing this particular case because of how much time had passed, how poorly it was investigated, and the risk of evidence having been mishandled, tampered with, or lost altogether. "There is no DNA that we know of because no evidence was collected at the crime scene," he said. "That's unfortunate, but it does not mean we will not find something to prove these men are innocent. If it's there to find, I will find it."

The clarity in our speeches turned intense scrutiny among the crowd to brighter and more tranquil gazes. Reluctance to embrace our enthusiasm softened as they appeared accepting of the possibilities. But they still had reservations about attending the Walk. Then, Johnny spoke volumes in his message to them. "It's time for the public to hear you, to see your pain—your anger—and to know the extent of how this tragedy has destroyed your lives," he said. "You are the unsung victims. You have been silenced with no one to support you." Two strangers were now giving them ample reason to once again hope for absolution.

In the time that followed and as Johnny's knowledge of this case increased, so did his cynicism. Often in reference to the Monfils case, the attitude "you can't make this stuff up" became the mantra of him and many other advocates of the six men. Johnny attributed his involvement to when he and I had met. "You reminded me of an ordinary housewife type, someone's mother or sister," he had told me more than once. "I saw merit in what you were trying to do. I am glad you appeared at the right time and place to help open my eyes. The Monfils book captured my investigative curiosity, which prompted me to read it multiple times." To this day, Johnny still shakes his head. "How could this prosecutor convict six innocent people?"

When we went to Green Bay to start a fact-finding operation, what Johnny discovered was a trail of deceit and fraud that led straight to the

Green Bay Police Department and the Brown County DA. His assessment confirmed that there was no physical evidence, no crime scene, no witnesses—only false statements camouflaged as evidence secured through police threats and intimidation.

The fabrication of a perceived truth took a toll on Johnny over time as law enforcement colleagues and friends labeled him a "turncoat" for standing by his well-informed understanding that this case was corrupt. It became a defining moment in his life as he became more aware that the oath of office he stood for had been tarnished by fellow officers who'd taken that same oath.

On our drive home, Johnny and I marveled at the experience of meeting the families. We also realized the uphill battle we faced. "It was too easy to make promises to them," I said. "We've got our work cut out for us if we're going to get this done."

Johnny replied, "Don't worry, Joan. We have resources and options. I still have people I can tap into. You and I will get this done."

I reluctantly agreed as I recalled the many rejections Johnny had continued to receive from lawyers. Seeing the pain in the eyes of the young adults at this meeting caused more urgency and a greater sense of obligation. Johnny sounded confident, but I could not dismiss a simmering sense of uncertainty about how we were going to pull this off. I felt inadequate and undeserving of their trust but even more determined than ever to never let them down.

Chapter 14
UNIFIED VOICES

The headline in the December 19, 2010, Green Bay *Press-Gazette* story read:

Friends and Families of 6 Convicted in Paper Mill Worker Tom Monfils' Death Form Truth in Conviction Group—'Conspiracy' Book Bolsters Mission

It started as a book proclaiming the innocence of the men convicted of the 1992 murder of Tom Monfils in a Green Bay paper mill. The book, The Monfils Conspiracy: The Conviction of Six Innocent Men, *helped bring together the friends and families (FAF) of the five men still in prison and the sixth man, Mike Piaskowski, who was freed in 2001 when a federal judge overturned his conviction. Now those friends and families and Piaskowski are hoping their unified voices will help spread the book's message, free the remaining five, and perhaps have an even wider impact on the criminal justice system.*

This was the first time that the community had heard about the formation of the FAF support group. The idea to formally organize was significant in light of the skepticism Johnny and I had witnessed at the meeting at the Oneida Nation High School.

The monthly FAF meetings were being held in Allouez, Wisconsin, at the home of Shirley DeLorme, a retired English teacher. When Shirley learned about the latest activities in this case, she realized that Michael Hirn, one of the six convicted men, had been in her speech class at De Pere High School years ago. Shirley's son had also shared with her his experience of having worked with Mike Pie and his unyielding defense of Pie's character when he had declared, "Mom, that man is no murderer!" Shirley offered to host the FAF meetings in her home, where she had served sandwiches, homemade Sloppy Joes, and fudge to her guests in the past as they engaged in planning fundraisers, fall rallies, and discussions about latest developments. It was at Shirley's house where we organized our first Walk for Truth and Justice.

Johnny was absent on the evening of our first Walk. He wanted to maintain a low profile because of his investigative probing. I was glad to have Clare with me to help calm my anxiety. I was concerned about how this would play out, if enough people were going to show up, or if we might encounter angry bystanders. I felt good about having created the renewed interest but inept at projecting confidence and strong leadership during this event. My certainty about wanting to help was equal to my uncertainty of how to be inspiring. Having been thrust out of my comfort zone and into the limelight, it truly was a relief when Denis offered to take the lead that evening. It was inspiring to witness his ability to exude confidence. Maybe someday I'd become more like him and overcome my fears. For now, I was happy just to get through this first event.

We met in the parking lot of St. Willebrord's Church near the courthouse in Downtown Green Bay. Mike Pie and John arrived earlier than Denis, who, no doubt, had a litany of personal commitments to work through before making his appearance. We knew and appreciated how Denis thrived on an insanely full schedule and how truly fortunate we were to have his participation for any event. I scanned the parking lot and saw a modest semblance of supporters. People I hadn't yet met were among a crowd of close to thirty people—a crowd indicative of fifteen years of futility. It struck me that a painful wound was being ripped open. I felt that this group made up the toughest and most courageous of the souls who carried this heavy burden.

I met Kim Johnson, Michael Johnson's wife and Joan Van Houten's mother, for the first time. Kim and Michael are the only couple among the "Monfils Six" who are still legally married. Use of the English language remains challenging for Kim, and her strong accent is hard for many to understand. She explained to me the reason why she had not been at the Oneida School meeting. "I don't live in Green Bay, and I work odd hours," she said. "But I wanted to be here tonight." I recall the sad, resigned tone in her voice when I asked her about life without Mike. "You know, you just go on, and you take care of those still at home. You make the best of the situation," she said. This made me realize that sometimes giving up the fight can almost come as a relief—or become a coping mechanism in a hopeless situation. She reminded me of a delicate porcelain doll, and I was consumed by the urge to reach over and support her tiny frame.

In 2016, I acquired some of the original Green Bay *Press-Gazette* newspapers from 1993–95 containing articles about the ongoing case. I came across one describing Kim and her immediate reaction following the verdicts on October 28, 1995. The Sunday, October 29, edition read, "Mike Johnson's wife, Kim Johnson, nearly had to be carried from the courtroom. She sobbed on the courthouse steps as her daughter, Dawn, held her." This had happened where we now gathered—on the same date as in 1995. It must have felt surreal to Kim and to those present who had experienced that fateful day. My words of comfort to Kim felt shallow. What did I know of the horrors she was reliving? Who was I to mess with the fragility of these individuals, forcing them to relive this nightmare? I had no clue of the courage it took for them to show up. I had pushed for this, but was it the best decision for them? Did they truly want this? Did they see merit in what I was trying to accomplish? Worse yet, were they just going along simply to appease me? "This had better count for something," I thought, "because I see no alternative." I had to believe that this rally was only the beginning of exposing the truth about this appalling injustice.

Byron Lichstein, an attorney for the Wisconsin Innocence Project (WIP), drove up from Madison to participate. Denis had invited him because of his current involvement in the case. Byron was representing Rey Moore in a post-conviction hearing that focused on James Gilliam, the jailhouse snitch who had testified against Rey at the original trial. Turns out, Gilliam had recanted his original testimony in an interview with John and Denis, as well as University of Wisconsin law students working at the WIP. This recantation prompted more recent legal action and was considered a last-ditch effort to help Rey.

I'd heard good things about Byron—that he was honest, caring, and a fighter for justice. When he arrived, I introduced myself. Byron was approachable and friendly, his smile cheerful and welcoming, and his words flattering when he told me, "I've heard about you." In his speech that evening, one phrase of his spoke volumes. "Persistence and determination will be the deciding factor to move this case forward," he said. He was optimistic and encouraging even though he knew all too well the obstacles faced when dealing with the Monfils case. His words provided great comfort and have stayed at the forefront of everything we try to accomplish.

Denis eloquently addressed the crowd, which included reporters from all four major news networks in Green Bay. He led with a compassionate and uplifting speech. "We're here tonight to commemorate six innocent men, five of whom remain behind bars," he began. "But just as Michael Piaskowski was released, we will continue to fight for the release of the other five men as well. There has been a groundswell of activity occurring within this community and in Minneapolis following the publication of our book, and we are optimistic about future possibilities."

Denis asked Mike Pie and me to also say a few words. I kept my message simple, reiterating my belief in the innocence of all the men and my commitment to stay involved in this mission and never give up or accept defeat, no matter what.

Mike Pie again hammered home his unwavering stance. "Whatever happened to Tom happened somewhere else, at the hands of someone

else, in some other way," he said. "What they said happened, did not."
Our voices echoed off of the courthouse steps, throughout the courtyard, and onto the stone walls of the building directly behind us that
contained the very bureaucrats who voiced their opposition to our efforts at every turn.

Denis then initiated a march around the block. We held homemade
cardboard signs that read, "Six Innocent Men," listed the names of each
of the wrongfully convicted men, or displayed suggestive phrases like,
"The authorities got it wrong!" In our hands, we cradled the now-lit do-
nated candles that had been fed through the bottoms of paper cups de-
signed to catch the hot wax and shield delicate flames from wind gusts.
The media followed alongside us as we left the courtyard and headed
north. We walked past the DA's office and stopped, chanting the names
of all five men and proclaiming, "Not guilty!" We continued around the
corner to the church entrance, where we paused to place seven candles
displaying photos of the six convicted men and Tom Monfils. At that
exact moment, the steeple bells chimed six times. We stared at each
other in awe of the implication that this event was being sanctioned by
unforeseen forces.

As the candles flickered, Denis recited a prayer. Afterward, we fell
silent. This moment was emotional—a shared bond to comfort heavy
hearts and to affirm our commitment to truth and justice. We then
marched on. Around the corner was our final stop in front of the police
department. We again paused to deliver our loudest chant. It felt good
to shout, to unload this burden, to scold. We poured all we had into a
final shout-out before turning the last corner and walking back to
where we had begun. This event was peaceful, powerful, and perfect.
The media witnessed deep emotion from anguished families and close
supporters of these men who had never been given the opportunity to
convey the level of suffering they had suppressed. Theirs were the
words that led on the evening's newscasts.

Byron, Mike Pie, Denis, and Joan were interviewed. Denis encouraged the media to get a statement from me, but I declined. This moment
belonged to those closest to this tragedy. They needed to have their say
and to have their pleas acknowledged by this community. They

demanded that the authorities own up to what they had done, a request that was long overdue.

Joan was courageous. She didn't shy away from the cameras. She stood firm, voicing an unrelenting and unapologetic appeal. "We will continue to fight for our men until we have no fight left in us," she said as tears flowed.

Mike Pie further stated, "By jailing the wrong people, justice was not served for our families or for the family of Tom Monfils."

Denis made his own provocative statement. "This grave injustice still hangs over the entire community like a dark cloud," he said. "Make no mistake: we will not rest until every last one of these men is released."

Byron spoke of the need to "acknowledge the system makes mistakes, and then work to correct those mistakes." Our intention to correct this injustice was made clear to a community long torn apart by controversy and opposing viewpoints.

Our group disbanded after the walk, but many of us gathered at a nearby restaurant to reminisce. For me, this event established a deeper connection with these folks than ever before. My commitment to stay involved became more resolute, and my fear of upsetting their lives dissipated. This rally had stayed positive, and we'd sent an important message of hope borne out of tribulation. We'd told the community that this travesty had not been forgotten and that we were proud to stand firm in our support for six innocent men.

The story led on each of the Green Bay news channels later that night. It also headlined on most stations the following morning. Voices silenced for too many years were broadcast loud and clear across the airwaves. Unfortunately, accompanying them were less savory opinions by the authorities themselves, who continued to defend their actions. Many naysayers masking themselves online behind social media pseudonyms also spewed hateful and uninformed rhetoric, mimicking outdated attitudes from long ago. Nonetheless, this event signaled to those within the legal community who continued to back their convictions that this long-forgotten case was shifting toward a new rebirth.

The courthouse steps that had once symbolized immeasurable pain and sorrow now signified positive energy for the families victimized by this tragedy. Thanks to inspiring leaders and exonerees in the years that followed, this place and these annual Walks for Truth and Justice became our platform of public defiance where all were free to speak out, to publicize announcements, and to broadcast new developments. In 2012, we unveiled the interest of a major law firm in Minneapolis. In 2014, the first in a series of legal motions was publicized. Hopeful letters from the men have been read there. Generous donations from people in the Minneapolis area have been delivered to the FAF group. Most importantly, this event serves as an annual reminder for a community more inclined to dismiss the realities of this grave injustice.

After each of these events took place, I thought of how fate had brought me to this place and time and how everything I had experienced had allowed me to accept this mission. Having a larger purpose had helped me to overcome many of my deficiencies and imperfections by accepting them and moving on to more pressing concerns. Taking a stand and believing in something teaches us that people will either love or hate us. In fact, we learn it is those who care the least who display the most contempt. But believing in oneself and dismissing those who try to tear us down only empowers us to find the strength to withstand adversity.

Chapter 15
TESTIMONIALS AND VISIONS

In acknowledgment of a well-known phrase, "The heart knows truth before the brain," my heart continued to compel me to promote John and Denis' book. This path ultimately led to an opportunity at a large congregational church in Minneapolis called Mount Olivet Lutheran Church. Mount Olivet is recognized for numerous community-based outreach programs including elder care, a children's camp, and counseling services. Its parishioners also participate in a monthly book club. Being asked to appear at a book club event at this church was appealing to us because it guaranteed readership, unlike events we had tried in the past.

This event was set up through Melissa, one of the move managers at Gentle Transitions. After reading the Monfils book, she offered to approach her book club at the church. "I think the club members would be interested in reading this book," she said.

"If you can convince them to add this to the agenda, I'm certain I can persuade the authors and the exoneree, Mike Pie, to show up for a later discussion," I said.

Melissa confirmed the book's approval. "I asked Michele, the church librarian, to contact you to work out the details for the discussion meeting," she said. A date was set, books were purchased, and the authors, Mike Pie, and Joan Van Houten made plans to attend.

The drive for those coming from Green Bay on the day of the event via Freedom Highway was taking longer than expected due to the rush-hour traffic they had encountered as they entered the city. I was too energized to care if they were a little late because Joan was with them this time. By then, she was president of the FAF group and was eager to represent the members during this trip. I was excited for Joan, and I had a feeling she'd do well in this setting. I respected how she never had minced words when speaking about her stepfather's conviction and how effective she was at reaching those in an audience setting. In her delivery, there was unmistakable sincerity and deep emotion conveyed through her words. "The more you know about this case and what was done, allowed, and accepted by the authorities, the more frightening the reality becomes," she would tell the audience at the church. "There were many gross and intentional lies coming from them . . . and nobody stopped them." What fell on deaf ears in Green Bay became widely embraced in Minneapolis.

Seven of us entered a small room at the church. Johnny's wife, Linda, accompanied us and sat in the audience. Michele directed the rest of us to sit in the semicircle of chairs provided. I closely observed the gathering of about twenty people, mostly women. They were scattered throughout the seating area as they focused their attention on us. This many participants came as a pleasant surprise. They waited patiently as Michele addressed them. "Let's give our guests a warm welcome, shall we?" Their clapping created a hospitable atmosphere.

A few of my coworkers were there also. Candee was not a member of the church, but she had read the book and was one of my most enthusiastic supporters. Barb was a church member who supported this cause as well. I didn't see Melissa but learned afterward that she had had a conflict that evening. I felt bad for her because of her role in making this event possible.

I was in charge of making the introductions. After sharing a little about each person, Denis then took over. He gave a brief synopsis of the case and addressed the crowd. "Since you all read the book, rather than us providing additional details, why don't you ask questions and lead the direction of our discussion?"

Mike Pie was asked a question. "Could you describe the events leading up to the victim's death and explain what your life was like both in prison and since your exoneration?" As Mike Pie spoke, it brought back memories of the day I had met him. My initial fear of offending him with my ignorance seemed silly now. He was not the type to discredit or show disrespect for anyone, no matter the level of understanding about his circumstances. Mike Pie was his usual relaxed and genial self that evening.

Joan was asked, "How has this affected you as a family member of the accused, and what effect has it had on your entire family?"

Joan became emotional as she talked about the fear and humiliation of having accusatory fingers pointed at her family. "We didn't know how the system worked," she said. "We were thrown into a situation foreign to us. We were law-abiding citizens who knew nothing about what was happening. We trusted our attorneys and the system. Because we knew Big Mike (a nickname Joan used to distinguish her stepfather from her stepbrother, Michael) was innocent, we didn't expect he would get convicted. But it didn't matter how we felt. The overall opinion within our community was that he was guilty."

The time flew by, and our session ran well over the usual two-hour limit. It was getting late, and Michele moved to end the meeting. Rather than leave, however, the audience gathered around and expressed dismay at the injustice. There were hugs and handshakes. Paula, one of the women in attendance, was particularly inspired by our presentation. She promised to take action on our behalf. "I'm going to write to *Dateline* and tell them about this case," she said. Michele offered to facilitate an exchange of contact information between us.

Mike Pie and Joan received many praises for their courage and resilience. Joan's face spoke volumes. What I had hoped for was happening. She was allowing herself to trust strangers and embrace their sincere appreciation of what she had faced since the trial. In this setting, she was finding something she had lost long ago—an ability to believe in others' acceptance of her pain.

Back at our house following the event, Joan reiterated her gratitude for this opportunity and for the welcomed reception from the attendees. She expressed readiness for whatever was next on the agenda. She also shared something that her stepfather had written and sent to her some time ago. It was his testament of a vision he had had and could not dismiss. It serves as a guiding light for the calling I've been chosen to pursue.

The vision in Big Mike's own words:

> *I spent approximately eight months in Brown County Jail. While I was in county jail waiting for the jury to return its verdict is when the Lord gave me this vision. This [was] a very stressful time in my life, having been stripped of everything that was dear to my life. I believe the Lord was comforting me with this vision. The vision was in a time in the future, and I did not yet understand it. I believed at the time it was of the Rapture. It was ten years before I correctly understood the vision. It began with me walking amid rubble. As I looked down, I wondered why I wasn't being cut or hurt by what I was walking on. The presence that was with me said: "It is because I am guiding your feet." I then looked up and it was a summer day. The grass was green and the sky was blue with puffy white clouds. Before me was a blacktop road with a woman running on it up to a control tower screaming and waving her arms in the air. Then I looked up and the clouds were rolled away and Jesus was looking down at me and was smiling. This vision was of the institution I am currently incarcerated in (Stanley Correctional Institution), yet this institution had not yet been built at the time I had this vision. I believe this woman was running to the authorities with some kind of information, the truth about the Thomas Monfils murder. I was reminded that a woman holds the Scales of Justice in front of the courthouse.*

My next question, "This is about you, isn't it?" begged for clarification.

As Joan spoke, the implication became crystal clear. "Big Mike and I talked about this vision many times," she said. "Both of us always felt the woman in the dream was me because of my self-proclaimed mission to help free him. There was never any question of that. Not until recently. Now both Big Mike and I firmly believe the woman is not me. We don't think it ever was. We believe you are and always have been that person." At that moment, time stood still. Silently I rationalized this to mean I had been chosen to further the mission until I found the next person who could bring it to the next level. I surmised that Johnny was this person and that he and I were the ones who would be handing it over to the next one in line.

The following week, I received this email from Michele, who had sent it on behalf of the entire book club:

> Sent: Monday, October 18, 2010
> Subject: Thank you
>
> *Hello Denis, John, Mike, Joan, Johnny, and Joan:*
> *I just wanted to thank all of you again for coming to talk at our Church Book Club meeting last Wednesday night. We appreciated you taking the time to share your story with all of us, and we look forward to hearing that justice has been served and the remaining five men are free.*
>
> *Listed below is the email address for Paula that Denis and John requested. I spoke with Paula on Sunday, and she has already begun writing her letter to Dateline. Also, I noticed that* The Monfils Conspiracy *is not available for checkout at any library in Minnesota, so I have suggested to several book club members that they put in a request at their local library that this book be added to their collection.*
>
> *Take Care and God Bless.*
> *Thanks again,*
> *Chelle*
> *Michele*
> Librarian

Letters were written to *Dateline*, but no replies were received. And requests to add the book to library shelves went unfulfilled. However, in 2016, we were contacted by a producer at Peacock Productions, an NBC subsidiary, due to the buzz created by the Steven Avery wrongful-conviction case from Manitowoc, Wisconsin—a city located just forty-five minutes from Green Bay. Interviews were conducted, and the Monfils case was finally going to have national exposure on a show called *Deadline: Crime with Tamron Hall*. The segment aired on Sunday, June 12, 2016.

Additional book events in the Minneapolis area failed miserably despite our most sincere efforts. However, not all had been lost. Prior to one event, I'd performed an online search and found the website for the Innocence Project of Minnesota, which, as of 2020, is recognized as the Great North Innocence Project (GN-IP). This is the organization Melissa had mentioned at work. Its mission appeared to be about aiding the wrongfully convicted, which was the essence of what we were trying to do. I had sent an email inviting them to our events and was pleasantly surprised when I received a welcoming reply from the current legal director, Julie Jonas. Julie thanked me for the invitation and said she would do her best to attend. Unfortunately, we did not meet her at that time due to unforeseen circumstances. But this brief encounter represented a vital connection that we would be able to revisit at a later date.

For the time being, we pursued a more direct approach to reach key legislators, senators, and representatives in Wisconsin who had the power to initiate critical legal actions in this case. Johnny's insight provided an ample number of fact-based details that we could take to Madison, Wisconsin—a more progressive area of the state—to generate the kind of interest that might unlock doors typically beyond the reach of crusaders like us.

Chapter 16
FISCAL APPEAL

Our new agenda became a targeted letter-writing campaign. One specific letter I wrote was sent to the then Attorney General of the State of Wisconsin, Mr. J.B. Van Hollen. I expressed my angst about the case, pointed out its most alarming flaws, and suggested an urgent reinvestigation. I also appealed to his fiscal side by addressing the costs of housing a single prisoner per year and the unnecessary expenditures burdening the State by continuing to incarcerate five innocent people. Based on current data and location, the annual taxpayer costs can range from $30,000 per prisoner to $60,000. Given these figures, the cumulative costs incurred from incarcerating these men since 1995 are staggering, and the unnecessary incarceration of innocent people across the board, simply put, causes an unnecessary increase in state taxes.

In the letter, my stance was clear: "In the long run, it will cost the State dearly by the time this is really over," and, "Be aware that it will most likely take some time before we find the right people to take action, but we are searching diligently, and we will find the one person that will do something."

Within weeks, I received this response from Mr. Gregory M. Weber, the assistant attorney general and director of the Criminal Appeals Unit of Wisconsin. It reflects a typical attitude of those in positions of power who prefer to play politics rather than take seriously a possible err in the criminal justice sector:

December 17, 2010
Dear Ms. Treppa,

Thank you for your letter to our office regarding the 1992 murder of Thomas Monfils, the subsequent criminal prosecution in Brown County, and the recent publication of a book about these events. I serve as Director of the Wisconsin Department of Justice's Criminal Appeals Unit.

As you know, multiple courts have reviewed the case and confirmed the guilt of all but one of the men originally prosecuted and convicted. One of those men, Reynold Moore, has an appeal pending in the Wisconsin Court of Appeals. If the remaining men believe they have viable legal challenges to their convictions, they remain free to bring those challenges in the appropriate courts.

Sincerely,
Gregory M. Weber
Assistant Attorney General
Director, Criminal Appeals Unit

I was more annoyed than anything to have my efforts so flippantly dismissed. I wrote back to Mr. Weber to express my displeasure. The letter, written more for my benefit than his, remained dignified. In it, I highlighted a remark he had made that infuriated me, when he had referred to "the guilt of all but one of the men." I reiterated the significance of Mike Pie's exoneration and my resentment toward his attitude. I resisted revealing my deepest wishes—how I longed for the day when he and Van Hollen would be forced to witness the eventual freedom granted to these men. I wanted them to experience discomfort as news reports revealed full exonerations for all the men, and I wanted it to happen on their watch. To my dismay, this was not meant to be.

In January 2015, Van Hollen was replaced by Brad Schimel, the new attorney general, who also refuted any new findings in this case. In a Green Bay *Press-Gazette* news article from May 2016, Schimel argued that the new evidence is "so flimsy and unconvincing that no reasonable jury could have seriously entertained any doubt that he [Monfils] was murdered."

No second response was forthcoming from Weber, who was also replaced in 2015, but I was content to have received his first. My letter was acknowledged. My voice was heard. And though it wasn't nearly as satisfying as receiving a positive response, what I did receive is all any of us can hope for. Furthermore, because my letter is in their permanent records, anyone who holds the office knows *someone* is paying attention.

In addition to correspondence sent out to media outlets, newspapers, philanthropists, online organizations, and radio personalities in Wisconsin, we widened our range to include Minnesota. We received a small number of replies, but none that opened potential doors. Few had an appetite for this cause, and we found ourselves in limbo once again. We were discouraged and weary . . . again. Book sales diminished, and we felt the sting of impending doom . . . again.

I highlight these low points in our mission to illustrate the constant frustration of every wrongfully convicted person fighting for his or her deserved freedom. As Johnny and I talked about these letdowns, always in the back of our minds was the relief that it was not our immediate loved ones we were fighting for. Being able to step back and keep things in perspective for that reason alone was extremely helpful to us. We did still have plenty of added worries through all of this. For instance, what effect was the latest failure having on the families and the men? Was each letdown another enormous blow, or was it business as usual for them? Did it lessen their hope? Did it solidify a belief that their situation may never change? Letters from the men always said otherwise— that they would never lose faith in us, in possible freedom, or in the very real hope we had provided. As troubled and disenfranchised as we'd become, deep down, we believed in these people, and we never tired of doing what we could to help them.

Johnny and I spent a fair amount of time sulking in my family room, where we'd rack our brains looking for any new ideas. We'd sit in silence and stare into our cups of green tea as though we'd find answers there. And as luck would have it, we would soon find another avenue to pursue.

Chapter 17
THE MADISON ATTORNEY

"This case probably represents the greatest travesty of
injustice in Wisconsin history" — Ed Garvey

Johnny and I continued to engage in activities with John, Denis, and Mike Pie, hoping to find ourselves in the right place at the right time with someone willing to help us. While these thoughts were purely wishful thinking at this stage, one major event came our way that triggered optimism. And we were given a rare opportunity to meet the event's founder, who happened to be based in Madison.

Denis had an ongoing rapport with Ed Garvey—a well-known and respected attorney with political connections. In 1986, Ed had been the Democratic nominee in Wisconsin for US Senate. In 1998, he had been the Democratic nominee for Wisconsin Governor. Ed had been in the legal field for decades, and he had connections that could further our cause. According to Denis, Garvey was an outspoken supporter of the Monfils defendants. In fact, the brochures we tucked inside each book included the above-mentioned quote.

We met with Ed at his office shortly after Johnny joined the group. Denis wanted Ed to meet Johnny to hear his latest findings. This meeting was also a way for us to discuss future actions regarding our mission.

We entered the modest office building where Ed's practice was located. The friendly receptionist on the second floor was expecting us. "Mr. Garvey will be with you momentarily," she said. "Please make yourself comfortable in the conference room."

The cozy room was furnished with a large wooden table and chairs in the center and a tired old couch pushed up against the wall. Upon entering, Johnny and I were immediately drawn to a portrait hanging on the far wall. We stared, mesmerized by an almost life-sized image of Paul Wellstone, the late Minnesota Senator who was known as a progressive Democrat and was often a lone voice that stood firm against status-quo policies on both sides of the aisle. Wellstone had died in a plane crash alongside his wife, Sheila, and one of their daughters on October 25, 2002, while campaigning for a third term as senator. The incident had happened eight years prior to the day we visited Ed's office and, although the painting reignited memories of the horrific deaths, its presence gave Johnny and me a good feeling about meeting this attorney.

Ed appeared and greeted us enthusiastically as he joined us at the table. His white hair and seasoned face revealed years of experience as a practicing lawyer.

Johnny spoke to him first and explained his impressions of the case based on what we had discovered. "For my own level of comfort, I did my own mini-investigation," he said. "Joan and I visited the GBPD, and I conducted private interviews with witnesses. I then compiled an entire case file. My conclusions as a former detective are as follows: this case is full of corruption. I'm convinced it was a community conviction involving the police, the prosecutor, and the news media all working in collusion to seal the fate of these men. My biggest concern is the lack of evidence, and I am dismayed at the absurdity of Mike Pie having been the only one released to date." He gestured to Mike Pie. "Look at him. He served his time in Vietnam only to come back and serve time unlawfully in prison. I submit to you that what he experienced in prison equates to being on active military duty in relation to having post-traumatic stress disorder."

"That's very true," Mike Pie agreed.

For the majority of the meeting, I remained quiet. Having earned the respect of my colleagues, both as an outsider and a woman, I conceded to them as the experts, knowing that I was still learning. Besides, my perspective leaned more toward how this had affected the families on an emotional level following the convictions. At some point during the discussion, Ed turned to me and said, "Why don't you share how you feel about all of this and what compelled you to get involved."

I collected my thoughts and replied, "I was bullied as a child, and this entire situation boils down to bullying on an enormous scale. It disgusts me to know that others have been treated this way and that the bullying continues as innocent men waste away in prison. I share the sense of duty you've witnessed among this group today to get the men out of prison and reunite them with their families. I choose to be here and to be a part of this unified voice for them."

Ed nodded and said, "Thank you. That is quite commendable." He listened for a long time to what everyone had to say. He then scanned the room and said, "Well, what do you want me to do? I can contact some people I know to see if they can help. I cannot promise anything, but I can certainly try. If you'd like, I'll see to it that there's a space reserved for you at the next Fighting Bob Fest."

"That would be great," said John.

"That could allow us to put books directly in the hands of public officials," said Denis.

Our meeting ended. We felt grateful for Ed's assistance. His pledge to make phone calls on our behalf had begun, even before we left his office. "Keep me informed of any news, and stay in touch," he said. "And I'll let you know about Fighting Bob."

As we left Ed's office, I was overcome with curiosity. I had to ask, "What's a Fighting Bob?"

Chapter 18
A FIGHTING CHANCE

This truncated press release announced our first Fighting Bob Fest event and depicted our ongoing enthusiasm despite discouraging setbacks:

FOR IMMEDIATE RELEASE:

Lakewood, Wisconsin – September 7, 2010 – Authors, Experts, and Activists Will Gather at Fighting Bob Fest

Denis Gullickson and John Gaie, authors of The Monfils Conspiracy, *will be promoting their book and the innocence of Dale Basten, Mike Hirn, Mike Johnson, Keith Kutska, and Rey Moore at an annual gathering of progressive activists this coming Saturday, September 11, in Baraboo, Wisconsin.*

Along with exoneree Mike Piaskowski, Midwest Marketing Director Joan Treppa, and crime scene expert Johnny Johnson, Gullickson and Gaie will be talking to progressives at the Sauk County Fairgrounds. Keynote speakers at the event will include Rev. Jesse Jackson, Tammy Baldwin, Jim Hightower, David Obey, Mike McCabe, and others.

"This will give us an opportunity to take our cause to the progressives from throughout the state and the

Midwest," said Gullickson. It also gives us a chance to support Ed Garvey, who has become very involved in our cause."

Garvey, a highly respected Madison attorney and political activist, is the founding force behind Fighting Bob Fest. The Fest is an annual political event that has grown from 1,000 attendees in 2001 to over 8,000 in 2009. In July, Gullickson, Gaie, Piaskowski, Treppa, and Johnson met with Garvey to explore avenues for pushing for new trials or the outright release of the five men who remain incarcerated in Wisconsin prisons. Garvey—who serves as emcee for the event—will be plugging the book and the cause from the stage throughout the day.

"At the very least, we intend to hand a book directly to the main keynote speaker, Rev. Jesse Jackson," said Gaie. "Rey Moore was a delegate for him when he ran for president. We've had a pretty successful summer expanding our circle through Ed Garvey. If we can get this person involved, we can take our efforts to the next level."

According to the event's website, Fighting Bob Fest is "an old-fashioned Chautauqua" named in honor of "Wisconsin's most famous hell-raiser, Fighting Bob La Follette. La Follette fought for democracy and economic fairness; he busted trusts, railed against the robber barons' control over the political system, called for open primaries, workers' compensation, and unemployment insurance. He thought people and ideas should rule instead of Big Money."

The potential to participate in this event was a step up from sending letters or mailing books, many of which were most likely shelved or ignored altogether. Having a booth could land books in the hands of politicians and activists alike, and the potential to forge deep connections with them was a distinct possibility. Ed's generosity afforded us a significant new avenue of support.

Clare came along for a specific reason. She and I anticipated an encounter with the Rev. Jesse Jackson. We planned to engage him by sharing an important connection of his with the Monfils case. Clare was the bridge linking the two. In a letter to Clare in 2010, Rey had shared these words about delegating for Rev. Jackson during his 1988 presidential campaign:

> When we were on strike at Nicollet Paper, he [Jackson] came to a rally I organized and spoke at the Brown County Arena. While we were on stage together, he also took my cap and never gave it back. I worked throughout the 8th district to get out the vote for Rev. Jackson. I was with him in Oshkosh onstage with other workers in the campaign. I also helped organize a rally at St. Norbert College. I emceed both this rally and the one at the Brown County Arena. His advanced person stayed in my home. As I said before, I would have been a regular delegate, but Paul Tsongas had a person he wanted at the convention, so my spot was taken and I became an alternate, but I never stopped working. I am hoping Rev. Jackson will get involved.

All of Rey's past kindness to Clare was going to be compensated on this day through a rare opportunity to speak on his behalf to this political figure. To make sure Jackson understood Rey's current plight, Clare and I formulated a simple plan—to literally stop Jackson in his tracks so that Clare could explain Rey's dilemma and hopefully tap into Jackson's emotional spirit. All we needed was a small window of opportunity.

We grabbed a bite to eat while waiting for Jackson's arrival. As we finished, Clare declared excitedly, "Joan, come on! There he is! Let's grab the book and get into position!"

I jumped up in time to see three black sedans in succession turning the corner and heading toward the parking lot. My hopes soared. We only had to wait a few moments before our sole target came into view.

As he headed our way on foot with Secret Service men surrounding him, we vowed to be assertive yet nonthreatening.

Fortunately, getting close to Jackson was easier than anticipated. I stayed back to watch while Clare, having received permission, stepped directly in front of him, obliging him to stop. She began her narration while resting the book on Jackson's chest. All eyes were on her as she looked boldly into his eyes and spoke, "Rev. Jackson, I have a book for you to read about Reynold Moore, a friend of mine who aided in your 1988 presidential campaign. He was wrongfully convicted of murder a few years later and remains behind bars to this day. I am here to ask that you help him gain the freedom he deserves. Please take this book and read it. Then you will understand what this is all about. I thank you, sir."

As fast as she had stepped in front of him, she now backed away and allowed him to grasp what she had said. He paused and repeated her message, to which she nodded affirmatively. He then handed the book to the Secret Serviceman behind him and commenced walking toward the main stage. The person holding the book leaned toward us and said, "I promise to make sure Rev. Jackson gets this back."

Later that day, after Jackson's speech, Clare and I verbalized our hope that this encounter would be a turning point in helping Rey and the others. As I paused to watch the caravan of black sedans pulling out of the fairgrounds, I prayed Rey's chance for release did not exit along with it.

Despite our efforts to contact Rev. Jackson afterward, we never heard back from him or his associates. I still wonder if he thought about us—or took the time to read that book. My reasons for telling this story do not rest on what Jackson did or didn't do but are rather intended to illustrate the lengths we went to accomplish our mission. Although our effort proved unsuccessful, we had done our best, and we held onto the belief that we'd eventually be successful.

Chapter 19
ENCOUNTERING AN ADVERSARY

Trips to Green Bay during the summer of 2010 put many miles on Johnny's vehicles. For me, this experience became a lesson about the complexities of researching an old case. For those who were being researched, I suppose we became a bit of a nuisance. One trip in particular illustrates this point, as we created quite a stir at the GBPD and the courthouse.

While Johnny and I were making inquiries related to the case at the police department, we received undivided attention from police officers who began to gather and watch us from a windowed room behind the reception desk. As Johnny continued to request documents from a list he had compiled before our arrival, the clerk became increasingly reluctant to release them. She then excused herself, saying she'd return momentarily.

Soon, a police officer entered the lobby from another glass-enclosed room off to the side. We both immediately recognized his face. In his research, Johnny had acquired an official police video that documented the recovery of Tom Monfils' body. In the video, a young police officer's face appears in the camera lens. He is pointing to the top edge of the vat where a disturbance has been found. His face suggests a look of indignation about who may have done this horrible deed. Standing before us on this day was that same officer.

Fifteen years later, this officer, now a lieutenant, escorted Johnny back into the room he had emerged from. I could see them, but their conversation remained private. As soon as Johnny exited the room, he motioned for us to leave. We quickly got into the pickup and drove off. "He was cooperative," Johnny said, acting surprised. "He told me I can have access to whatever public records I want. But he was curious about why I was looking into this case. I wanted to leave before divulging too much just yet."

On our visit to the courthouse, we met up with a woman unfamiliar with the initial investigation. "Isn't that case over and done with?" she asked.

"Not as far as I'm concerned," said Johnny.

"Well, here's what you asked for." She handed him a paper containing the oath of office from the DA's office. "I'm not sure what you plan to do with that."

Johnny found the encounter amusing. Back in the vehicle, he explained. "I did that just to get a rise out of those people," he said. "Makes 'em wonder what you're up to." But Johnny's true aim was to make a statement about the importance of this oath.

By the end of the week, Johnny felt certain he had obtained all of the information he needed. We talked about heading home the next morning.

My sister Clare suggested we dine that evening at a place called The Fox Harbor Pub and Grill. "It has a great outdoor patio overlooking the Fox River," she said. "It's on South Washington Street in Downtown Green Bay, roughly half a mile from the courthouse and police department. A lot of people from both places go there on Friday night to have dinner. We can ask the guys to join us."

The day was pleasant, so we opted to sit on the patio. Johnny wasted no time in checking out his surroundings. He always went into what I call "observe and detect" mode because of his fascination with people's behaviors and insatiable desire to study them up close. He was quite intrigued with the people living in this area who were, as he said, "more obsessed with the status of their football team than the fact that their county had wrongfully convicted six innocent men."

As we placed our orders, Clare spotted John Zakowski, the former prosecutor in the Monfils case who had since become a judge in the same district. He was standing near the bar chatting with a likely colleague, their attire suggesting they had just come from work. We were not surprised to see Johnny standing quite close to them—in stark contrast, wearing khaki shorts, a polo shirt, and sandals. A huge grin covered his face when he realized that we had spotted him. Johnny had, of course, also recognized the familiar face of the former DA from the many news clips he had reviewed.

Zakowski went to sit with a group of middle school-aged students at a nearby table and left the restaurant soon after, but it was enough for Johnny to have encountered him. "Wow, I got to stand next to the man who orchestrated this whole travesty," Johnny said. "What a fitting way to end the week." We then relaxed in the company of good friends before heading home to Minnesota.

Chapter 20
GAINING MEDIA ATTENTION

During periods of time when little progress was being made, we'd recharge our mental batteries while keeping an eye out for opportunities to once again spur us in a new direction. In the meantime, small ones popped up here and there.

In 2012, we attended a second Fighting Bob Fest in Madison, Wisconsin, at the Alliant Energy Center. The venue was well-attended. We had hung a large banner promoting the book and this cause behind our table, which caught the attention of many passersby. One notable person who stopped to chat was Gil Halsted, a Wisconsin Public Radio (WPR) personality. Halsted reported on criminal justice issues, with story shorts airing between longer segments. He expressed interest in doing a spot on the Monfils case. After interviewing John and Denis, he promised to let us know when it aired. We were delighted to hear his informative piece shortly thereafter, which summarized the case and our latest efforts. Receiving this kind of exposure was gratifying because of the potential awareness it could bring and because media attention outside of the Green Bay area was about as inaccessible as legal help.

At the Alliant Energy Center, many who approached our table expressed interest and dismay as we described the story. We sold numerous books that day. In the afternoon when the crowds thinned, Denis asked if I'd watch the table while he, John, and Mike Pie listened to Senator Bernie Sanders' speech.

"No problem. I'll be fine," I said.

I strained to hear Sanders when a man walking by caught my attention. He halted abruptly in front of our table. He tilted his head to one side, staring at the banner behind me for many seconds. He then looked at me and, in a distinct British accent, spoke, "What's this all about?" he asked.

Following my summarization, he introduced himself. "I'm Bruce Bradley. I'm from the UK, but I'm currently living in Spring Green, Wisconsin. I'm a screenwriter. I work with a local theater company, and I'm trying to figure out why I am not aware of this particular story. I absolutely love writing about anything crime-related." Bruce's face lit up as he uttered an idea. "I may be interested in writing a screenplay about this case," he said.

"If you come back in about an hour, the authors will be back," I said. "They can fill you in on the more intricate details." Bradley suddenly remembered that he was on his way to meet up with someone. "I will return later to speak with the authors and purchase the book," he said as he hurried off.

When the others returned, I told them about Bradley. "He said he'd stop back here," I said.

"Sure he will," said Denis with a hint of sarcasm.

Glances agreeing with Denis' supposition appeared on the faces of both John and Mike Pie. "You guys have no faith," I said. "I'm telling you, this guy will be back. Mark my words."

As the event drew to a close, we began to pack up our belongings. I was quiet and feeling quite defeated until Bradley appeared out of the blue, just like before. "Guys, this is Bruce," I said excitedly. I was relieved but opted to enjoy my small victory by interjecting a bit of my own sarcasm.

The guys picked up on it as they all sent an apologetic look my way. Bradley became thoughtful. "From what Joan has said, I think I'd be interested in working with you on a screenplay about this story. Can you tell me more about it?" The guys relayed details. Bruce purchased a book and said, "Let me read this and get back to you." We exchanged contact information and made plans to get in touch.

The guys followed up by sending additional information to Bradley, and sometime later, he contacted us to inquire about a meeting to discuss his vision for the screenplay.

Chapter 21
DISCOVERY OF HIDDEN
TRUTHS

Months later, John hosted a meeting with Bruce at his house. Also in attendance were Mike Pie, Denis, Johnny, and I. Cal Monfils, the younger brother of Tom Monfils, and Byron Lichstein were there as well after having expressed a similar enthusiasm toward this endeavor.

Johnny met Cal and Bruce for the first time that day. I had only met Cal briefly on one other occasion, so I broke the ice by giving him a book my son, Jared, had written and illustrated titled *MEGA 99: Adventures of an Appalachian Trail Thru-Hiker*. "It's a journey in the outdoors depicting my son's five-and-a-half-month excursion into the wilderness," I said to Cal.

Cal was appreciative and accepted the gift in a reserved and quiet manner. Prior to this meeting, I learned that Cal had reached out to John, Denis, and Mike Pie when he had heard about the Monfils book being published. He had been curious about their views on the case. In their discussions, they had all been in basic agreement about what may have happened. Cal believed that the case had been mishandled. He believed that the convicted men could possibly be innocent. Cal had even written a forward for *The Monfils Conspiracy*. I admired him for his objectivity and honesty.

Johnny had driven us to Green Bay for this meeting, this time in his twenty-eight-foot RV. He and Linda had bought it for family trips, but Johnny used it often as an office space for his ongoing investigation. It became a convenient place to conduct interviews privately. Inside John's house, we sat around the dining room table as our discussion got underway. After we listened to Bruce's artistic vision for a screenplay and shared our viewpoints, Johnny asked Cal to accompany him outside. After a short while, Johnny returned and asked Byron to join him and Cal. When they returned, Johnny seemed agitated and was quieter than usual.

Johnny confided in me later. "You're not going to believe what I found out," he said, the intense look on his face suggesting its significance.

"I'm listening," I replied.

"Cal told me about a conversation he'd had with Detective Randy Winkler early in the investigation regarding the knots used on the rope found around his brother's neck," he began. "Winkler had shown him photos of the rope and weight. Cal had then told Winkler that the knots in the picture looked like knots his brother would have tied. He then said Winkler had assured him that the idea had been considered and that it was determined that the knots had not been tied by his brother. Cal told me he feels uncertain about what Winkler said and shared his concerns that the photos are important because they were the only evidence he knew of that the prosecution had."

I stared at Johnny in disbelief.

"Wait, there's more," Johnny warned. He paused, sighing deeply before dropping another bomb. "Cal also told me about a conversation that took place at his parents' house shortly after the body was found. He said Tom's wife, Susan, had told their (Cal and Tom's) parents that she believed Tom had committed suicide. In fact, she had insisted that this was what happened. But Cal said his mother had rejected the idea as nonsense. If this information was unveiled, it could bring new life to the entire case!"

Johnny's voice rose to a familiar high pitch as he continued. "See, this is what I keep saying. Damn it anyway! These were things that should have been brought up during the trial! The lawyers should have known and used these details during the trial. They could have helped to debunk the prosecution's murder theory. The jury could not have convicted these men because of the reasonable doubt that would have been raised about their innocence. This information could have cleared them! Look, this case has nothing to do with murder. It was a suicide, plain and simple! The guy jumped in the vat! I was convinced of that from the get-go, and this proves it!"

Johnny had predicted this would happen—that crucial evidence would materialize. He had said as much at the Oneida Nation High School. This was it. But there was another concern. "We have an even bigger dilemma," he said. "We can't do anything with this information right now because Cal did not say these things under oath." Johnny explained that "in order for it to be legally binding, Cal will need to give a deposition. A lawyer will have to interview him, and he'll have to sign a statement. Until then, the only thing we can do is sit on it until we find someone who is qualified to handle this. Oh, and one other thing, you cannot discuss this with anyone. Not even Clare."

My heart sank. I wanted to scream it from a rooftop or, better yet, alert the press. But Johnny was firm about keeping it quiet. "We need to go through the proper channels and do this right. That was not done the first time," he said. I knew he was right, but it was still one of the toughest things I'd ever been asked to do. "You may tell your husband, but no one else can know. We cannot risk the backlash of too many people finding out."

Keeping this from my sister felt like a betrayal of her trust. So I approached this predicament by having a frank discussion with her and apologizing for not being able to share with her what I had learned.

"That's okay if you cannot tell me," she said. "If it means helping Rey and the others, I don't want to know."

Chapter 22
THOUGHTFUL SENTIMENTS

By this time, Johnny had collected a treasure trove of information about the case, such as videotapes of the crime scene, autopsy reports, various photos, witness statements, and detail sheets from the original investigation. If it was accessible, he acquired it. He continued interviewing former mill workers and family members. He searched online for news clips and poured himself into finding the one thing to prove these men were innocent. He spent many hours digging deep, compiling, reviewing, and cross-referencing stacks of files, looking for a single key piece of tangible evidence to blow the lid off of this case. Now he had it—and from the most unlikely source.

From his standpoint, the statement from Cal was beyond significant and an indication that there was more to be discovered. "If that was never disclosed, what else are they hiding?" Johnny said. "If you smell one rat, there's always more."

Even though he felt adequately armed with this new information, Johnny was wary of who might get involved. "No lawyer from Green Bay is going to touch this case. It's too controversial. We'll have to keep searching here in Minneapolis for someone who is financially able and whose judgment is not clouded." We both knew it was a long shot to find a lawyer who could take this case on, but we had to keep trying. Johnny's optimism was met with added caution. "Whomever we find will have their work cut out for them," he said. "The work I've done is merely the tip of the iceberg."

I remember problem-solving with Johnny about this one day in the family room. The euphoria of uncovering this new evidence kept us hopeful, but we still had the lagging monetary problem. "That's always the dealbreaker for lawyers," Johnny said. "As soon as the discussion about money comes up, that's the end of it. Everyone wants to get paid. It's understandable but frustrating as hell." We sat there saying little as we again sipped tea. I hardly tasted its mild burst of sweetness as I focused on the bitter reality that this could be the end of the road. Neither of us wanted to believe it and talking about it helped.

"To make things more complicated, we cannot hire just any attorney," I said. "It will have to be someone who understands wrongful convictions and who will be focused on the best interests and welfare of the men."

I paused to think about something my mom used to say to us kids. It made me smile and seemed appropriate given the slump we were in. "When I was little, my mom piled all of us kids into the car and took us on adventures," I said. "She was a new driver, so she had this knack of getting lost. She'd act like it was no big deal and then laugh as she proudly declared, 'I know where I'm going. I just don't know how to get there.' We'd get so mad at her, but now it's funny to think of how her carefree attitude and misguided sense of direction never hindered her determination. It behooves us to maintain a similar attitude." This insight sparked a good laugh between us. Even in our doldrums, we could find something to brighten our spirits and make us feel like nothing was going to defeat us. With renewed vigor and a stubborn determination to succeed, we eagerly put our thinking caps back on.

A connection I'd made previously dawned on me. "Remember me telling you I contacted someone from the Innocence Project when we had those book signings?" I said. "They did respond to the email I had sent, so maybe I should contact them again."

We decided that it was worth a try. "Maybe they can give us some direction," said Johnny. "Maybe even some leads on attorneys."

Chapter 23
VITAL CONNECTION

In 2012, I reached out to the GN-IP for a second time to learn about what they did, who they represented, and whether they could point us in the direction of a suitable attorney.

I sent a general email again inquiring about a visit to their office. "Can anyone just stop in?" I wrote. I included my phone number in the message. I received an email again from Julie Jonas. In it, she included Erika Appelbaum, the executive director.

Erika decided to call and speak to me. "What can I help you with?" she asked.

"My friend and I want to learn about the organization and meet your staff," I said. "We also want to share our story—and hopefully get some advice." I explained our predicament. Erika was surprised but impressed that we'd taken on this mission. She stated how unusual it was for outsiders to get involved in something that didn't affect them personally. We became fast friends when we learned of our mutual acquaintance with Byron Lichstein, and we then set a date for a visit.

The front desk was vacant when Johnny and I entered the office. We peeked down the hallway as someone walked by. A young woman, an intern, acknowledged us. "We're here to see Erika," I said. The woman nodded and disappeared down the hall.

Erika soon emerged. Her face lit up when she saw us. "Come on back," she smiled. We entered her office, and after introducing ourselves, Erika asked about the Monfils case.

We shared most of the details—our frustrations about the book signings, the failed search for legal assistance, and Byron's involvement in the efforts on Rey's behalf. We said nothing about what Cal had told Johnny. Erika was sympathetic but explained upfront how understaffed and backlogged with cases their office was, which prevented them from helping us. It was more of a relief to us than anything to share our woes with someone who understood our predicament.

Julie Jonas took a quick break to say hello. It was great to finally meet her in person. Fascinated with the legalities of the case, she reluctantly returned to work before hearing all that we had to share. However, as she walked away, she mentioned an upcoming gala called a Benefit for Innocence. "You both should think about coming," she said. "Maybe you will meet some attorneys who can help."

Erika filled us in on the details, describing it as an annual event typically scheduled for the fall. "Hundreds of guests including attorneys, judges, media personalities, and exonerees will be in attendance," she said. "An event page will be up on our website soon."

We thanked Erika for her time and left with a sense of hope and eagerness about this new adventure.

Chapter 24
DOSE OF REALITY

The 2012 Benefit for Innocence listing appeared on the organization's website. This gala was scheduled for October 11 at the (former) Graves Hotel in Minneapolis. The keynote speaker was someone named Damien Echols. I made a note to myself to read up on him.

We wanted to invite a few family members from Green Bay, but the event costs were prohibitive. However, exonerees received free admission. That meant at least Mike Pie could attend.

In a conversation with Mike Pie, he agreed to attend and asked a favor of me. "Since you are taking charge of signing us up, could you invite some friends of mine? I think they'd come. They are fellow Wisconsin exonerees Audrey Edmunds and Fred Saecker. It would be great to see them again."

We discussed overnight accommodations. "Johnny says you can stay at his place, but do you think Audrey and Fred would feel comfortable staying with us?" I asked.

"I don't know, but you can ask them," Mike Pie said. "Fred's kind of quiet, but he's a really good guy, and I think he'd be okay with that."

"What's Audrey like?" I asked.

"She's easygoing and has a positive attitude," he said. "I'm sure you girls will get along great."

I took Mike Pie's advice and contacted Audrey and Fred. They responded, saying they planned to come. In his email, Fred said he appreciated the offer to stay at our house. "You are kind by making this trip affordable for me," he wrote.

Mike sat on the couch reading the newspaper as I searched the internet for information about Fred. Based on our brief communications, he seemed thoughtful and polite. I was shocked when I Googled his name and began to read the numerous articles about his case. "Mike, listen to this," I said. "Fred, the guy I just invited to stay with us went to prison for burglary, second-degree sexual assault, and kidnapping!" We both made light of this, but honestly, if we had told others who were not familiar with wrongful convictions that we had invited him into our home, they would have thought we were crazy. "It says a woman was kidnapped from her home, raped, and abandoned on the side of a road in Bluff Siding, Wisconsin. The cops arrested Fred even though he didn't fit the description given by the victim, simply because he was in her neighborhood. It says here that Fred is six feet, three inches tall. Even you'll be looking up to him," I teased.

During Fred's trial, a truck driver testified to seeing Fred with a bloodstained T-shirt. A forensic analyst also testified that pubic hairs found on the victim were "microscopically similar" to Fred's. "What does that mean?" I wondered as I looked it up. *Microscopically* just means something is invisible or indistinct without the use of a microscope. "So, it was small. But how was it relevant? And how does using a *fancy* word that most people don't understand make the results conclusive?" I mumbled angrily to myself.

I read deeper. In 1993, Fred's mother had paid for DNA testing, which excluded him as the perpetrator. But his request for a new trial was still denied. It wasn't until three years later, in 1996, that the charges were dismissed and Fred was exonerated based on the DNA evidence. "Why on earth did it take so long?" I thought. "How do you convict someone who's obviously the wrong guy? And where is the right guy? Did anyone ever think about that?" I fumed over the circumstances of a guy I hadn't even met yet. And to add insult to injury, I found no articles to confirm that the actual perpetrator had been arrested. I assumed this meant that this person was most likely still out there. "How often does this happen?" I wondered. "And how safe are any of us?"

Audrey shared in her email that she lived about half an hour south of us in Lakeville, Minnesota, so she would meet us at the hotel on the night of the event. She didn't expect that she'd be spending the night.

I wondered about Audrey's circumstances. I was also curious about the total number of female exonerees. My research took me to the website of The National Registry of Exonerations. Founded in 2012 in conjunction with the Center on Wrongful Convictions at Northwestern University School of Law and the University of Michigan's Law School, it lists every known exoneration since 1989. Their statistics indicate that females make up about 10 percent of all wrongful convictions. To date, 226 women have been exonerated since 1989. Analysis from The Women's Project at the Center on Wrongful Convictions also shows that false or misleading forensic evidence played a role in more than one-third of those exonerations. Many of these cases were based on situational prosecutions in which a female caregiver was blamed for someone's injury or death. About 40 percent of those female exonerees had been convicted of harming or killing a child or loved one in their care. An alarming 73 percent of them were wrongfully convicted of crimes that never took place, such as events determined to be accidents, deaths by suicide, and crimes that were fabricated. DNA evidence rarely proved their innocence, as it had in more than 25 percent of male exonerations. Only eleven women were exonerated with the help of DNA evidence.

In 1995, Audrey was married and had three girls under the age of five. Their family lived in the small Wisconsin town of Waunakee. She ran an at-home daycare, and in October of that year, a baby fell ill while in her care, shortly after being dropped off. The baby died later that day. An autopsy showed traumatic brain injuries. Audrey was convicted of first-degree reckless homicide for Shaken Baby Syndrome (SBS).

"Audrey was called a monster in court," I said to Mike. "She spent eleven years in prison." Audrey had been given an eighteen-year sentence, but the Wisconsin Innocence Project had secured her release in 2008. Interestingly, the same forensic pathologist whose testimony had helped to convict her had also testified on her behalf when more factual information had come to light about the symptoms present when a baby has been shaken. "It's a rare occurrence when an expert comes forth to admit they were wrong," I said. "How fortunate for Audrey to have finally been freed. But how sad for her girls to have essentially grown up without their mom."

By the time Audrey was released, her daughters were young adults. Her case was another instance in which authorities hadn't correctly determined what had actually happened to the victim. And the parents had never been investigated, despite the fact that old bruise marks, which had already begun to heal, were found on the baby's body when examined.

Mike and I looked forward to meeting Audrey and Fred. "This is a bittersweet way to make acquaintances," I said. "These people have gone to hell and back, and their circumstances are beyond anything I can comprehend. To imagine the trauma—the anger—of being labeled as something they were not, to be called a sex offender or baby killer and then to lose your freedom, is unfathomable to me. Mike Pie was open, albeit emotional, about his experience, but I wonder how easy it will be for these two to open up about theirs."

Audrey's story made me appreciate Jared's childhood—how I had never had to worry about when I would see him again or who was going to take care of him in my absence. "So, what do we say to Audrey and Fred?" I said to my husband.

As always, Mike's advice was simple and practical. "Be honest," he said. "Tell them what you just told me."

In an earlier conversation, Mike Pie had shared what many exonerees face after being released. "They have no money to live on, and they either end up with low-paying jobs or none at all. Many find themselves without housing," he said. "People don't realize that job opportunities and government compensation are hard to come by—or nonexistent. Because of the beliefs about us being guilty and the screwed-up way that compensation laws (the few that do exist) are set up, there are few payouts."

How many times had I heard others say that everyone in prison claims to be innocent or that an offender was released on a technicality? Consider this idea shared by Julie Jonas—that it may actually be innocent people who are being kept in prison on technicalities advanced by authorities who resist any admission that mistakes have been made.

Uninformed attitudes from the public add to the problem, putting exonerees in the center of these unresolved controversies. "The injustices do not end just because we are released," Mike Pie said. "For many, it creates a whole new set of problems."

Mike Pie's statement alluded to a matter still being resolved between individual states and those proven to have been wrongfully convicted—monetary compensation. On average, exonerees have spent more than fourteen years behind bars. The agony of prison life and the complete loss of freedom are accompanied by thoughts about what their lives might've been like without a wrongful conviction. The nightmare is compounded by years of separation from family and friends and by the inability to establish oneself professionally. The feelings of complete loss don't end because the person is released. An exoneree still has to face the reality that he or she typically has no valid ID or driver's license, no money or bank account, no housing, no transportation, no health services or insurance, and is forever linked to a prior criminal background, whether or not the wrongful conviction is removed from court records.

After these individuals have been freed, I believe states have a responsibility to assist and compensate them as best they can because of the difficulties they face when reentering society. Because they often have no funds available for basic necessities, failure to compensate them in this manner adds insult to injury. I feel that it is our duty as a society to assist them. This can be achieved through a number of ways: 1) compensation through a set dollar amount for each year spent in prison; 2) providing access to services like basic housing, medical/dental care (that was substandard or nonexistent in prison), counseling, assistance with education, job counseling and training, and legal services (to assist them with expungement of their criminal records and regaining custody of their children); and 3) a means of obtaining public benefits (since compensation has to be applied for, and those wrongly accused often must prove actual innocence to the State's satisfaction or in court in order to receive it).

The admission by the government that no system is perfect is crucial. When it's willing to take responsibility for its wrongs or errors and publicly recognize the harm inflicted upon a wrongfully convicted person, this helps to foster healing. To date, the federal government, the District of Columbia, and thirty-six states have compensation statutes. These fourteen states do not: Alaska, Arizona, Arkansas, Delaware, Georgia, Kentucky, New Mexico, North Dakota, Oregon, Pennsylvania, Rhode Island, South Carolina, South Dakota, and Wyoming.

Each state that does offer monetary compensation determines the conditions that must be met and the specific amount. Compensation packages range from $5,000 per year with a cap of $25,000 in Wisconsin to $80,000 per year in Texas, along with a matching annuity. Former President George W. Bush endorsed an overall recommendation by Congress of $50,000 per year, with an additional $50,000 for each year spent on death row. But many exonerees do not receive a dime because of various legal obstacles.

Some of the lawsuits filed against the state by exonerees are successful. One example of a large settlement awarded to an exoneree is the case of Jeffrey Deskovic from New York. He was wrongfully convicted of rape and murder in 1990, at the age of seventeen. He remained in prison until 2006, when he was thirty-two. DNA evidence ultimately helped to overturn his conviction.

Upon his exoneration, Deskovic filed and won lawsuits against the entities that were involved in his wrongful conviction. For example, Westchester County settled with him for $6.5 million for the fraud its medical examiner had committed. The Legal Aid Society of Westchester settled for an undisclosed amount for legal malpractice. The city of Peekskill settled for over $5 million because its police officers coerced a false confession out of him and fabricated a statement against him. He went to trial with Putnam County, but with what's called a "high-low" agreement in place. This meant that if he won, Putnam County would have to pay $10 million. On the other hand, if Putnam County won, they would have to pay $6 million. The jury was not aware of this agreement and came back with a $41.2 million verdict, which, in essence, was a moot point. He was never going to receive that much money.

All of those figures clearly represent sizable amounts of money. However, Deskovic has expressed his frustration over the public's misunderstanding of the fact that the amounts awarded to him in each of the settlements are a fraction of what he actually received. For example, he was responsible for paying all of the legal expenses in each case. Additionally, his lawyers took the standard one-third for their fees. The net effect of these expenses typically results in plaintiffs only receiving 55-60 percent of what was awarded in court.

The real reason for Deskovic's frustration about this has less to do with being able to buy fancy cars and boats or living the high life. Rather, Deskovic's dream, and now reality, was to become an attorney so that he could help to exonerate other wrongfully convicted people. The main vehicle by which he accomplishes this today is the Jeffrey Deskovic Foundation for Justice. He actually used a significant portion of the settlement money to launch this nonprofit organization.

The misconception of how much settlement money he received has unfortunately hindered fundraising efforts for his foundation. Why? Because everyone thinks he's sitting on 41.2 million dollars!

All of that said, Deskovic carries on. The mission of his nonprofit organization is what he calls the "three Rs."

1) Reversal: freeing the wrongfully convicted
2) Reform: pursuing policy changes aimed at preventing wrongful conviction
3) Recovery: helping exonerees reintegrate back into society through a combination of emergency funding and training to perform advocacy work

To date, the Jeffrey Deskovic Foundation for Justice has freed ten wrongfully convicted people. Additionally, it has helped to pass numerous laws that thwart the recurrence of wrongful convictions.

A disturbing reality that connects Deskovic's case with the Monfils case is that law enforcement's preconceived theory of what occurred replaced logical thought and the actual evidence in order to support its assertions of guilt. Deskovic was convicted of rape and murder. But the DNA results proved he was not the source of the semen in the victim's rape kit, so the State moved the goalpost by arguing that the semen had actually originated from a prior consensual sex partner of the victim. Then, in a purported jealous rage, Deskovic had killed the victim.

When Deskovic was exonerated years later, the DNA from his case was retested. This time it identified the real perpetrator, who was in prison for the murder of schoolteacher and mother of two children, Patricia Morrison. In Deskovic's situation, not only was an innocent man sent to prison, but the true criminal went on to commit another murder.

To learn more about Jeffrey Deskovic, watch the documentary titled *Conviction*. This short film is about his advocacy work and life post-exoneration. To date, *Conviction* has been selected by eleven film festivals and has won three awards for its candid indictment of the criminal justice system. In the film, Deskovic speaks passionately and highlights many of the injustices within the legal system.

Chapter 25
GRAVE TESTIMONIALS

F red arrived at our house on the day of the Benefit for Innocence. He and I were relaxing in the family room when Mike came home after work. As Fred stood to introduce himself, Mike took notice of Fred's most distinct characteristic—his height. As in the articles describing him, Fred was exceptionally tall and thin. But neither his size nor his nature was overbearing. Fred was soft-spoken, shy, and humble. "I struggle with being in large groups," Fred admitted. "But I wanted to come to this event so I could see my good friends Mike Pie and Audrey. I don't get to see them very often."

During our brief discussion before Mike's arrival home, Fred asked me, "Did Mike Pie tell you about my situation?" Fred seemed at ease as he talked at length about his experience. The authorities are not always interested in going after the truth," he said. "Look at the description of the perp in my case. It wasn't even close to what I looked like. But that didn't matter. They arrested, charged, and convicted me anyway."

I saw many similarities in both Fred and Mike Pie. Neither of them seemed capable of committing the heinous crimes for which they were convicted. In fact, they both exhibited genuine, unselfish, and sincere attributes. Like Mike Pie, Fred still harbored distrust for the authorities, which was the basis for his concern for others he had met while in prison. "I'm grateful for my freedom," he said. "But I know lots of innocent guys who are still in prison. In fact, the prisons are full of them, and it makes me sad to think of how many will never have their cases looked into."

Before long, we heard a vehicle pull up to the house. Johnny, Linda, and Mike Pie were all decked out. Mike Pie was even wearing a suit he had borrowed from Johnny. "Wow, don't you look fashionable," I said as he and the others strolled in.

"Not too shabby," Mike Pie remarked.

Johnny smiled at Fred, giving him the once-over. "I don't think I have anything to fit you, Fred," he teased as he strained to look Fred in the eyes.

"I'm okay wearing what I have on," Fred replied as he shook Johnny's hand.

Fred definitely towered over Johnny's short and stocky frame. "Hmmm . . . Mutt and Jeff," I said, poking fun at Johnny's expense.

Johnny could be quite entertaining. But when necessary, he knew how to conjure a more serious mindset to effectively work a room, something he'd illustrate later that evening. Off we went on this new adventure. On the way out, I grabbed a tote bag filled with gifts I had packed earlier. When I had started meeting exonerees who had been forced to live in small cells for years at a time, I had thought that they might especially enjoy my son's Appalachian Trail book and appreciate reading about the freedom to roam in the open wilderness. I felt that this event was the perfect place to hand more of them out.

During the ride to the hotel, I studied Fred. You'd never guess he had such a traumatic past by looking at him. Exonerees resemble all of us. They could be the neighbor mowing their lawn, the person in line at the grocery store, or someone riding a bike down a busy street. I thought they'd stand out for some reason, but they don't. It's an uneasy feeling to realize that what happened to them could easily happen to any of us. I wondered how I had been so ignorant about wrongful convictions and about the number of people affected by them.

We entered the hotel lobby and signed in. I scanned the room looking for Tori, another of my coworkers who had promised to meet us there. Tori's excitement was evident as she rushed over to us. "I cannot wait to meet Audrey," she said. "She is coming, right?"

"I hope so," I said. "I'm not seeing her here. Maybe she's at the reception already."

The elevator ascended and opened to a large room filled with small groups of people engaged in conversation. I immediately spotted Audrey. There was no mistaking her. She was tall, slim, blonde, and beautiful, like in the pictures I had seen of her online after she'd been released. She was visiting with two other people. Tori and I separated from the others and approached them. I touched Audrey's arm. She turned to offer hugs before introducing us to Panghoua Moua and Koua Fong Lee, who smiled politely and nodded amiably. "Koua is an exoneree too," explained Audrey.

In June 2006, Koua Fong Lee was driving his family home from church. While on an exit ramp in St. Paul, Minnesota, the 1996 Toyota Camry he was driving accelerated out of control. It reached a speed of ninety miles an hour, crashing into a stopped car in front of them. Three people were killed, and two others were injured. In 2007, Koua was charged with intentional vehicular homicide and sentenced to eight years in prison. Two years into his sentence, more Toyota drivers reported similar acceleration issues. Toyota started to recall millions of cars, but not the 1996 model. Based on this new evidence and errors by his trial lawyer, Koua filed a motion for a new trial. The lawyers representing Toyota fought the motion, claiming that his vehicle was not flawed. But Koua was granted a new trial and was exonerated in August 2010, after serving three years of his sentence.

Despite this frightening experience, Koua emphasized his appreciation of others' support. "We are very grateful for the help we receive from many good people," he said.

Theirs was a perplexing battle. In ongoing efforts to receive monetary compensation from a resistant automotive company, Koua and his family fought for normalcy while raising four beautiful children. Having seen Koua and Panghoua on many occasions since, the trauma they had experienced is still evident and overwhelming.

Tori and I excused ourselves to catch up with the others who were gathered around another exoneree. Damon Thibodeaux was quiet but receptive. We understood why when we learned that he'd been released from prison only two weeks ago. Mike and I also learned he was the same age as our son. For that reason alone, I found it difficult to stomach his disturbing story.

In July 1996, Damon was a twenty-two-year-old deckhand on a Mississippi River barge in New Orleans, Louisiana. During that month, his step-cousin was found strangled and beaten to death. He aided in an extensive search to find her before being brought in for questioning. Already exhausted from helping in the search and with little sleep for roughly thirty-six hours, Damon was interrogated for nine hours. Due to police coercion, intimidation, and being threatened with the death penalty if he did not confess to raping and murdering his step-cousin, he falsely confessed to what the interrogators demanded he say.

The case against him was built upon this confession, even though there were discrepancies between what he had stated and the facts and evidence that was later found. For example, his confession of rape was plainly false since there was no physical evidence a rape had even occurred. However, this fact had not stopped the authorities from including it in the charges brought against him.

Damon had also been misidentified. A week after the crime, two women picked him out of a photo lineup. At the trial, they pointed to him as the perpetrator. However, during a later investigation of his case, it was revealed that the women had seen Damon's face on the news prior to identifying him in the photo lineup. Additionally, the date they had claimed to have seen him was incorrect because by then, he had already been taken into custody.

Damon spent fifteen years on death row at Louisiana's Angola Prison, one of the nation's worst. He was isolated in an 8x10-foot cell for twenty-three hours a day. He was the three hundredth person nationwide and the eighteenth from death row to be exonerated largely by DNA evidence. He was released in September 2012.

Standing near Damon was his attorney from the Minneapolis law firm of Fredrikson & Byron, PA, a firm known for its generosity in contributing pro bono services to clients and nonprofits in the Minneapolis area. Standing beside both of them, talking up a storm, was Johnny.

With Johnny's keen ability to zero in on the right person at the right time, I was curious to meet this attorney.

As I approached them, Johnny declared, "Hey Joan, this is Steve Kaplan. He was instrumental in helping with Damon's exoneration. I've been telling him about the Monfils case."

Steve was soft-spoken and charming. He talked about Damon with pride and about spending the last twelve years working on his case. He expressed his relief that it was over and that Damon was free. It was inspiring to hear such dedication for his client, and I wondered if we could find someone like him to help us.

About halfway through the reception, Damien Echols, the keynote speaker for the evening, appeared alongside his wife, Lorri. There was no mistaking his identity due to the dark glasses and long trench-like coat that he wore, which is how he is typically portrayed on various social media sites. Lorri was striking, with deep blue eyes and a bright smile. They both stood in the center of the room as a crowd slowly surrounded them. With my son's book in hand, I waited my turn to speak with them. Damien had a calming effect on those around him. His personable and relaxed composure paired well with Lorri's outgoing social nature.

I had become familiar with Damien's story through watching the three-part documentary *Paradise Lost*, a deeply disturbing tragedy in which Echols and two other teenage boys, Jessie Misskelley Jr. and Jason Baldwin, were convicted of murdering three eight-year-old Cub Scout boys in West Memphis, Arkansas, in 1994. Echols, Misskelley, and Baldwin were dubbed "The West Memphis Three." Echols, the leading suspect, received three death penalties. Baldwin and Misskelley, both of whom had low IQs, were also given life sentences despite no physical evidence linking any of them to the crime. The authorities failed to pursue every possible lead, and they fabricated evidence and even enhanced the storyline, labeling the deaths as satanic killings to terrify and infuriate a prejudiced community.

I found the films compelling and fascinating because of the distinct similarities to the Monfils case. Echols was seen as a troublemaker, like Keith Kutska. The court of public opinion had all three boys charged, tried, and sentenced before any of them saw the inside of a courtroom.

Finger-pointing and cruel epithets came at them from every direction. In addition, the teens were mischaracterized and accused of being involved in satanic rituals and human sacrifice simply because they wore black clothing and listened to heavy metal music.

Although watching the documentary series leads viewers to speculate about other possible suspects, no one else has ever been investigated or charged. To this day, reasonable doubt about the guilt of these three men remains high, yet the police have shown no interest in examining other potential leads.

An eventual twist in this case introduces a disturbing aspect of the criminal justice process. Years into their sentences, all three of these boys agreed to change their original pleas from not guilty to guilty in exchange for immediate release. This is known as an Alford Plea. It's a legal maneuver some describe as a "wink and a nod" allowing someone to be released from prison while maintaining his or her innocence but pleading guilty to an agreed-upon charge based on the possibility that prosecutors have enough evidence to convict. According to Echols, it was his only option because of his inability to survive in prison any longer. For him, it literally meant the difference between life and death. Some see an Alford Plea as a source of worry due to the implications it places on overall exonerations. I see it as another way of bullying innocents and maintaining control over their fates and a last-ditch attempt to satisfy a prosecutor's unrelenting position before releasing someone.

Echols spent eighteen years in prison, and he refers to that experience and his legal battle for freedom as an "absolute living hell." In 2012, he wrote a memoir titled *Life After Death*. Copies were available for purchase at this benefit.

Damien was alone when it was my turn to speak with him. I offered him the copy of Jared's book. "This is for you," I said. "My son wrote it. I'd like you to have it."

He was delighted. "Thank you," he said.

"I'm deeply sorry for what you've been through," I said.

Damien explained the dark glasses he wore. "My eyesight was destroyed from being in a small, dark room for so many years," he said. The sadness in his voice broke my heart.

"Could we have our picture taken together?" I asked to lighten the mood.

"Sure," he said, "but no one can use a flash."

We searched for a suitable spot. I worried that Damien might become irritated when it took longer than expected. He didn't. And as we stood there amid a barrage of camera clicks, I felt his reassuring hand rest on my shoulder.

When I spoke with Lorri, she was open about her deep love for this man. She's modest about her role in Damien's redemption and about having lifted him out of the depths of despair while he was in prison. They had started a relationship through letters that eventually developed into marriage. It was a situation that called for great courage and devotion on both sides. Because of her compassion, Damien was liberated from his hell on earth.

We entered a dining hall full of tables covered in white linen. Hundreds of guests flocked to their assigned seats. The atmosphere was ripe with laughter and conversation as Audrey, Fred, and Mike Pie joined us at our table. In fact, we received favorable mention for having the most exonerees at a single table.

After dinner, Damien shared an eye-opening and infuriating story through an informal Q&A session. The fear-based hate he experienced, the biased judicial process that took place, and the constant beatings and years of isolation while on death row were inconceivable to an audience who sighed in disbelief at his stark reality. Once you hear these things, they never escape you. If you truly care, you will never dismiss them. And if you are wise, you will never forget them.

After dinner, a last-call announcement was made. A table had been set up outside the dining room entrance for those who had not yet purchased Damien's book. Linda leaned into me and said, "Joan, let's go and buy our copies." This gave us a chance to also express our sincere sympathies and gratitude to Damien for the deeply personal experiences he had shared.

We walked over to a small group that had congregated around a young man named Mike Hansen. He was a client of the GN-IP who had been exonerated in 2011. Hansen was young enough that his wrongful conviction had not completely stolen his youth. He was fortunate to have many years ahead to create a new life and a new future. His shaved head resembled my son's, and his face lit up when he laughed. He was self-assured and seized the attention of those around him, looking each of us squarely in the eyes as he offered a firm handshake. His story was similar to Audrey's. As he shared details, his tone defied and scolded the authorities who had caused catastrophic harm to him and his family years earlier.

In 2006, Michael Hansen was convicted of murdering his three-month-old daughter, Avryonna. On the morning of her death, he had found her unresponsive. He called 911, but she could not be revived. An autopsy was performed, and the medical examiner testified at his trial that the infant had died of a skull fracture from an intentional blow to the head, even though he had found little evidence of swelling, bleeding, or brain injuries. He dismissed the idea that the fracture could have been caused by a fall she had taken out of a shopping cart six days prior to her death.

The case was reopened by the GN-IP, and they hired a team of experts to reevaluate the autopsy. These experts testified that a skull fracture alone does not cause death and that to do so in an infant, it must be accompanied by significant bleeding, swelling, or some type of brain injury before death can occur. It was determined that Avryonna most likely died of accidental suffocation or Sudden Infant Death Syndrome (SIDS) while sleeping. Hansen served five-and-a-half years of a fourteen-and-a-half-year sentence before the charges against him were formally dismissed.

Despite convincing research, there is much dissension and debate in the scientific world about the circumstances surrounding infant deaths, leaving parents desperate to find peace with the death of their child. Often, parents are sent to prison or face separation from their children when genetic anomalies are present and misdiagnosed. Osteogenesis imperfecta is a group of genetic disorders mainly affecting the bones that causes imperfect bone formation or frequent breakage due to mild trauma, or in many cases, with no apparent cause. Often, this disorder is mistaken for child abuse. The 2016 film titled *The Syndrome* seeks to address these issues and features Audrey's case as a way to educate the public on the facts surrounding infant deaths.

As we drove home from the benefit, the car was quiet, but my mind was unsettled. Johnny, Linda, and Mike Pie agreed to stop over for a nightcap, a welcomed way to decompress from what we all had seen and heard. During the evening, I realized that all of the exonerees we had met had one thing in common—none of them appeared angry. I found this odd. These situations were beyond horrific, so how could they be so cheerful, so calm, and so damned peaceful?

A stark contrast to this attitude comes from family members I've spoken with over the years who have their own sets of worries. Jenn, Keith Kutska's niece, whose spirited nature matches that of her uncle, puts it this way: "There are some family members who won't mention him anymore—as if he fell off the face of the earth. That is what breaks my heart. The ones who miss him are the ones who have lost out—not to mention Keith himself, who has been robbed of his absolute freedom. His name has been dragged through the dirt. Those who didn't truly know him thank God for sending such a 'beast of a man' to prison. That pains me as well. And his reputation as a wonderful man is forever shattered even if he is found innocent. People are going to hear the name Keith Kutska and cringe because of the mess up in the judicial system. His life will never be the same. When the day comes that God decides it's his time to die, and I pray it's not soon, I will bawl my eyes out, as will his family. I just want to scream to the world, 'He's not who you think he is! He's not a murderer!' But my fear is that no one will listen."

Jenn's "beast of a man" quote compelled me to search online for a possible reference. That search led me to an article in the *Deseret News* out of Utah, dated October 29, 1995. In the article, the then District Attorney John Zakowski had referenced the following quote by Ralph Waldo Emerson as a characterization of the men convicted in the Monfils case: "A mob is man descending to the level of beast."

The GN-IP benefit had been about people traumatized unnecessarily within a criminal justice system that had failed miserably by shattering the ideals, the hopes, and the dreams by which we all live. But for those we met, miraculous changes had occurred. They were fortunate to be free. And they knew it. Because of their good fortune, they were making peace with their circumstances and doing their best to educate others through the sharing of their personal stories.

Among those I spoke with, a common theme lingered of trying to reconcile our imperfect criminal justice system with why it tolerates wrongful convictions even in the face of compelling evidence of innocence. I thought about Damien and his plea deal. Though this wasn't an ideal option, it was the only viable one for him at the time. At least for the time being, it allowed him his freedom until he could find a way to achieve formal exoneration. Damon Thibodeaux knew how lucky he had been to be liberated from death row with the help of the Innocence Project of New York and a remarkable legal team. Audrey and Mike Hansen expressed gratefulness for the guidance they had received through the Minnesota GN-IP and WIP and for new scientific advances. Fred had the benefit of DNA testing, and Koua received enough support through collective information from other victims and advocates alike, which prompted new legal action.

The uncertain challenges they all now faced were more about survival on the outside, in a whole new world. The most important thing they would have to rely on was the support of family and true friends who could pull them through difficult times ahead.

As uplifting as this event was, the reality of what we lacked in our mission to free our five incarcerated men was still quite real. There was no DNA. The WIP had recently lost an appeal for Rey Moore, and we had no apparent leads on the legal front. Our biggest hurdle also remained—the absence of funds to pay for a decent attorney. Three years into this and we had barely made it out of the starting gate. The constant stress and urgency of an unknown future weighed heavily on my mind. The stories we heard that evening all proved that goodness prevailed through miracles. But where was ours?

Chapter 26

A GATHERING OF FRIENDS

After the benefit, Audrey and I met for lunch occasionally. Her free spirit, strength, and ability to wear a smile despite her circumstances were attributes that inspired me to reject the negative aspects of my life and to embrace only the positive. My husband always says it best when he describes Audrey as "one of the most positive people I've ever met."

Our first lunch date was before Thanksgiving 2012. It was then that Audrey told me about a book she was writing. "It's called *It Happened to Audrey: It Could Happen to You*," she said. "It'll be published soon."

"I'd like to have a copy," I said. "Why can't we host a book signing for you at my house?" I asked. Audrey was delighted.

"Let's schedule it for early December before people are bombarded with Christmas activities," I said. "Mike and I will turn it into a festive event."

On December 8, 2012, Mike and I hosted a gathering of approximately twenty people at our house. Beforehand, I had sent online invitations to a few close friends and to Erika and Julie from the GN-IP. Although I was unsure if Steve Kaplan would remember me after such a brief introduction at the benefit, I decided to send an invitation to him. I extended the invitation to include his wife, Norma, and Damon. Responses came back, and the turnout was looking great. Then, the one response I had hoped for appeared.

An email from Steve came with good news. He had accepted the invitation, and although Norma could not come, Steve planned to bring Damon. He also asked about inviting one other person. After sending my reply, I told Johnny, "Steve remembered me."

"Well, of course he did," he said. "Joan, I told you before. I keep tellin' you. You have this ability to get people's attention, and now you have Steve Kaplan's. Someday, you'll learn there isn't anything you can't do."

We received positive responses from the majority of those who had been invited. Johnny had the flu, so he and Linda did not attend. Steve and Damon were among the last to arrive. I noticed a positive change in Damon since the benefit. He was more at ease and self-confident. He conversed with the other guests, and we learned that he possessed a hearty laugh. He was doing great considering he'd spent the past fifteen years in solitary confinement. Since his release, he had been living with the Kaplans so he could focus on getting his GED. Steve had also facilitated finding a job for him at the firm. My admiration for Steve continued to grow. The level of generosity he'd shown in setting this young man up for success was unusual and commendable.

When Damon completed his studies, he was all smiles at his high school graduation. He went on to enroll in commercial truck driving school. He now spends his days on the open road as a professional truck driver—something he used to dream about in a tiny cell.

Steve introduced me to Pam Wandzel—the director of the Pro Bono and Community Services program at the law firm. The three of us chatted briefly before Mike reminded me of the time. "We should get Audrey's presentation started," he urged.

"We can talk later," Steve remarked.

Before I could formally introduce Audrey, she greeted the crowd from her seat at the large table. "This woman needs no introduction," I thought as I quickly grabbed a plate of food and joined the other guests.

Audrey was as delightful as her story was disheartening. We listened intently as horrific details unfolded. Most disturbing was her description of being separated from her three daughters and of how she had worried about their well-being while she was "away." Audrey uses noncommittal words like this because in her mind, she had never allowed herself to become a *prisoner*. She had never catered to being a number, and she had never given up on the idea of someday being released. In the meantime, she had maintained a normal routine as best she could, with exercise and a healthy diet. She had seen the devastation happening to other women around her who abused themselves with drugs, cigarettes, junk food, and a lack of exercise. She had avoided any type of violence and was thankful that she had never been threatened.

The mood in the room was somber as she explained how she had been labeled so outrageously in court and that no one had believed her side of the story. Her experience was representative of four primary themes in all wrongful convictions: 1) unwarranted character defamation; 2) an incomplete or inaccurate depiction of what happened; 3) neglect by law enforcement to look into all possible suspects; and 4) narrowly focusing on a specific person despite evidence that proves his or her innocence. When Audrey finished, the group applauded her for sharing this nightmare, knowing it had taken great courage to relive it.

My friend and coworker Candee then spoke up. "I'm not familiar with Damon's story. I was wondering if it's okay for him to talk about his experience."

Everyone liked the idea, and with a little encouragement, Damon shared details of his arrest and confinement. He talked about confessing to a crime he had not committed. "Until you've been placed in a situation where you are coerced into confessing to something you didn't do, you cannot know how that feels," he said.

Over time, I learned the rationale behind the absurdity of confessing to a crime you did not commit. Suspects are supposed to be interviewed but instead get interrogated, which is a more aggressive tactic known as the Reid Method of Interrogation. It's used by law enforcement when closing a case becomes more important than going after the truth. The suspects are fed lies. They are told that they can go home after being questioned or that they will get a better deal from the courts if they admit involvement. They are scolded and continually fed facts about the crime known only to the police and to the actual perpetrator as a way to cause confusion. The interrogator will say, "We know you did this." They use scare tactics and lies, such as falsely saying they have a witness who has identified him or her or that they have physical evidence proving guilt when, in fact, they do not. The goal is to convince the suspect that he or she has no realistic option but to confess. The sheer length of the interrogation combined with the threats of greater legal harm if the suspect does not confess may not only exhaust the suspect emotionally and physically but succeed in convincing him or her to confess.

In death-penalty states, interrogators may use the threat of a death sentence as leverage to coerce suspects into confessing. Suspects are told of the risks of putting their fate in the hands of an unsympathetic jury. Many are offered the possibility of a shorter sentence in exchange for a guilty plea.

Damon was threatened with the death penalty, which he was ultimately sentenced with because of, rather than despite his confession. He talked about his experience on death row—the overwhelming heat during the summer, the long days, and how it felt to be stared at as people from various tour groups, including religious organizations, schoolchildren, and tourists taking side trips from their vacations, walked past his cell. He talked about how Steve Kaplan had come into his life and became not only his lawyer but also a friend and mentor and mentioned his gratitude for the consistent contact with Steve while his case was in litigation.

Afterward, I said to Damon, "I cannot begin to understand what you went through."

His reply to me was profound. "I hope you never do because that will mean you didn't have to go through what I did."

To lighten the mood, I fetched gifts for our guests. I asked Damon to stay at the table while I motioned for Audrey to stand next to him. "Since we're entering the harshest part of our Minnesota winter, I'm gracing each of you with a practical gift," I said as they pulled thick knitted hats from their gift bags. We shared hearty laughs as they each playfully donned them.

Damon teased, "I definitely needed one of these." Afterward, we celebrated their freedom with laughter, hugs, and good cheer. Audrey proceeded to sign books.

The time was slipping away, and I still needed to talk to Steve about the Monfils case. I wished Johnny was there to help explain in terms an attorney could better understand why it was imperative that this case be revisited. I knew enough to answer the basic questions, but my lack of knowledge about the legalities prevented me from taking on more complicated procedural ones about the investigation and appeals that the men had filed afterward.

No amount of knowledge could answer the one question Steve eventually asked: "Why was one released and not the other five?"

I'd learned from Johnny that no attorney asks a question he or she doesn't know the answer to, but this one had *no* answer, let alone a rational one. "That is the big mystery," I said. "It should have ignited a reinvestigation into the case, but it didn't."

After a while, I broached the subject of legal assistance. I tread lightly. Since Steve had only recently finished with Damon's case, I felt it unwise to ask him outright to represent our men. I was also aware that Steve was planning to retire soon. I settled on asking for any attorney recommendations he might have. He suggested I talk to Pam about making an appointment at the firm.

Pam advised me to call the office and set up an appointment. I was elated for having just been handed the proverbial olive branch—an invitation to one of the largest law firms in Minneapolis. I had done my part; now all Johnny had to do was go through the mountain of documentation he had gathered over the past two years and decide what to bring along. I took great pleasure in sharing with him this game-changing news.

Chapter 27
UNLOADING A HEAVY BURDEN

Sometimes our plans took unexpected turns, and we would find ourselves scrambling to recover, like the day in January 2013 when Johnny and I had a scheduled meeting with Pam at Fredrikson & Byron, PA in Downtown Minneapolis. Johnny circled the block a few times before we finally located the entrance to the underground parking garage. We quickly found a parking space and rushed toward our destination, managing to arrive with minutes to spare.

The firm occupied the upper nine floors of the twenty-two-story US Bank Plaza tower, with the reception desk being located on the top floor. After carrying the heavy, clumsy cardboard box full of case files as we made our way through the parking garage, the main floor plaza, and up the elevator, Johnny made it perfectly clear, "There is no way I am carrying this box back home. That simply is non-negotiable."

As soon as we walked off of the elevator, Johnny set the box down on a nearby coffee table with a thud. I approached the receptionist with the widest grin I could muster, making light of the commotion behind me. "We're here to see Pam," I said. "She's expecting us."

We waited as the receptionist made the call. After she hung up, we received devastating news. "Pam is not in today due to an illness," she said. "Can you reschedule?"

Johnny and I looked at each other, panic setting in. I leaned over to him and said, "This is our moment. We cannot leave without talking to someone. Hang on—I have an idea." I turned back toward the desk. "Is Steve Kaplan in today?" I inquired.

She offered to check as she picked up the receiver once again. We both crossed our fingers and paused. She hung up the phone and said, "Steve will be right down." I thanked her with an enthusiasm that may have sounded over-the-top.

Then Johnny stated loudly, "I hope he remembers us."

"Hush," I said, giving him a dogged look. "You can be so embarrassing sometimes," I scolded under my breath. But Johnny only reveled in this new twist. "Way to go, Treppa," he whispered.

There were advantages to speaking with this compassionate and generous lawyer. But we would have to exercise restraint in getting our hopes up or appearing overly anxious. I also hoped we were not upsetting Steve's busy schedule while in the midst of his last month at the firm.

As we waited, we marveled at our surroundings. Large paintings of the firm's founders adorned the walls. The view overlooking the city of Minneapolis from this vantage point was stunning. The sheer size of this space where we now stood was daunting. Maybe the audacity of expecting a favorable response from a firm of this magnitude felt surreal. But there we were, driven like desperados, equipped with nothing but a tattered box of documents and an unrivaled determination.

After standing for some time in that lobby, it began to feel as if this was meant to be. An affirmation washed over me that miracles are real and that our dreams could somehow come true.

I thought about how Steve had expressed his intrigue with the case. "Maybe he *will* decide to take it on," I thought. "It does need the attention of someone like him." But I also thought it futile and a little bold of us to ask. My thoughts were interrupted as Steve exited the elevator and walked toward us. He greeted us with the warmth of old friends. We both immediately felt the burden of our troubles slipping away. As Steve quizzed the receptionist about an empty conference room, Johnny and I caught each other's glances. Johnny nodded reassuringly that this was somehow going to work out just fine.

"The second room on the left is open," the receptionist told Steve, and off we went. We talked for an hour, then two, and well into a third. Steve's professionalism and knowledge of the law allowed him to unravel the confusing details with which he was inundated. We were relieved to finally have an outlet to share our coveted information from Cal Monfils.

Johnny explained everything he had discovered over the past two years. I shared my connections with the family members and the five men. I assured Steve of my ability to facilitate trust between them and whoever took the legal reins. Johnny and I stressed our concerns about future mismanagement of the case and the level of ineffectiveness of the lawyers who had represented them in the past. Steve, in turn, established his intent to complete a thorough examination of the documentation Johnny had supplied. He added that if an evaluation of the evidence affirmed the guilt of the men, he would discontinue his inquiry into the case. Johnny and I readily agreed to this reasonable ultimatum.

Before we wrapped up our meeting, we reluctantly declared that we lacked the funds to pay an attorney. We did not detect hesitation from Steve when he again agreed to look at the information Johnny had supplied. We were grateful for his time, and we walked out of the meeting feeling heard and understood. I was ready to hire Steve Kaplan right then and there. All he had to do was say the word. Nevertheless, we said our goodbyes and left, and we waited patiently for what we might hear back.

Chapter 28
OVERCOMING MAJOR HURDLES

S teve Kaplan retired in February 2013. As much as we wished him well, we silently prayed that he would respond with good news. Up to this point, we had refrained from saying anything to the Green Bay folks about our affiliation with Steve until we had an idea of the outcome, in case things didn't work out.

While we waited, we tried to muster enthusiasm for a next move, keeping in mind the distinct possibility that our search for an attorney was not over. Time passed with no word from Steve. Still, we resisted the notion that he was enjoying retirement too much and that the Damon Thibodeaux case was going to be the capstone on his well-deserved legacy. "He's not going to jump back into a big case like this," I said. "He's going to realize it's another long-term commitment."

Johnny countered those remarks with, "One never knows what he will do. Let's be patient a little longer." Even though I questioned Johnny's optimism, I remained hopeful. Aside from my certainty that Steve was the perfect candidate to take on this case, I questioned our rationale for believing he'd get involved, especially for free.

My concern for the families was ever-present. They'd be the losers if we failed to bring Steve or anyone else from the firm onboard. Clutching to any positive means necessary, I kept reminding myself that Steve had alluded to contributing minimal assistance after he retired. It was not the preferred outcome, but it was something. If he did decide to help us, how long would he allow it to invade his life? What if this case became too overwhelming or time-consuming? I wondered about the travel and unforeseen expenses along the way, and I feared he would have inadequate assistance. It had been easy to get caught up in the moment of that meeting where anything had seemed possible. And though there was no shaking this inner battle between optimism and apprehension, I chose to embrace a more favorable outcome.

My faith in the impossible was confirmed one day as I turned on my computer to check emails. In my inbox was a message from Steve. I read furiously through to the end, looking for an indication of his intentions. There it was—verification that he was willing to help us! After a brief retirement of about three-and-a-half weeks, Steve and the firm decided that he should return in late March to work on the "Monfils Six" case. The words took a moment to sink in before I jumped up to call Johnny. "It took us two long years, but we've done it," I said.

"This changes everything," said Johnny. "Now we can see about getting this case back into the courts. I'm coming over. We have things to do. The first thing you should do is let the folks in Green Bay know and have them organize a meeting at Shirley's."

I agreed. "I'll get an email sent out right away," I said. "If the media gets wind of this, there's no telling how they might react, and we don't want them to catch the families off guard."

Johnny and I also ran over to see Erika and Julie to share the good news. They had already been notified, but it was still great to celebrate with them. Even with their extremely busy schedules, they would always make time for us. We spoke briefly with Erika, and as we walked back toward the front door to leave, we passed Julie's office. We peeked in for a quick "hello," and she called us in to chat about the latest development. Our success had generated many questions from Julie, who was always interested in the latest. And on that day, she wanted to find out exactly how we had managed to get Steve involved.

A few hours after our visit, I received a message from Steve with a significant development. In essence, it said that Julie had contacted him and wanted to sign on the GN-IP as co-counsel for the Monfils case. I was overcome with emotion when I read the part where Steve gave Johnny and me credit for Julie's actions. To add to the excitement, soon after the GN-IP signed on, the WIP did likewise because of their connection to the case through Rey Moore and his appeals process.

I had initially learned about the legal activity on Rey's behalf from Byron at our first Walk for Truth and Justice. Approximately a year before Fredrikson & Byron's involvement, he and attorneys from the WIP had pushed for a new trial for Rey in light of the recantation by James Gilliam, the jailhouse snitch who had testified against Rey during the original trial. However, while Denis and John were conducting their research for the Monfils book, they had interviewed Gilliam, who summarized Rey's involvement in a significantly different way. Below are brief summaries from the January 26, 2012, transcript of Rey's post-conviction hearing, as told by three witnesses:

(Paragraph 21): *Denis testified that, during the course of the interview, Gilliam said Rey told him in jail that Rey had tried to help Monfils on November 21, 1992, and specifically "tried to stop the alleged confrontation" of Monfils. In other words, Denis understood Gilliam to say during the interview that Rey told Gilliam he was present when Monfils was confronted by coworkers, but that Rey tried at that time only to help Monfils, not to harm him.*

(Paragraph 24): *Nicholas Schwalbach, a University of Wisconsin law student, working on behalf of Rey through the WIP, learned from John that Gilliam "was now saying something different than what he testified to." With two other law students, Schwalbach visited Gilliam in prison, informing Gilliam that they were with the WIP. During the course of the interview, Gilliam said that Rey "had tried to break up the fight and that he did not punch anybody." Gilliam told the students that this account was the same one he had given in his trial testimony. [But of course, it directly contradicted Gilliam's trial testimony.]*
(Paragraph 25): *Another of the law students working with the WIP, Anthony Rios, testified that "Gilliam said that when he testified at the trial that he was really trying to*

help [Rey], and that he knew [Rey] was innocent . . . [H]e
said that [Rey] saw a commotion, went over there, and
tried to break it up. He said the whole incident was about
drugs, that everybody knew it was about drugs, and he
went on for quite some time about how drugs were run-
ning through Green Bay and running through the plant
from Sheboygan up to Green Bay."

My understanding was that this post-conviction petition was a final attempt by the WIP to help Rey in overturning his conviction. They
had not yet dropped his case, however, and the news that a law firm
was now involved came as an enormous relief. They, too, were enthusiastic about the prospect of working in conjunction with the Minneapolis team.

This instance of a law firm partnering with an Innocence Project is
a typical initiative for many wrongful-conviction cases. It is beneficial
because of the inadequate financial situations of many smaller projects.
In order to provide free services, they align themselves with law
schools, with much of the staff consisting of a handful of paid lawyers
or law instructors and law students who volunteer their time while
earning class credits. Projects similar to those in Minnesota and Wisconsin tend to be understaffed and unable to field and assess many of
the calls they receive monthly from potential clients. Aside from being
able to finance executive director and staff attorney or legal director
positions, the out-of-pocket expense associated with the litigation process, including filing motions, testing DNA or other evidence, and hiring expert witnesses, can be great. Rather than charge fees to their clients, they rely on state grants and donations from the public to pay for
these crucial services. Additional funding provided by law firms con-
tributes to the likelihood of success in any given case.

Johnny was ecstatic and immediately began working with Steve on
what is referred to as the discovery phase—the period of fact-finding
and fact-gathering before a post-conviction petition is filed in court. In
this instance, it was a reevaluation of known facts that had never been
presented during the trial and a search for new evidence that may have
been overlooked during the original investigation.

They found that the facts had been there all along but had been blatantly ignored. Factors inhibiting a fair and unbiased trial, such as ineffective legal counsel, incomplete disclosure of known facts that could have caused a different verdict, and the coercion of certain witnesses were examined and included in the final analysis of the case. What was ultimately found was a corrupt police detective, a web of deception by an overzealous but charismatic prosecutor, obvious and questionable autopsy testimony by the state's forensic pathologist, a shamed police force, and ineffective assistance of defense counsel. What followed was the manipulation of the facts filtered not only through the courts, but also through the media, thereby misleading the public.

The Fredrikson & Byron law firm decided to represent Keith Kutska, the main suspect in the case. Even though he was picked as their sole client, establishing and substantiating credible new evidence could benefit all of the men. Strong indicators supporting the conclusion that this death was a suicide became apparent. Once discovery was complete and all of the old and new evidence, including all relevant witnesses, could be evaluated by the defense team, a petition could then be filed and presented at an evidentiary hearing in the Brown County Circuit Court, where the case had originated. The objective of the new defense team—headed by Steve—would be to request a new trial for Kutska.

Chapter 29
BROADCASTING OUR MISSION

While Steve and Johnny oversaw the legal end of things, I continued to bridge the communications between Green Bay and Minneapolis. I participated in all annual Walks for Truth and Justice and orchestrated a presence of those associated with the Monfils case at future Innocence Project benefits.

My first experience with discussing this case in a televised interview took place in the spring of 2012. Jared's friend, Erik Stewart (who had read the Monfils book and begun exchanging letters with Keith Kutska), offered to produce a segment while taking a video production class at Northwest Community Television (Channel 12), a small public-access cable channel based in Crystal, Minnesota. "The video production class is free, and they allow channel time to residents and organizations in a specified area," Erik told me. "From the time I first read the book, I've wanted to help out in some way. I'd like to set up an interview for you, which I can do while taking this class."

The segment that Erik had titled "Seville Disobedience" was scheduled. The name was derived from the initial image that appears on-screen as the video begins. The sound of a French horn is heard as an off-balance Buick Seville appears onscreen. The camera then shifts to the discussion between me and the host, Eric Olson. Knowing that I was being filmed and having a camera pointing directly at me was terrifying. Although I was extremely nervous and felt clumsy throughout the interview, I felt that the final product that was edited and produced solely by Erik Stewart was outstanding.

Denis and I collaborated on a written piece titled "Walking without 'Treppa-dation'" later in 2014 for *Scene* magazine, a Green Bay monthly publication. For the first time, an article touched on personal and unpleasant characteristics of my childhood, specifically highlighting the parts of my childhood when I had experienced bullying. This was something we had discussed at length because of the risks involved in putting oneself in the spotlight, especially while immersed in a major controversy like the Monfils case. "I think I can handle myself," I told Denis. "I think of my past as an important facet of this mission because it explains why I became involved and why I'm able to empathize with the folks I advocate for. I'm beyond worrying about what people might think or say."

In a development that fell in line with the many small miracles we witnessed along the way, days before the December 2014 issue was to be published, Denis received word that the article was not going to appear in the Green Bay edition but in an expanded issue accessible to readers across the entire state. We were elated—and fortunate that the article produced no negative feedback aimed at either of us.

A strategic move also prompted by Jared helped to bring the message about this injustice to a global audience. Sometime during the process, Jared described the benefits of social media and stressed the importance of having an online presence. "Great things are starting to happen in this case," he said. "This is becoming a success, and you need to let people know." This made sense, but I was unsure of my ability to maintain these sites considering I was unskilled beyond the basic functions of a computer.

Jared explained standard concepts behind managing social media pages and recommended that I start with a basic site called about.me. This site was a single webpage allowing subscribers to post a bio and photo, along with related virtual links. There were countless about.me pages being used by people around the world to promote themselves and their interests. The page I built was easy to navigate and maintain and a good way for me to get comfortable with having a website while connecting with people from all corners of the world. It also helped with another difficult task—self-promotion. This concept conflicted with my growing up in a household that had associated exhibiting pride in one's accomplishments as bragging.

I don't remember my parents offering much encouragement in that regard. I do remember something my dad had done to let me know he disapproved of my spirited personality. There had always been a bounce to my step, no matter where I went—up and down the aisles in church, in the grocery store, at home, and at school. But whenever I walked past my dad, he would rest the palm of his hand on the top of my head and apply pressure to lessen the bounce. Then he'd say, "It's more ladylike to maintain a steady stride." As much as this angered me, I'd reluctantly comply. But to this day, I've not mastered that ladylike gait.

Thousands of people in the about.me community visited my page over a three-year span. Many expressed an interest in my personal mission. I received messages from people who had been similarly victimized and wanted to share their experiences. I heard from those who were looking to be educated and others who simply wanted to express their dismay.

Awareness surged and I was inspired to start writing a blog to document my observations and experiences regarding the Monfils case and to highlight those whom I had become acquainted with over time who had been wrongfully convicted and exonerated. It was unsettling to learn that there were many more cases than I could possibly write about.

Jared agreed that this was a great move. "Blogs are growing in popularity and are considered great resources for information on anything and everything," he said. "You can then share those posts on Facebook and Twitter to expand your audience."

In 2017, it was time to evolve, to upgrade to a new domain site with a fresh new look. Jared helped with the transition to this new site which I had named *A Matter of Facts: Social Justice Advocate for the Wrongfully Convicted*. The combined analytics for both sites indicate my blog has been viewed in more than ninety countries.

Joan Van Houten and I formed a bond that later developed into a partnership. We put together a *Voice of Innocence* Facebook page—a platform to promote awareness about the Monfils case. Joan was the brains and technical support behind this page and used it to share her personal experience as a family member of a wrongfully convicted person. She readily embraced my efforts. "I'm so glad someone other than us family members has taken up this cause," she said. "It gives our situation credibility when someone from outside our inner circle speaks out on our behalf."

Joan and I called ourselves *sista-flames,* indicating the way to a brighter future for the five men as we created a consciousness about this tragic ordeal. Our personal writings and ongoing activities regarding this case can still be accessed on the *Voice of Innocence* site.

Having an online presence triggered invitations to be a guest on blog talk radio shows. Friends I had met through the about.me site approached me with requests to do interviews. The first was with Suzanne Wigginton, who was based in Phoenix, Arizona. Our conversation on her blog talk radio show, *Souls Aloft,* aired in June 2014. It centered on the importance of finding and enacting ways to overcome emotional trauma and how to achieve inner peace through advocacy.

I also met Nina Bingham, a life coach and writer, through about.me. She connected me with a friend of hers, Alex Okoroji, who was an actress, writer, and host of the blog talk radio show, *The Naked Talk,* which is based in Lagos, Nigeria. Alex hosted Joan, Johnny, and me in February 2015. We focused on the Monfils case and the challenges of dealing with the wrongful conviction of a loved one. Alex invited us back for a follow-up interview a year later.

The three of us were invited to appear on a third blog talk radio show based in Charlotte, North Carolina, called *Charlotte View.* The segment, also made possible through Nina, aired in March 2015. The conversation with cohosts Claudia Pureco and Nina centered on the Monfils case and the emotional turmoil surrounding wrongful convictions.

Chapter 30
COUP D'ÉTAT OF SORTS

When Johnny and I occasionally met with Steve, he would supply updates and recite a litany of tasks yet to be completed. Steve sometimes included difficulties he had encountered. Prior to one of those meetings, Steve had experienced major resistance from a private lawyer associated with the Monfils case. While making arrangements to send a photographer to take photos of the primary pieces of evidence—the rope, rope knots, and weight—as part of the re-investigation process, Steve learned that the items were not where they should have been—in an evidence-storage locker at the GBPD or at the Brown County Circuit Court. They had, in fact, been released in 1997 with the court's approval to a private lawyer for a stated purpose but had never been returned to the clerk's office or to the police for safe-keeping. Rather, this critical evidence remained in the possession of a private law firm.

When Steve contacted the lawyer in September 2013 to inquire about the whereabouts of these items, he received a hostile response. So in November 2013, Steve commenced a civil action seeking injunctive relief against the lawyer and his law firm directing them to return the evidence to its proper location. Soon after the petition was served, the items were delivered to the GBPD, and a photographer was able to photograph them.

Steve always summarized what had been accomplished since our last visit. I was amazed at the lengthy and convoluted process of reversing a single miscarriage of justice, let alone one that was compounded by four additional defendants. There were times when we left Steve's office with a sinking feeling that this process may never end, let alone end favorably. Having him on our side during those times and knowing that he had successfully solicited additional help from a hand-picked team of fellow attorneys from the firm who were also willing to work pro bono kept us hopeful. It was a privilege to have them, in addition to attorneys from Wisconsin, who eventually came on board to represent the other four men. Since the case had originated in Wisconsin, it was necessary to hire additional legal representation from that state to work in sync with the attorneys in Minnesota. Their collective compassion, attention to detail, and obvious capabilities were a blessing and a miracle. For once, attorneys representing these men were committed and fully engaged. They were, by far, the best representation the men had ever had.

The topic during one of our meetings was about hiring expert witnesses. They, of course, can be expensive. Johnny and I grew concerned about the cost.

Johnny was always helpful in explaining the whys and hows of this process. After our meeting with Steve, he clarified the importance of expert witnesses. "These experts are crucial to us and to the case because they can evaluate the evidence, like the autopsy report and the knots on the rope and weight," he said. "They will give credence to the evidence at hand. I think Steve is also planning to hire an expert to assess the lawyers who misrepresented these men."

Explaining this, however, triggered frustration over a growing list of things deeply troubling my friend. "So many facets of this case were never addressed, and those lawyers sat on their pompous asses and did nothing," Johnny said. "They should have been jumping out of their seats objecting to everything put forth by the DA during that trial! And now these guys have to deal with more bureaucracy because of the inadequate representation they had back then. The judicial wheels grind slowly, and this case will take so much time because of the number of defendants involved."

Out of his frustration, Johnny came up with a daring idea. "What would you say to you and me jump-starting the fundraising process?" he asked.

"How do you mean?" I replied.

"Well, in the military, we have a saying. It's called 'coup d'état.' In military terms, it has to do with overthrowing, or a sudden forced seizure, usually instigated by a small group," he said.

"Okay," I said. "How is this relevant to what we are trying to do?"

"It's simple," he said. "What if we plop some dough-re-mi onto Steve's desk and see what happens? Let's seize this opportunity and get the ball rolling."

I thought about it for a moment. "The idea is tempting, but I don't know if Mike will go for it," I said. "We're talking a lot of money."

"Mike's a generous guy, and I know you can talk him into anything," Johnny teased. "I tell you what, let's each talk to our spouses and see what they say."

"Fair enough," I said.

I broached the subject with Mike that evening. "Sleep on it before you give me an answer," I proffered. "But Johnny has a good point. It will take too much time to organize some type of event, and Steve is ready to move on this now."

I'll never forget the look on Mike's face when he agreed to it the next morning, saying, "I cannot think of a reason not to."

Linda's answer was the same. So later that day, I contacted Steve to see if Johnny and I could stop by his office for a few minutes. "We can't stay for lunch," I said. "This is strictly business."

We met Steve by the reception desk, and he again asked for a conference room. "This won't take long," I said. "Only a few minutes." After entering the room, and without sitting down, Johnny and I placed two checks on the table in front of Steve. It took only a brief discussion regarding his acceptance of them before we exited the room. Steve walked us over to the elevator. As the doors closed, we saw him run into Pam and hand the checks to her.

What happened afterward was humbling and significant. When the WIP caught wind of our contribution, they responded by contributing funds of their own. And although the law firm was more than willing to fund the litigation expenses itself, we still wanted to contribute to that effort in a meaningful way. We began considering possible fundraising ideas.

Chapter 31
SOLICITING FUNDS

Whenever the slightest hint of warm weather arrived in Minnesota, Johnny would rescue from storage his bright yellow classic car—a 1934 Ford three-window coupe. He was proud of his lemony wonder, with its dark painted stripes tracing the fine lines on both sides and a purple heart sitting on the top right side of the trunk door—a medal he also took great pride in. He would take me for rides sometimes while we brainstormed. I'd chuckle at the stares from other motorists.

Johnny drove over in the coupe one sunny day to discuss fundraising options. This time we sat in my dining room admiring the car when a thought materialized in his head. "How about hosting a car show and using that platform to raise money?" he said. "I'm a member of the MSRA (Minnesota Street Rod Association), and I have friends with classic cars that love to be in shows. They might even be interested in helping us plan this type of shindig."

I didn't know much about car shows but figured what the hell. However, I saw one big problem. "Who's going to donate money to us?" I asked. "We will need to come up with a legitimate organization that people feel comfortable giving money to."

"Why not ask Erika at the GN-IP?" Johnny said. "Maybe they will partner with us."

"It's a great idea," I said. "Let's make some inquiries to see if this idea will work." After some thought, we developed a plan of attack and hit the pavement.

We drove to a place Johnny knew of called Route 65 Classics—a nearby consignment shop for classic cars. We talked to Sue Stang, the general manager, about our predicament and shared our vision to highlight stories about exonerees while collecting funds through car entry fees and donations from spectators. She was intrigued by the idea and immediately set up a tentative date for the event. We then held a meeting with Erika, Audrey, and Steve. We defined two basic but important aspects of this event: 1) to raise funds; and 2) to educate the audience about wrongful convictions. Our pitch was unanimously agreed upon. We decided we'd do the bulk of the work, with the Innocence Project lending their name and participation on the day of the show.

Mike and I attended a few car shows to get a feel for how they were structured and to find either a band or a DJ to provide music. We found Chuck Brost, a DJ we liked who was willing to charge a reasonable fee. Then, at a planning meeting with our newly formed committee, we gave this event a proper name: Hotrod Breakout.

Prior to the first show, I contacted our local Blaine paper, *Life*—a free weekly circular with a potential audience of approximately 61,000 Blaine residents. For the interview, I offered to coordinate with two exonerees who would be at the show, Audrey Edmunds and Damon Thibodeaux. A few days later, staff writer Eric Hagen contacted me to set up a date for the interview.

Eric looked to be in his thirties. He placed a handheld tape recorder on the coffee table and looked at Audrey and Damon. "Is it okay to have this going during the interview?" he asked. Eric was absorbed and visibly moved by his subjects and the horrific stories they shared. In addition to having the recorder going, he scribbled notes on a notepad, intent on capturing every last bit of information from his subjects. He took statements from Johnny and me and used Johnny's classic car as a backdrop for a photo to go with the article.

The following week, the story appeared on the front page with the headline: "Blaine Residents Host Car Show for Those Exonerated."

The article was extensive, filling the front page plus an additional full interior page. Eric had done us a great service by placing most of the emphasis on Audrey and Damon.

Many who attended the event were unaware of the organization and its mission. Some expressed concern over the idea of wrongful convictions. Some attendees opened up about their personal stories of dealing with the "system." In the next few years, informative panel discussions were set up with the Innocence Project staff, exonerees, and advocates for the wrongfully convicted. These events brought favorable reviews, one of which came from the mayor of North Branch, Minnesota, Kirsten Kennedy. One couple, deeply touched after listening to one of the panels, made a rather large donation. Despite the time and effort we put into these events, overall, they failed to solicit the level of interest and donations necessary to supplement our mission. And as each successive show failed to gain traction, we called it quits after the 2016 Hotrod Breakout event. Not all was lost, though, as the sincerity of our efforts was recognized by those at the firm who continued to move forward with the legal process in this case.

Chapter 32

LEGAL WOES FOR THE OPPOSITION

Halloween, October 31, 2014. A fitting day to illustrate an unearthing of ghosts still lurking through the halls of the Brown County Courthouse. Finally, twenty-one months of effort put forth by a dedicated legal defense team came to fruition when they filed a 152-page motion, more than one hundred exhibits, and several affidavits in Brown County Circuit Court requesting an evidentiary hearing for Keith Kutska. Close to twenty years later, this modestly populated city in the Midwest was thrust back into legal upheaval. There were a flurry of news reports on local TV stations and in print. One Green Bay *Press-Gazette* headline read: "Defense: Monfils Death a Suicide. New Legal Team Seeks to Have Conspiracy Conviction Thrown Out."

When this motion was filed, Johnny and I took great satisfaction in knowing that we had played a monumental role in a significant milestone. The families were hopeful. We all felt great knowing real progress was being made. The historical outcome was no longer being accepted as the absolute law of the land. This new and unambiguous legal action was a kick in the legal shins for Brown County. They had most likely never expected we would get this far or that this case would actually make it back into the courts. But there it was. I imagined them clambering behind closed doors to keep their wits about them because the further this moved forward, the more media attention they'd receive. There'd be no escaping public scrutiny or the tough questions that followed. And it would be a cold day in hell before those questions stopped. This was no longer merely a movement of family members, close friends, and two crusaders from Minnesota. This motion was spearheaded by a respectable law firm armed with unrelenting dedication and impetus to move toward a more just ending.

The main points of this motion were extracted from the original 152-page brief:

- *Defense counsel provided ineffective assistance by conceding the State's homicide theory without consulting an independent forensic pathologist and investigating the evidence of suicide*
- *The State denied Mr. Kutska due process by relying on erroneous forensic pathology and perjured fact witness testimony*
- *Mr. Kutska has presented "sufficient reason" for this motion*
- *The court should vacate this conviction in the interests of justice.*

The following excerpts were taken from the same document. They reveal major aspects of a failed investigation in a massively flawed case:

At approximately 7:42 a.m. on November 21, 1992, Tom Monfils—despondent, shamed, and angry—left his work area at the James River Paper Mill and walked toward an entrance of a nearby airlock passageway. As he neared the airlock, he picked up a 49 lb. weight and proceeded through the airlock. He then entered a storage area where his jump rope was hanging on a railing. With both the rope and weight in hand, Monfils walked over to a large vat containing approximately 20,000 gallons of liquid. There, he tied one end of the rope around his neck and the other end to the weight, and entered the vat where he suffered traumatic injuries and died from drowning in the liquid.

After a two-and-a-half-year investigation, Kutska and five other mill workers were convicted of first-degree intentional homicide and sentenced to life in prison for Monfils' death. The prosecution's theory was that after Kutska had learned that Monfils had reported him to the police for stealing a piece of electrical cord from the mill, Kutska fomented "an angry mob" of his "union brothers" that viciously beat Monfils at the water bubbler at approximately 7:45 a.m. and then disposed of his body in the vat at approximately 7:50 a.m. on November 21, 1992. That theory embraced the conclusions of the medical examiner Dr. Helen Young, who concluded that Monfils had been beaten and then placed in the vat where he died.

Dr. Young's homicide determination was, however, erroneous and rested on a series of provably false assumptions, as well as her ignorance regarding the engineering design and operating factors impacting the movement of Monfils' body in the vat. As Forensic Pathologist Dr. Mary Ann Sens states in her report, Dr. Young also lacked any scientific or medical basis for reliably and accurately determining that Monfils' death was the result of a homicide and not a suicide. Indeed, there is ample and compelling evidence that Monfils had taken his own life.

Unfortunately, residents and law enforcement officials in Green Bay remained unappreciative of the implications surrounding the firm's findings that supported a possible suicide. This first round of filings caused the county to push back . . . hard. They resisted the notion that the case had been mismanaged. They remained as steadfast as ever in a dying effort to uphold all of these convictions, including Mike Piaskowski's, in spite of his exoneration in a federal court. At every opportunity, former District Attorney and now Judge John Zakowski defended the biggest case of his career with toxic statements that still fuel a vengeful public. In the present day, his most vicious attacks are still aimed directly at his worst nightmare come true. In reference to the exoneration of Michael Piaskowski, he flatly states that Michael Piaskowski "was not exonerated," rather, he was "mistakenly let go" due to a poor appeals argument by the attorney general's office. Also, in a recent interview for an upcoming documentary, he offers this assessment to validate his most revered case, "People tend to say, well, it's only circumstantial evidence. Circumstantial evidence is many times stronger."

To date, this judge has two overturned convictions on his record as former prosecutor of Brown County. The exonerations of Michael Piaskowski and Mario Victoria Vasquez represent circumstances that have achieved the highest standard of proof required to declare each of them *factually* innocent.

We waited for a reply from the State. Their response argued against every measure of the firm's brief. However, it was again the defense team's turn to have one last say in the matter before a final decision was to be reached. The firm was ready, having prepared their reply brief in less time than had been allotted.

Chapter 33
ADDITIONAL MEDIA
CONNECTIONS

M edia opportunities in Minneapolis surfaced as legal action pushed through the courts in Wisconsin. In 2014, Johnny and I made an important connection at a GN-IP benefit. We met reporter Ted Haller from KMSP Fox 9 news. Ted, an enthusiastic and good-humored individual, was the emcee for this event.

Of course, Johnny managed to zero in on him during the reception. And when Ted shared that he was pursuing becoming an attorney, Johnny told him all about our activities. Ted was interested to learn more. Being nearby, Johnny called me over for an introduction. We shared our dual efforts since 2010, which prompted Ted to make an irresistible offer. "I'd like to do a news story about the both of you," he said. "I cannot promise anything, but I think I can convince the station to let me highlight you as the Minnesota link to the Wisconsin case."

"I've been trying to engage reporters in the Twin Cities," I said. "If you can make this happen, the folks in Green Bay will finally have their story told in a meaningful way, unlike the negative coverage they're accustomed to." Mike Pie was at this event, so we introduced him to Ted as well.

Months later, Ted reached out with great news. He had been given the green light for the story and was ready to set up interviews. He worked with Johnny and me first and then traveled to Green Bay for additional interviews. While in Green Bay—and to our complete surprise—Ted was granted an on-camera interview with Judge John Zakowski.

In April 2015, an eight-minute feature story aired in the Minneapolis area. It provided a new perspective on the Monfils case by focusing mainly on the struggles of the families, with minimal time devoted to the opposition's views. The story brought forth the silenced voices affected by an ongoing injustice. It highlighted the fact that wrongful convictions shred the very fabric of our society and destroy families despite claims by the authorities that their intent is solely to protect and serve.

When I'm asked why wrongful convictions should be a concern for all Americans, my response is simple—because it can happen to any one of us, with no warning or conceivable reason. For decades, the innocent citizens who make up our neighborhoods, towns, and cities have been taken from their families and sent to prison with no credible evidence or sometimes fabricated evidence, for being poor, uneducated, *different*, or simply for being in the wrong place at the wrong time. Law enforcement sees them as easy targets and convenient scapegoats.

In an email from Ted sometime later, he said our story had been nominated within the media circuit for a Regional Emmy Award in the investigative crime category. The story didn't win, but he said it was a great honor to be nominated. He expressed gratitude for the opportunity to help people through his reporting. He ended with a touching remark, thanking me for being on the front lines of those who help others, which is one of the reasons he was able to cover these kinds of stories. Ted remained a valuable resource for additional stories as developments occurred. I am both happy for him and a little saddened that he has since left the station as a full-time reporter, having achieved his goal of becoming a full-time lawyer.

Another significant connection came about through social media. I ran across Mark Saxenmeyer through Facebook. Mark had an extensive background in journalism as a reporter in various cities, including Minneapolis and Chicago. Mark left news reporting to delve into producing longer-form stories, like documentaries, that address important yet rarely covered topics. He decided to form his own visual media production company based in Minneapolis called *The Reporters Inc.*

When we finally met in person, Mark asked about the Monfils case. He told me about a related project he was working on that addressed wrongful convictions. "It's a documentary called *The Innocent Convicts*," he said. "I'm working with a Texas Tech student who wanted to do a film about the posthumous exoneration of a former student from the same college. Timothy Cole was wrongfully convicted of rape at the age of twenty-five but died in prison of an asthma attack before he was exonerated. It's a very tragic story. The film will also feature a number of other wrongful conviction cases as well."

Mark had asked me to write an article in relation to the film for his website in November 2016. Its title read, "How I Became a Citizen Advocate: Wrongful Conviction of Six Wisconsin Men Captured My Attention, Changed My Life."

Because of that article, I became acquainted with the film's director at the time, Okoruwa (Ossy) Osagie Nations. Both Mark and Ossy decided to include the Monfils case in the film. In March 2016, Mark drove his film crew over to Green Bay for a week of conducting interviews for the project. And in September of that same year, Johnny and I, Steve, and North Dakota Forensic Pathologist Dr. Mary Ann Sens were interviewed for the project in Minneapolis. This was another boost toward a wider range of awareness and real potential for this case and our mission, with the film's eventual release to film festivals and various public and private screenings upon completion.

Another intriguing connection to this documentary dawned on me in September 2016. I remembered that while my about.me page had been active, I had seen a number of Texas Tech student logos showing up as viewership of my page. This had me curious because of the large number of them that had appeared almost daily for about a month. Ossy suggested the possibility of these visits had come from law students at Texas Tech who were working with the adjoining Innocence Project of Texas. "They were most likely doing research for the Timothy Cole posthumous exoneration," he indicated.

Although this project is still in the works, structural changes have occurred in the past few years. Ossy and Mark have since parted ways. Ossy is solely promoting the Timothy Cole segment and has maintained *The Innocent Convicts* title. Mark has renamed his portion of the documentary *Guilty Until Proven Innocent* and is hoping to complete it in 2021. Mark also approached me about becoming a board member for *The Reporters Inc*, a position which I accepted.

A second documentary covering this case is also being produced in Madison, Wisconsin, by father and son team Dave and Michael Neelsen. The film, *Beyond Human Nature*, is dedicated solely to the Monfils case and delves into the emotional aspects on both sides of this tragedy. According to the film's website, "*Beyond Human Nature* is about the conflict that erupts between mankind's inherent need to make sense of the world and his limited capacities to do so."

I met the Neelsens in 2016 while they were filming at our seventh annual Walk for Truth and Justice. At that time, production of the documentary had been in the works for two years and was ongoing. The film was completed in 2020, just prior to the outbreak of the pandemic. Plans to hold a private screening in Green Bay before eventually releasing it to the public were in the works. Those plans, however, were put on hold. To date, a new plan to expand the film into a four-part series with additional footage and interviews is being considered.

Chapter 34
SPINS, SLANTS, AND BIASES

The latest attempts in Minneapolis to cover this case were refreshing, but they formed a distinct contrast in my mind to how slanted much of the news reporting in the Green Bay area was. In regard to our annual Walks, I couldn't say for sure whether or not details in local broadcasts were misstated on purpose to lessen our significance. Actual video from our speeches was often omitted, and coverage of our latest developments in the case would be replaced with incorrect or outdated information. I also noticed inconsistencies in the facts most favorable to our mission. One such instance was when Denis made a public announcement in 2012 that Keith Kutska had acquired legal representation by a Minneapolis law firm. This detail was included in initial news reports, but in later coverage of the same story, it was left out. The story would instead indicate that Kutska's legal team was comprised solely of the Innocence Project.

In my opinion, whenever this organization is mentioned in a story related to the Monfils case, it results in a flood of controversy. This is because of the well-known case regarding a previous client of the WIP—Steven Avery. People were incensed when Avery was exonerated by the WIP in 2007 and then sent back to prison two years later for a heinous murder. Even though DNA had clearly eliminated Avery as the perpetrator in the first offense, a sexual assault costing him eighteen years of freedom, news of an indictment for this second crime angered the populace in the state—an anger that is forever aimed at the WIP.

In my quest to remain optimistic, I believed that as developments and shocking truths about our case surfaced, reasonable doubt about the guilt of these men might start to resonate with the residents of Green Bay. I hoped that the real facts could sway overall opinion. After all, the information was forthcoming from an independent source. But as new details surfaced—no matter their relevance—the media inhibited our ability to make headway by continuing to downplay them and focusing on the negative characteristics of the story. Another example of this occurred in news coverage in 2015. At our fifth Walk, an announcement was made about a possible evidentiary hearing for Keith Kutska. The story highlighted new evidence uncovered by the firm that suggested the death of Monfils was actually a suicide. But as substantial as this information was, it was overshadowed by simultaneous reports covering Kutska's first-ever parole hearing, which resulted in a denial of his release. And while most first-time parole requests are typically denied, the news of Keith's misfortune became the bigger, more prominent headline.

The tide did eventually start to turn, and we did come across two open-minded reporters in Green Bay. On the day of our Walk in 2015, I was interviewed by Raquel Lamal of NBC 26 in Green Bay a few hours prior to the event. This opportunity arose through default. Denis was not available, so I was asked to speak with her instead. Raquel was the first reporter from Wisconsin who was as open to sharing the real tragedy as Ted had been. For this type of story, I was the likely candidate, being the kindhearted outsider who had taken the time to get to know the families and share the depth of the pain they continued to endure. I felt that this interview was a great outlet to communicate what I truly believed, "that these men and their families had been bullied."

Another opportunity surfaced in April 2016 after I had initiated a connection with Rey Moore's daughter, Kayce. She had asked if I would like to do an interview with Mark Leland, an investigative reporter and weekend co-anchor for WLUK FOX 11 news in Green Bay. He was working on a story about wrongful convictions and had interviewed Kayce. The story focused on a recently exonerated Green Bay man named Mario Victoria Vasquez. Mario had been wrongfully convicted for the sexual assault of a four-year-old child and had served seventeen years for this crime. The piece, approximately eight minutes long, was a great platform for Mario to share his story—a story which needed to be told because of the horrific way the case had been investigated and because of the inhumane way he had been treated after his release.

Early in the investigation, Mario had hoped to clear himself of suspicion of an assault on a four-year-old girl. He asked to be tested for herpes, which the four-year-old had developed after the assault. But an old scar found by the examining doctor led him to conclude that Mario could have had the disease, which led to his arrest. However, no herpes test was ever performed on him. No DNA evidence was given to Mario's defense even though he had willingly given samples of his blood, hair, and saliva for comparison. In addition, the nurse who had examined the child at the hospital had never completed a full examination on her, according to court records. These tests could have eliminated Mario as the suspect right away. Each time he pushed to have his samples tested, he was assured that it would be taken care of. It never was. Another contributing factor was testimony from the child. At trial, she had referred to her perpetrator as "Mario." But what was never revealed was that the girl also referred to her uncle as "Mario." Mario's attorney failed to present an expert witness to challenge the child's testimony, even though it was something he had said he would do in his opening statements to the jury.

It was nearly two decades later when the authorities learned from the victim who her actual abusers were. There were, in fact, two people, neither of whom was Mario Victoria Vasquez. A hearing was scheduled in light of this new information. But during a second hearing meant to determine if there was going to be a new trial, the former assistant DA argued that they still believed they had convicted the right person despite the girl's testimony. He also said that the State would not be seeking a new trial. This information elicited a puzzled look from the judge overseeing the hearing, who then stated for the record that the victim had positively identified her abusers and that Mario had not been cited as one of them.

After this second hearing, Mario was unexpectedly released from the county jail. It happened that evening at approximately 7:00 p.m. The expectations at the hearing were that because of the weight of the child's testimony, he would be released the following week after the paperwork had been filed. But unbeknownst to anyone, Mario was sent out into a cold, dark, and blustery night in January with temperatures in the teens. Lacking adequate clothing or a means to call a relative to pick him up, Mario had no choice but to go back into the county jail and ask to use their phone to call his son. There were no media present to hear his side of the story. No apologies were forthcoming from the authorities who had robbed him of so many years for one of the worst offenses possible, an offense that the vilest of criminals find distasteful.

What infuriated Mario the most was the likelihood that because he had been convicted and because the real abusers were family members, the assaults on the child had continued. And even though he has been exonerated, neither of those abusers have been held accountable. His overall concern was for a child he refers to as an "angel" who hadn't understood what she had done by pointing the finger at him.

What is equally infuriating is twofold: 1) Three months after Mario was convicted, a woman filed a complaint against one of the child's uncles. The uncle had denied under oath at Mario's trial that he had herpes. But this woman alleged that he had given her the disease during a sexual assault that same year—evidence that was buried until it was uncovered in 2014 during the investigation of Mario's case by attorneys from the WIP; and 2) The main reason I've written as extensively as I have on this case is the fact that the original prosecutor and former assistant DA (at Mario's hearing), are the same as in the Monfils case.

I was eager to be included in Mark Leland's segment because I had become acquainted with Mario while he was still in prison. This was another connection that I made through my sister, Clare, who was friends with Mario's ex-wife, Darcy. I had expressed interest in writing to him after talking with both Darcy and Clare about his case. At the time, Mario had already retained legal representation from the WIP, and at one of our Walks, I mentioned my communications with Mario to Byron Lichstein. Months later, in January 2015, I was notified that Mario was being exonerated. His was the first and only exoneration I've witnessed so far.

In the final moments of Leland's piece, Judge John Zakowski is asked to comment on the possibility that there could be others who have been wrongfully convicted. He acknowledges this with these re-marks: "It's possible. It could be possible; we don't know that." In the story, he admits that he doesn't fully recollect Mario's case. He claims that he hadn't been aware of Mario's release or of the fact that his re-lease was based on the victim's new testimony. In spite of these deeply troubling and, frankly, unbelievable declarations, I felt the overall story was sufficiently detailed, informative, and enlightening.

Chapter 35
ROUSING A NEW GENERATION

An encouraging realization moving forward is that we've reached a new generation of supporters. In 2015, I became acquainted with two thirteen-year-olds who supported our efforts. One of them contacted me online, which led to a phone conversation. She said that she had heard about the case in the news and wanted to do a school report on it. While conducting research for her project, she contacted me. "Your name kept popping up, so I wanted to talk to you," she said. I asked her how her peers viewed the case, and she said, "They were sad mostly."

Before school let out for the summer in 2016, she was granted permission from her teacher to invite me into their social studies class. I asked my sister, Clare, to assist me. We met with nineteen inquisitive, smart, and open-minded students. We discussed the mission of the Innocence Project and addressed the bullying aspect. We talked about individuals who had been wrongfully convicted and covered some of the pitfalls of wrongful convictions, such as faulty eyewitness identification. We showed them photos of exonerees and asked them to share their impressions of the kind of people they saw. They were amazed at how normal the faces looked.

To make things interesting, we engaged them in two exercises involving eyewitness identification. We asked for their feedback on two actual cases. The first addressed the wrongful conviction of exoneree Ronald Cotton. A brief case summary was read to the class. They learned that Cotton was convicted solely on the eyewitness testimony of a rape victim, Jennifer Thompson—a young college student assaulted in her apartment who had had the presence of mind to study her attacker's face close up. When it came time to identify him in court, Jennifer was 100 percent sure she had picked the right man. As a result of her testimony, Cotton was convicted. He spent eleven years in prison before DNA evidence exonerated him and led the authorities to the real assailant, who was serving time at the same prison as Cotton for another crime. We showed photos of both men to the class. Their jaws dropped at the facial similarities of each. "They could be twins," one of the students said.

In one other exercise, the students were asked to identify the correct perpetrator in a case in which a police sketch had been publicized on the news prior to an arrest. In this case, the suspect that had been arrested was guilty, but the exercise we conducted was more about how an innocent person could easily have been arrested if the circumstances had been slightly different. It's a case that hits close to home.

In 1996, US headlines brought news of a horrific bombing in Oklahoma City, Oklahoma. Former-war-veteran-turned-domestic-terrorist Timothy McVeigh detonated a truck bomb in front of the Alfred P. Murrah Federal Building in Oklahoma City on April 19, 1995. The blast killed 168 and wounded nearly 600 people. Back then, it was classified as the largest terrorist act ever committed on US soil.

When the story hit the news, the sketch of the suspect looked a lot like my son, Jared, who was in the military at the time in California. When McVeigh was finally caught and his face appeared in news clips, our first impression was that his facial features didn't match the police sketch as well as Jared's did. We wondered if Jared, had he been in that city during the investigation, could've been arrested based on his resemblance to the sketch—a possibility that will always haunt me.

While I was preparing the latter exercise for the class, I found out from Jared that he had never seen the sketch. When I sent it to him, he was shocked by the resemblance to a photo of his from his military days. For the students at the middle school, and at future venues with audiences too young to remember the incident from 1995, the majority picked my son's military photo over McVeigh's as the one closest in likeness to the police sketch.

The class was surprised at how easy it was to misidentify someone. They were equally concerned when we brought up the idea that when innocent people are convicted, the guilty go free and may continue to commit additional crimes.

We were quite honored to have met this class, and I must admit that they were not the only ones to receive an education that day. Learning about the intuitive nature and basic understanding that these students had at their age was refreshing and far outweighed my own level of awareness at that age.

I also met a young man who came to our 2015 Walk with his father. He was shy and didn't say too much. His dad told me that when he read the Monfils book, his son was able to see the flaws in the case and was adamant about supporting this movement. It's hard to measure the effects of these instances. If they are any indication of what's to come, then it means our message is resonating with an important portion of society—future advocates, future lawyers, and future prosecutors who won't be so quick to convict without adequate and reliable evidence. I see these young people as the brains and compassion behind many future innovations, and I'm encouraged that because of their knowledge of this problem, they'll be the ones to reform our judicial system and, hopefully, eliminate wrongful convictions altogether.

Chapter 36
PRISON VISITS

After a few years of correspondence with the five men, I considered visiting them. I saw the visits as beneficial in providing a more personal level of communication. I discussed this idea with Mike. He was unsure about me going alone and expressed concern for my general safety. While we all hear about the riots, violence, and mayhem within prisons, Keith told me once that in all of his years in prison, he had seen few altercations. Julie Jonas reassured me that visits to prisons are quite safe because of the safeguards in place.

Mike offered a quick solution he could live with that wouldn't restrict my plans. "I'll go with you," he said. We filled out the necessary paperwork and were added to four of the five men's visitor lists. There was a cap of ten to twelve visitors allowed at any given time, and we found out that Rey's list was already full. Visiting him would require a different form that allowed a one-time special visit. We needed to decide on a specific date, so we elected to address this visit at a later date. At the time, we had every intention of following through with the visits, but they didn't happen right away. Life got in the way, and it was not until a few years later that I was motivated into action by a good friend.

In December 2014, shortly before I left my part-time job to focus on this cause, Mike and I attended a holiday party for Gentle Transitions employees. These events gave me a chance to share the latest regarding my mission. This year, I was bombarded with questions as right before the party, my boss, Diane, had posted in the employee newsletter the *Scene* magazine article that Denis had written.

A conversation I had at the party with one of my move managers, Kathleen, struck a chord. Kathleen had a shared interest in this work because of a family member who had been incarcerated. She remarked on something in the article that had bothered her. "You stated you've never met the five men," she said. "This troubles me because I understand the importance of them having outside contact. I think you should consider visiting them. You will not regret it."

I thought about my neglect to follow through with the visits. "Why had we not taken the time?" I asked Mike after the party. "Because we were too busy, that's why," I said, acutely aware of the answer.

It is not a simple process to get on visitor lists. The requirements are painstaking. We first needed to contact the men and have them request the necessary forms and mail them to us. We would receive the forms, fill them out, and send them back to a specified mailing address for processing. Finally, the men would receive confirmation and let us know if we had been approved. In one instance, our names had been removed from one list in order to make room for another visitor, which required us to complete the process all over again. "We simply disregarded the inconvenience we'd placed on them, not to mention the disappointment we most likely caused," I lamented, "We have to follow through this time."

We decided that our first visit should be with Keith Kutska. This time, we committed to visiting as soon as we received word that we had been approved.

Our visit was on Saturday, February 21, 2015. As much as Mike and I looked forward to it, the worrisome part was the instruction sheet accompanying the visitor forms. Each lengthy list of rules and restrictions of what constituted proper dress, appropriate conduct, and so forth also varied greatly from prison to prison. Certain types of shorts, short skirts, sleeveless and strapless tops, revealing or see-through clothing, spandex, and obscene or profane messages and images on T-shirts were strictly prohibited. Luckily, before we showed up on that day, I learned of the advantages of wearing a sports bra. The metal clasps on a regular bra trigger the highly sensitive metal detectors. If you are wearing one, you'll be sent to the restroom with a brown paper bag to remove it, store it in the bag, and then shove it down the conveyor belt before going back through a metal detector. And to be clear, you do not get to put it back on until *after* the visit. I was lucky to come across a related story prior to this visit that described a woman's experience after having been fitted with a breast prosthesis inside of a regular bra. In spite of her unique circumstance, she was forced to go braless during her visit at a prison, which caused her undue embarrassment. We also learned that visitors have three tries to successfully make it through the metal detector before being sent away. Wallets, purses, and cell phones go into tiny lockers. The only item allowed in the visiting room is a clear plastic bag with no more than ten dollars' worth of quarters. The quarters are for the vending machines in the lounge that only visitors can retrieve refreshments from.

The two-and-a-half-hour drive there gave us time to mentally prepare for this experience and to double-check that we had fulfilled the necessary requirements.

We entered the building and were greeted by a guard who readily explained all we needed to know for entry into the visitor's lounge. After fulfilling our duties, we lined up to go through the metal detector. "I'll definitely relax once we get beyond this contraption," I thought as we approached the towering orifice. Partly due to a miracle and partly due to a little planning, both Mike and I breezed through with no problems on the first try. The guard even commented on the rarity of that happening.

We proceeded to the exit door, which led us outdoors to the building where our visit would take place. I don't remember feeling especially frightened, even with the loud clanging of the heavy metal doors that unlocked and relocked as we navigated our way to our destination. When we finally entered the visitor's lounge, Mike and I took a moment to observe our surroundings. I marveled at how normal everything and everyone looked. The atmosphere was pleasant. The lounge looked similar to those in the free world, except for the long desk off to the side where the prison guard sat. Each table was occupied by one individual clothed in drab green garb who conversed with friends and family members in a remarkably relaxed manner. According to the instruction sheet, as many as twelve people (a mixture of adults and children) could visit at a time. Although the message was clearly stated regarding the limits on making physical contact with the incarcerated individual, there were children on laps, and we saw lots of hand-holding. I approached the guard desk to receive our table assignment, which was #7. We then waited patiently in anticipation of seeing a face that was only familiar to us from news articles.

After a few minutes, Keith, who was sixty-three years old at the time, entered a far door. We recognized him immediately and waved when he looked in our direction. He indicated that he had to check in with the guard. When he approached us, we shook hands and hugged. Seeing him felt familiar because of how well we had gotten to know each other through letters. Keith shared an anecdote as we sat. "It took me longer than usual to get over here because I was eating lunch," Keith said. "But I did a good deed. I gave my brownie to my cellmate." Keith beamed, and he made no effort to hide a sudden outpouring of emotion. His eyes welled up as he shared information about his recent visit with Steve Kaplan. At that time, Steve was making regular visits to see Keith regarding the motion for a new trial. During their last visit, they had discussed my presence at Mario's exoneration, which had taken place on the same day. Keith said how touched he was about my support on Mario's behalf.

As expected, Keith was not shy. He led a conversation that didn't stop for the next two hours—the maximum time allowed for weekend visits. After we covered current activities in the Monfils case and Mario's exoneration, Mike and Keith discussed shared topics of interest. Only once in a while was I able to get a word in edgewise.

It was great to finally meet Keith. Those who know of him only through news articles about the case see him as a bully. But to those who know him on a personal level—the woman who loves him to this day, a proud son and daughter-in-law who look up to him with respect, and grandchildren who look forward to spending time with him after his release—his character is adamantly defended. Keith is educated, with diverse interests including astronomy, history, gardening, and politics. He reads books and keeps up with the latest news and world events. He's well-versed in many subjects. I enjoyed hearing Keith's observations as we talked about the Monfils case. There was no mistaking it: this man knew exactly what had gone down in that courtroom in

1995. And he was not one to shy away from expressing his views on the matter.

"As I have often said," he began, "the question is not whether these convictions are right or wrong; they are indeed wrong. But the real question is, how wrong are they? As you well know, the deeper you look into how wrong this is, the more sinister the answer becomes."

"All of us at this table are in agreement about a few things," I said in response. "We know Steve would never have agreed to look into this case if he had not found adequate reasons for doing so. With all that he and Johnny have uncovered so far, I have every confidence that they *will* get to the bottom of this. To use your own words, Keith, in Johnny's pursuit to find out exactly how wrong this is, he brought forth enough evidence that convinced Steve of the urgency to pursue this case. And allow me to point out one other thing. After close observation of Johnny's investigative abilities, I feel qualified to say how unlikely it is to pull the wool over the eyes of a seasoned investigator with his level of credentials." A hopeful exchange darted back and forth between three ardent souls.

I wanted to make sure this experience was documented, with photos taken of the three of us. I noticed a sign warning us about requesting photos at least thirty minutes prior to the end of a visit. To my dismay, it also said, "The cost will be charged to the prisoner's account."

"Don't you worry about that," Keith said. "What else do I have to spend my money on?" He walked over to get the necessary form from a guy who was sitting at a small desk off to the side. "He'll be the one taking the photos," Keith said after he returned. We were summoned within moments of completing the form to an area with a backdrop depicting eagles soaring in the mountains. I was struck by how faded the scene looked, obviously due to the constant exposure to fluorescent lights. In my mind, I couldn't help but compare it to the vibrancy of the photos our son takes of the Lake Tahoe area, where he lives.

We were permitted to stand arm in arm with Keith, which Mike and I later learned was not permitted at every prison. After the photo was taken, the photographer showed it to us. Keith wasn't smiling, so I chided him. His reply was, "I'm a prisoner, and prisoners shouldn't smile."

We made light of his comment, and the three of us posed for a second photo. Again, Keith wasn't smiling. This time neither was Mike. "What am I going to do with the both of you?" I scolded. "I guess these will have to do," I told the photographer, who appeared sincere in his concern over my exasperation.

"I'll have these ready in a few minutes and will bring them to your table," he said to me reassuringly. We reviewed the glossy images, which Keith and Mike found acceptable. I shot one last critical glance toward each of them, with both appearing more amused than troubled over my obvious displeasure.

This visit was bittersweet because, within a two-hour span, we had managed to become the best of friends. Dread set in when the guard stopped by to inform us that we had five minutes left. Two hours had gone by in what seemed like minutes. It was during that flicker in time when I thought about testimonials from family members with incarcerated loved ones who say that the hardest part of visiting is going home without them. Experiencing this harsh reality churns your insides. Having only met Keith that day and not even knowing he existed until four years ago did not ease this hardship. I imagined that being a blood relative makes one feel ten times worse.

In our final moments, Keith became thoughtful. "I have to tell you something," he said as he looked me squarely in the eyes. "In the span of time between the failed attempt at a new trial for Reynold Moore and the start of the legal proceedings by the law firm, your letters kept me alive." My heart sank as his eyes welled up with tears once again. The sight of this big, cuddly, teddy bear of a man (as opposed to "a beast of a man") sitting before us was gut-wrenching. In a different setting, it was he who had provided comfort for his family. Now he was the one in need of the same. I was desperate to provide at least a fraction of that for him until this nightmare came to an end.

This experience was a glaring example of what these injustices do to the strongest of souls. Angry over the cruel circumstances but more determined than ever to see this mission through, I felt forever indebted to Kathleen for stressing the importance of this and other eventual visits.

We visited the other men throughout 2015 and 2016. Michael Hirn was next. He is the youngest of the six men. He was fifty-six years old when we met him on April 18, 2015. When this case was originally investigated, he readily took four polygraph tests and passed them all. He also pushed to get the FBI involved in the investigation. Although they did initially get involved, their inquiry was brief. Why? The reasons for this are still unclear. But one thing does seem clear to me: that a guilty person would not push for FBI involvement.

The process was different for this visit. We were categorized as "special visitors" due to Michael's now full visitor list. We filled out the necessary form and sent it in. But when we arrived at the prison, the form was nowhere to be found. The guard apologized as he thoughtfully acknowledged our long drive. After a short time, he found the form, which had been placed in the wrong folder. He promptly sent us on our way. As we waited at table #30, we remarked on the difficulties of scheduling this visit. While that paperwork was being processed, Michael had been transferred to this new place, and it had gotten lost in the shuffle. Thanks to the assistance of his social worker, the paperwork was filed expeditiously.

To this day, Michael is kind, thoughtful, courteous, and outspoken about the judicial system. Like Keith, he understands how they were wronged. He, like Keith, keeps his anger in check and focuses on future goals. "I'm serious about my intentions of being an advocate for prison reform once I'm exonerated," he said that day.

During our visit, we discussed developments in the case and talked about his activities in prison. I mentioned the picture he had sent us of a wooden storage unit that he had made in woodshop. "It's obvious you love working with your hands and that you pay attention to detail," I said. Michael also mentioned his love of the outdoors and the enjoyment he got from prison sports. At one time, he was the umpire for the prison softball league.

Forty minutes into our visit, a guard approached our table to ask if it was okay for two other visitors to join us. Michael thought it was his Aunt Marlene and Uncle Terry who had arrived at the front desk. "We're excited to meet them," I said. I had previously met a couple of Michael's closest family members—his son, Tyler, and stepfather, Mike

Dalebroux. I had walked alongside Dalebroux at one of our Walks and listened as he shared the unwavering pride he has for his stepson. A staunch supporter of his dad, Tyler also attended one or two of our Walks.

We learned that day that Marlene and Terry had supported Mike over the years by driving long distances to visit him. When they walked into the lounge, Michael introduced us and mentioned my involvement. Marlene was full of gratitude and hugs as tears filled her eyes. Looking at Michael, she remarked, "I don't know how you maintain such a positive attitude under these circumstances." Michael said it is the support from all of us and many others that has kept him strong.

Michael readily smiled in the photos we took. Marlene and Terry opted out of having any taken with him. "We are waiting until after he is released," Marlene said.

We purchased ice cream bars, enjoying them and the few moments we had left before our visit ended. We said our goodbyes to Michael, and in the lobby, the four of us exchanged contact information. Marlene and Terry were grateful for our willingness to visit. We expressed our admiration for their outstanding courage.

We visited Reynold Moore on July 11, 2015. Rey, who was sixty-nine years old, spotted us at table #9 in the visitors' lounge. He waved excitedly, wearing a grin that stretched from ear to ear. He walked over with arms wide open as he towered over us. Hugs were like gold to these men. We felt it each time we visited them. Rey's hearty laugh exemplified warmth and helped to release the tension I always felt about having to enter these prisons for visits.

We discussed the disturbance in the courtroom on that fateful day in 1995 when the guilty verdicts had been handed down. "Those screams came from my daughter, Kayce," Rey said. He shared how difficult it still was for his family to accept what had happened.

We asked Rey about the original trial and when it was that he had felt certain he would be sent to prison. He said it wasn't until the guilty verdicts were read. His fear became absolute when Mike Piaskowski was found guilty. "The belief among all of us was that Mike Pie would go free since there was no evidence to convict him," said Rey. "The moment his verdict came back as guilty was when we all realized our fate."

As with the others, Rey's false sense of the integrity of the system and his belief that the truth would prevail instead created a new reality that prison was imminent for all six of them. This reality had sent shock waves throughout the entire courtroom. The betrayal they all felt in that moment on October 28, 1995 was beyond the comprehension of outsiders who had merely witnessed the events of that day.

Rey had told us he had divorced his wife as a result of his conviction but that he had maintained a close relationship with his children. He had asked me on many occasions, including the day of this visit, to find a way to connect with them. It wasn't until a year later that I would find the opportunity to connect with Kayce. After doing the Mark Leland piece I had introduced her to Mario and then to Mark Saxenmeyer, who had eventually interviewed her for the Guilty Until Proven Innocent documentary. As these events unfolded I sent corresponding photos of them to Rey, who was pleased with the important connections being made.

Our final visit was on June 26, 2016, with Michael Johnson, who was then sixty-eight years old. He waved to us and was all smiles as he approached us at table #9. "Bless you, my sister," he said as we shook hands. Many individuals find God during their incarceration. Michael already had, long before this ordeal had begun. He continues to be a steadfast Christian. Reading the Bible daily helps him to cope, to forgive, and to find peace. It helps him to isolate the existence that truly defines him from the one given to him.

When we met, we discussed his stepdaughter, Joan Van Houten, and the vision he had years ago. Thinking of Joan and his family brought tears, forcing Michael to regain his composure. We talked about the time in 2010 when Joan had described the vision to me. "Joan said both of you thought the woman was her at first, but then changed your minds," I said. I fell silent, thinking about the uncertainties we had faced back then and how far we had come since.

Michael spoke of his family with longing—the unfairness and the consequences of being absent from their lives. He somehow knew God was watching over them and that he had a plan to reunite them one day. Freedom was a concept, a hopefulness that each of these men desperately clung to.

Mike went to purchase drinks for us while Michael went to the restroom. After both returned, Michael looked down at the palm of his hand and chuckled. He then turned it outward. "I wrote some things down I wanted to talk about, but I smeared the wording when I washed my hands," he said. The topics we covered triggered his memory, allowing him to recall most of his notations. I reassured him that the law firm representing Keith Kutska had turned the case on its side to learn everything there was to know about what happened. "They are quite capable," I said. "They will continue on with this fight for as long as they are needed."

In a 2016 podcast interview with host Lorraine Dmitrovic of *The Ultimate Movies Broadcast*, Joan had described an incident that should have been used to prove Michael's innocence. "During the investigation, Mike was approached by a local reporter who asked him if he knew Tom Monfils," Joan had said. "Mike told him he did and that Monfils was a nice guy who brought homemade popcorn into work to share with everyone. He stated that at work, Tom Monfils was known as the popcorn man. It was later determined that Mike was incorrect and that the popcorn man was someone else. The video of this conversation was never introduced as evidence during the trial."

Mike and I are grateful for having met Keith and the others and for the lessons these men have taught us—that in a fast-paced world, it's easy to waste precious time and take everything for granted. This isn't a luxury afforded anyone behind prison walls. Because they had thought they could count on their innocence to vindicate them, there's an element of mistrust that they developed toward anyone and anything resembling good intentions. When communicating with outsiders like us, a bond needed to form before trust could be established.

After meeting these five men, I believe those involved in prosecuting the Monfils case had to have known that these men were not criminals and that they didn't fit a typical criminal profile. These men had healthy long-term family relationships. They engaged in activities within their communities. They held good jobs and owned decent homes in respectable neighborhoods. Most of them didn't even know each other at the time. It did not make sense for them to all of a sudden risk losing everything by conspiring with strangers simply because a guy had made a phone call. They certainly would not continue to profess their innocence for decades when admitting guilt meant possible freedom. I've asked many different people whether they would falsely admit guilt to gain their freedom, and to date, I've not found one person who said they would. I feel justified in believing that the idea of "the conspiracy of silence" was concocted by the authorities overseeing this case and that the urgency to solve this case at any cost arose following the realization that the police had erred in releasing the tape that Keith later played for Tom Monfils shortly before Monfils disappeared from his workstation. But who's going to admit that?

Chapter 37
REQUEST FOR A NEW TRIAL

Eight months after filing the 152-page motion, Keith was granted
an evidentiary hearing to decide if the recent new evidence warranted a new trial. This bittersweet victory was encouraging for
all of us. Although it was a significant step, we knew in our hearts that
this action might not produce favorable results. My heart sank when I
learned that Judge Bayorgeon, the original trial judge from 1995, was
coming out of retirement to oversee the proceedings. I was surprised
and dismayed to learn how common a practice this is. It made more
sense to me to have an impartial judge take a fresh look. I had many
doubts that this judge could be open and objective enough to grant another lengthy and unbiased trial for Keith Kutska.

I learned so much throughout this process. Whenever a convicted
person files a motion for post-conviction relief, he or she is required to
present new evidence sufficient to warrant a genuine prospect of an ac-
quittal if the case were retried. It takes years, with much of the time
eaten up by prosecutors unwilling to admit mistakes were made. They
choose instead to discredit any new findings and go to great lengths to
explain why the defense has no case. It's a frustrating and exhaustive
process not for the impatient or faint of heart.

For an overview of the new findings in this case, I've included a
rudimentary summarization of the hearing that took place in Green
Bay, Wisconsin, on July 7, 8, and 22 of 2015.

Evidentiary Hearing for Keith Kutska, July 8–9, 2015

Day one:

9:00 a.m. – Two objections by DA David Lasee:

1. Discussion takes place about whether to sequester defense expert witness Attorney Steve Glynn or allow his presence in courtroom before he testifies. Glynn is then escorted outside and sequestered until he testifies.
2. Prosecution objects to a last-minute motion admitting testimony for the following day by retired coast guard and former Merchant Marine George Jensen. Ruling is in favor of the defense.

9:20 a.m. – First witness:

Dr. Mary Ann Sens – Licensed forensic pathologist and chair of pathology for the University of North Dakota who has been practicing since 1982 and has performed between three thousand and four thousand autopsies (including over one thousand autopsies involving suicide).

Her conclusion regarding the cause of death of Tom Monfils: "Undetermined," rather than "homicide"—contrary to what Dr. Young had concluded.

Condition of the body presents challenges. Evidence proves Tom was alive and still breathing after entering the vat. A police detail sheet is presented showing Dr. Young, the original medical examiner, making a determination shortly after the completion of the autopsy that the death was a homicide and could not have been a suicide. It is the opinion of Dr. Sens that, given the circumstances, Young could not have made that determination because it was impossible to recognize which injuries had occurred before and after death. Because he was alive when he entered the vat, every injury incurred before and after death could have occurred inside the vat rather than as a result of a beating. During the autopsy, determining which injuries had occurred before death versus after was also difficult because of the advanced state of decomposition, discoloration, and swelling of the body. There was no way to determine the exact moment when the death had occurred or if all pre-mortem injuries listed in the original autopsy report were caused before or after entering the vat. A professionally reliable conclusion as to a cause of Tom's death could not have been determined based solely on the autopsy. That determination required necessary toxicology tests and additional investigation by police, et cetera. In this case, it might not ever be possible to determine cause of death.

Dr. Sens agrees with how Dr. Young conducted the autopsy but suggests that she would have also weighed the organs. Discussion ensues about how current advances in science allow for different conclusions to be made.

DA Lasee presses that having another expert do an autopsy back then would not have necessarily garnered a different conclusion. Dr. Sens concedes that a pathologist might have agreed with Dr. Young regarding which injuries were present before death and which came after. However, she makes it clear that all pre-mortem injuries could have occurred in the vat.

11:30 a.m. – Second witness:

Attorney Royce Finne – Former Assistant DA in Brown County 1977–87. His career had focused on criminal cases, including approximately a dozen homicide cases. As an attorney, he had worked on prior cases with Detective Randy Winkler. He was Keith Kutska's trial attorney in the Monfils case.

Finne admits that he had never seen autopsy photos or consulted a forensic pathologist to challenge the autopsy, suggesting that he was satisfied with Dr. Young's conclusions and felt the autopsy report was accurate. He believed Tom was murdered and had no recollection of the other attorneys consulting a forensic pathologist. He is asked about his obligation to his client as defense attorney and responds by saying it is to defend his client as best as he can. Finne is shown a number of photos regarding the rotating blade dimensions and shape and is asked if he ever brought them to a specialist for comparison with Monfils' skull fracture. He did not. He did not attend all of the civil trial depositions in Susan Monfils' wrongful death litigation against Keith and the others, even though he was representing Keith. Finne states that he had inquired whether police had looked to see if there was blood evidence but had hired no experts to review evidence regarding blood and knots. He says he was not aware of a deal for David Weiner's testimony. He indicates that he did the best he could but reiterates that he did not question Dr. Young's conclusion that a homicide had occurred. He had worked with Dr. Young while at the Brown County DA's office and believed that whatever she stated was the truth. He felt that she was state of the art.

Finne states that he believed a beating had occurred but not by his client. He says that all of the attorneys believed someone else had done it. Finne felt each of the attorneys was competent. He did not investigate suicide. He felt that he could not prove this was a suicide and would not be able to find anyone to disprove the autopsy report.

1:30 p.m. – Third witness:

Attorney James Connell – Practicing attorney for forty years and retired in 2014. Did criminal trial work and represented Kutska on appeal and later in post-conviction proceedings.

Connell states that he had hired a private investigator to investigate Randy Winkler, David Weiner, and Brian Kellner. He did not consult or hire any expert witnesses. He knew that the body was "mangled" but was not aware of the extent of its decomposition. He suggests he felt that either Weiner had murdered Tom Monfils or that someone within the mill must have committed the murder. He never agreed with the State's timeline of when the death occurred. He had not believed Weiner's testimony was credible and had asked him about a deal. Weiner responded that there was none. Connell continues, explaining that he thought Weiner knew he was doing something that would get him out early and that he believes Weiner lied at the post-conviction hearing in 1997. Connell did not interview other mill workers regarding a suicide theory and didn't raise the issue of the ineffectiveness of Kutska's trial counsel either on appeal or in the post-conviction petition. He had thought all of the trial attorneys were sufficient in their client representation. He went to many of the appeals, and there was never any mention of suicide. He concludes that Finne did a reasonable or good job in defending Kutska.

Kaplan brings up the matter of a Brady rule violation. Under the United States Supreme Court case of Brady v. Maryland (1963), the prosecution must voluntarily disclose material favorable to the defendant in a criminal case that is known by the State. A letter that was not disclosed to the original defense is then introduced as evidence of a deal between an attorney representing Weiner and the DA's office that is directly tied to Weiner's testimony at trial. DA Lasee objects to the letter's authenticity. It is regarded as hearsay. Though it is not admitted, it is placed in the record under an "offer of proof."

2:30 p.m. – Fourth witness:

Attorney Stephen Glynn – Criminal defense attorney for forty-two years in Wisconsin. Helped with post-conviction appeals and has been involved with the Wisconsin Innocence Project. Has worked on approximately forty homicide cases with jury trials and on direct appeals for other serious felonies.

Glynn states that he reviewed both Finne's and Connell's work in the Monfils case and prepared a report regarding Keith's legal counsel. On the prosecution's side, Larry Lasee objects to the report, which is overruled. He then moves to strike related testimony. This is overruled.

Glynn testifies about the duties of legal counsel to aggressively investigate all avenues of evidence for clients, including retaining experts to create reasonable doubt, especially in homicide cases where life in prison is the most serious penalty allowed under Wisconsin law. He believes that the failures of the defense counsel undermined the trial and that Kutska, as well as the others, did not receive adequate representation. There is much discussion on a final determination of homicide versus suicide and how the trial could have been different. Counsel should have investigated Tom's mental state, coast guard experience, and family problems. The suicide theory would have explained a lack of blood near the bubbler. A short discussion arises about the prosecution's argument that washing away the blood was effective in ridding the area of any residue. Glynn states that this was not accurate due to the effectiveness of luminol (blacklight) testing and its capacity to expose residue left behind. Glynn refers to the commonly known SODDI defense acronym and why defense counsel's resorting to it undermined the outcome of this case.

Larry Lasee objects to Glynn's statement regarding luminol testing. It is stricken from the court record. Glynn states Kutska's appellate and post-conviction counsel was also negligent and should have brought up the deficiencies of trial counsel. A discussion between Larry Lasee and Glynn becomes heated when Lasee questions Glynn's conclusions regarding the ineffectiveness of upward of twenty attorneys involved in the entire case. Glynn stands firm in his assessment and adds a personal opinion about the likelihood of a different outcome had the case been tried differently, saying, "I don't think this case would have resulted in guilty verdicts, and I would bet money on it!"

3:55 p.m. – Fifth witness:
Ardis (Ardie) Kutska – Kutska's former wife.

Ardie testifies that she and Keith were friends with Verna and Brian Kellner. She says the four of them were together at the Fox Den Bar on the evening of the alleged bubbler beating reenactment that Kellner had testified Keith had performed at the bar in early July 1994. Ardie says there was no reenactment. When Kaplan asks if she had been called to testify at the trial, she states that she was not and was told by Keith's lawyer that no one would believe her because she was Keith's wife. She talks about Brian Kellner's character and says he was "a nice guy, but I think he wanted people to, I don't know, he wanted to make people like him or be important to everybody." Discussion takes place about Ardie's many conversations with Keith about the case. Keith first believed Tom had taken his own life but was later convinced that it was a murder after he read Dr. Young's autopsy report. Keith did not have any idea of who had committed the murder.

Hearing concludes for the day.

Day Two:
9:05 a.m. – Sixth witness:
Amanda Williams – Daughter of Verna and Brian Kellner. Also has older brother, Earl.

Amanda cannot recall if her parents were going through a divorce or reconciliation during the investigation but states that her primary caregiver at that time was her father. She was thirteen years old between the fall of 1994–95 and knew the Kutskas as close family friends. She had looked up to Keith as a father figure. She recalls when he had colored with her when she was young.

DA Lasee objects to Amanda's testimony about an experience she had with Det. Randy Winkler. This action is overruled.

Amanda continues, recalling being questioned by Winkler after getting off of the school bus and then spending a few hours with him during the Monfils investigation. Amanda suggests she was asked by him about her knowledge of the case. He asked if she wanted to stay living in the house with her dad or if she would rather live with her mom. She says she felt she was her dad's little girl. When asked if she felt threatened by Winkler, she describes physically backing away from him and his immediate and direct advancement toward her. He kept pushing her for answers. Winkler told her that if her dad did not cooperate, he would be in a lot of trouble. She felt at the time that this meant he would go to jail. She had been told by her dad to be mindful of whom she talked to and what she said. She describes her dad as being stressed about personal problems. The Kellners changed phone numbers and moved a lot. Her dad told her that he was being watched by the police. She says they would see cars sitting outside.

Amanda talks about a woman who appeared at her school one day and introduced herself as an Oconto County social worker who claimed that she was investigating possible abuse of the Kellner children at their home. Amanda says this experience felt weird and that the woman had produced no ID. It had bothered Amanda that the woman acted cold. The woman took her to the police station and left her in a room, but she was eventually allowed to go home. She later told her dad about it, and he fell silent. Amanda explains that her dad would get quiet when he was upset. Amanda says her father had felt threatened by law enforcement to make certain statements that supported the lead investigator's theory that Monfils was murdered. Kellner finally agreed to make the statements demanded of him. He later said those statements were false.

Judge states that he considers all of this testimony as inadmissible hearsay.

Amanda tells the DA that she had shared all of this information with Finne and that she does not know who the woman was who picked her up. She describes her as having tight curls and glasses. She believed then and still feels that Tom Monfils committed suicide.

DA Lasee suggests to Amanda that her life is better because her dad decided to recant his testimony about the Fox Den Bar reenactment and cooperate with the defense counsel. Amanda proceeds to lecture DA Lasee on the pain this experience has brought her and how it has *not* made her life better.

9:35 a.m. – Seventh witness:
Attorney John Lundquist – Has practiced law in both Minnesota and Wisconsin for thirty-seven years. He has concentrated on criminal and regulatory defense and is a certified criminal defense specialist. Is currently employed at Fredrikson & Byron, PA in Minneapolis and acts as general counsel for the firm. Interviewed Brian Kellner in the fall of 2014.

Before questioning begins, DA Lasee objects to Lundquist's testimony as hearsay. Kaplan argues that it is adverse to Kellner's interests and social standing. There is much discussion regarding the relevance and admissibility of Brian's unsigned affidavit. It is accepted.

Attorney Lundquist states that in February 2014, he met with Brian Kellner at Mike Piaskowski's house to interview him regarding his prior trial and post-conviction testimony. Piaskowski was not present during the interview. Kellner told Lundquist that the Fox Den incident did not occur and that it was complete fiction. Lundquist asked Kellner if he would be willing to sign an affidavit regarding their discussion. Kellner said he would. Lundquist says that he prepared the affidavit and was on his way to Green Bay to meet with Kellner a few weeks later to have him sign the document. Just east of Wausau on Highway 29, Lundquist received a phone call informing him Kellner had passed away earlier that day.

DA Lasee asks Lundquist if Kellner had ever seen the prepared affidavit. Lundquist replies, "He did not."

10:03 a.m. – Eighth witness:

Cal Monfils – The younger brother of the decedent, Tom Monfils.

Cal states that he felt close to his brother and that they never had a falling out. He looked to Tom with great respect but said Tom was judgmental. They shared a room after Tom returned home from four years in the coast guard. Cal talks about Tom's temper and how Tom would react by going off alone to cool off. He describes how Tom would always tie knots. Cal is shown photos of the knots tied to the weight found with Tom's body and describes them as knots that he saw his brother tie. Cal recalls a conversation he had with Winkler regarding the knots tied around Tom's neck and to the weight. He states that he had told Winkler those knots looked like knots his brother would have tied. He says Winkler assured him that they had already looked into this and determined that the knots were not Tom's. Cal feels these photos are important because they represented the only evidence directly relating to his brother's death that the prosecution had. Cal is asked about Tom's marriage, and he says it was "different." He says Tom would do many of the chores at home. Cal says that he does not know if Tom and his wife, Susan, were in marriage counseling. Both their father and uncle had retired from the mill. Cal states that Tom considered his job a large part of his life.

DA Lasee objects to Cal's comments about what he heard from Susan. Kaplan makes an offer of proof. Testimony is allowed to continue.

Cal recalls that shortly after the body was found, Susan had told their (Cal and Tom's) parents that she believed Tom had committed suicide. He says Susan's statement was known within the family but that his mother had thought the idea was silly. Susan had also mentioned notes she had found, and Cal suggests that he feels it was implied that they were suicide notes from Tom. Susan admitted herself into a psychiatric ward immediately after she learned Tom's body was found in the vat. Cal picked her up a few days later, after she was released. They were on their way to make funeral arrangements and were headed to a florist when they heard on the car radio that Tom's body had been found with a rope and weight tied to it. Susan then asked Cal to bring her to the bank instead of the florist. They both went in, and Susan went to check the safe deposit box. Cal states that he did not ask her why. There was a lot of media coverage after the body was found, and Cal's mother became the media spokesperson for the family. Susan remained silent. Cal talked to their mother many times about suicide, but she publicly stated that Tom would never kill himself. Cal then tells the court that their mother is deceased and has been for two years.

DA Lasee asks Cal if he had seen the notes. Cal says he had not. Cal indicates his surprise at the accuracy of the knots tied to the weight and around the neck. He tells the DA that he is convinced those knots were tied by his brother and that when Susan had described the notes, he was sure she was implying that they were suicide notes. Cal testifies he wants all possible information on the table.

10:55 a.m. – Ninth witness:

George Jensen – Retired from four years in the US Coast Guard. Was active duty from 1969–73 and involved in search and rescue. Was stationed in various locations including Wisconsin and was trained in knot tying, rigging, and firearms.

Jensen is asked about coast guard training requirements. He states that they included learning how to tie several types of knots, one of them being the two half-hitch knot, which was used as a slip knot for tying up boats. During training, they had learned to tie all of these knots without looking. Jensen proceeds to tie a two half-hitch knot for the court and makes a positive ID of this specific knot as being tied around Monfils' neck and to the handle of the 49 lb. weight as shown in Monfils' autopsy photos. Jensen also identifies this same knot as one that was tied onto some nails that Cal Monfils had found in Tom's home shortly after Tom's death.

DA Lasee asks Jensen if this kind of knot could also be learned in other branches of service, in Boy Scouts, or in Merchant Marine training. He replies that he did not know about the other branches of service but that he thinks it may be taught in the Boy Scouts and Merchant Marines.

11:10 a.m. – Tenth witness:

Steven Stein – Currently works at the former James River Paper Mill (now Georgia Pacific). He started in 1979 and is backtender on paper machine #7. Worked on this same paper machine with Tom Monfils and knew him for ten years.

Stein recalls Monfils did not have many close friends and describes his behavior as odd or strange. He says Monfils would make fun of others' circumstances. Stein relates the time when his wife had given birth to a premature baby and the Green Bay *Press-Gazette* had a story about it in the paper. Monfils had made copies, added derogatory comments, and posted several of them in various areas of the mill. The union consulted mill management about this, and management said they would fire Monfils. Stein asked them not to because Tom had a wife and children to support and suggested Monfils seek mental health treatment instead. Monfils wasn't fired, but Stein believes Monfils was off for a month to get the necessary help. Monfils would talk to Stein about how he had recovered the bodies of people who had committed suicide by drowning after tying heavy objects to themselves. He would describe the types of weights that were found tied to their bodies to commit suicide. Stein says Monfils seemed to have an interest in death and drowning and that they had conversations about how much weight it would take to submerge a body.

Stein had talked to Winkler about these details and had also told police that he thought Tom had committed suicide. At first, the police agreed it was possible, but a week later, they called it a murder. Stein states that he learned the weight used on Monfils came from the #7 paper machine and that he saw Monfils handling it just days before he went missing. He says Monfils was unusually quiet the week before his death. He says Monfils felt his job at the mill was important and was, in fact, his life. Rumors had surfaced at the mill before his death about Tom's troubled marriage and impending divorce.

Stein recalls the police presence at the mill during the investigation. He says the police didn't hold back their thoughts on what had happened and told workers that Monfils was beaten and thrown in the vat. Stein was asked repeatedly by Winkler if he thought Tom had been beaten. He felt pressured by Winkler to say that he thought there had been a beating. Winkler had called Stein a "scumbag" after he had refused to say there was a beating.

Stein says he feared for his job. He is asked about Detective Frank Pinto, who was working for the mill as its own investigator, but Stein says he had no direct communications with him. However, he says mill management told him that his cooperation with police was related to the security of his job. Stein was concerned because he knew of men whose jobs had been terminated due to a "lack of cooperation," which meant that those workers hadn't said what the police had insisted they say. Stein was never told within the mill to not talk to police. He recalls seeing the luminol and blacklights being used in an attempt to find blood residue.

Stein states that he knew Kellner a long time and that they became close friends during the last years of Kellner's life because they worked together on the same job. Kellner told Stein that he was troubled by his own statements to police about the case. He also told Stein he had sought out emotional and legal counsel. Kellner admitted to Stein that he falsely testified and lied on the witness stand because he was afraid of losing his family and his job. Kellner was also concerned about what people would think of him if he changed his story later on. Kellner told Stein he was having marital problems and was bothered that police had taken his kids out of school. Kellner said he was told that "this is how easy it is" to get to his family.

Stein recalls that he had testified at the trial but felt threatened beforehand. The authorities wanted him to testify that Mike Piaskowski told him that Piaskowski knew what had happened. Stein says this information wasn't accurate and that he wouldn't lie. Stein recalls, "An individual basically told me that they could take my life from me—not my life, but my job. Once I wasn't making any money, they could promise I wouldn't have a job in Green Bay. My family would no longer care for me. They wanted me to lie for them is what they wanted, and I refused."

At this hearing, Stein refuses to identify the person who threatened him but says it was an individual involved in the Monfils case. When asked by DA Lasee why he won't disclose the identity, Stein says it is because, to this day, he still feels threatened that he could wind up like the six men who were convicted. DA Lasee confronts Stein about the fact that even though he didn't lie on the stand, he didn't get fired or lose his family. Stein agrees he did not.

Hearing concludes and resumes on July 22, 2015.

Day three:

9:23 a.m. – Eleventh witness:

Attorney Bruce Bachhuber – Practiced business litigation and family law. He was legal counsel for Susan Monfils, wife of Tom Monfils, in a wrongful death lawsuit against all six of the defendants, and later in a separate civil suit against the Green Bay Police Department and City of Green Bay regarding the release of the audiotape to Keith Kutska prior to Tom Monfils' disappearance.

Bachhuber had been subpoenaed prior to this hearing by defense counsel to produce Susan's medical and marriage counseling records. Lundquist shows the court and Bachhuber a copy of that subpoena. Bachhuber verifies receiving the document. He is asked if he brought any of the stated documents with him. He says he has not. When asked why, he argues they are protected by attorney/client privilege and that he isn't willing to waive it. Discussion ensues about the relevance of the requested documents in regard to the Monfils case and why they should or should not be provided. Bachhuber adds that other documents listed on the subpoena were no longer in his possession. He states he had searched for them but couldn't locate them. The judge interjects by saying some of the requested documents hadn't been admitted as exhibits at the wrongful death case trial and weren't within the scope of what he had ordered Bachhuber's firm to produce at the hearing. The documents that Bachhuber did bring are of no relevance to the motion. Bachhuber is dismissed.

9:40 a.m. – Twelfth witness:

Jody Liegeois – Restaurant hostess in Abrams, Wisconsin, 1995–99.

Liegeois says she knew Verna Irish, formerly Verna Kellner, from the restaurant where she was employed as Irish worked at the adjacent gas station and had dined there often. She never met Brian Kellner but knew he was Irish's ex-husband. Liegeois says that Keith Kutska was a friend of her dad's and that she had met Keith at the family's home. She followed the trial and was aware of the Irish and Kellner testimony. She had a conversation with Irish about Irish's testimony. Irish said she was upset because she and Brian Kellner had been forced to lie about the so-called "bar reenactment" in which Kutska had allegedly showed them how Monfils was beaten at the bubbler.

DA Lasee objects to Liegeois' answer. It is overruled.

Liegeois says Irish told her the investigator in the case forced hers and Brian Kellner's testimony about the reenactment and that both she and Brian had lied.

DA Lasee objects to the statement about Kellner's testimony. Kaplan makes an offer of proof. The statement is allowed.

Liegeois again states that she was aware that Kellner's testimony was forced by Winkler but that she didn't report it back then because she felt the case was a "done deal." She contacted Kaplan after hearing news reports regarding the first two days of the current evidentiary hearing and the information stating that Irish and Kellner had lied during the trial. She did so because of what she felt she knew.

DA Lasee presses that Liegeois knew this twenty years ago but was only coming forth with it now. She answers yes.

9:50 a.m. – Thirteenth witness:
Gary Thyes – Employed as a barber in Green Bay, 1992–95.

Thyes states that he knew Brian Kellner and cut his hair for a number of years. He knew of Monfils' death and of the ongoing investigation. He says he had to kick detectives out of his shop when they brought in statements for him to sign about comments supposedly made by some of his regular customers who worked at the mill. "They made up stories . . . they made up what they wanted me to sign," Thyes says. Thyes says he refused to sign any of the statements. He had conversations with Kellner about detectives threatening to take Kellner's kids away. Kellner also told Thyes that he had signed a police statement he later felt bad about signing. They had talked about how Kellner eventually signed the statement when threatened with having his kids taken away. Kellner said he was very upset right after he signed it and had contacted an attorney about it.

DA Lasee asks if Thyes had ever contacted a defense lawyer. He says he had not and that he didn't start following the recent developments until he read Kellner's obituary (in 2014). Furthermore, he didn't contact Kaplan until he read about the recent evidentiary hearing. He also says that he didn't know Kellner had testified twice about the reenactment. He says he told Kaplan that he could pass a lie detector test in regard to what he knew about Kellner.

DA Lasee asks Thyes when his conversation with Kellner about signing the statement took place. He says Kellner came into the shop shortly after he had signed it and told him.

10:05 a.m. – Fourteenth witness:

Randy Winkler – Former Green Bay Police Officer and Detective Sergeant. In January 1994, he became the lead detective on the Monfils case.

Winkler was subpoenaed for this hearing to produce information about his disability settlement with the police department, along with other documents. He is shown a copy of the subpoena and verifies having received it. He is asked if he brought documents specified on the subpoena to the hearing. He says he hasn't. When asked why, he states attorney-client privilege and doctor-patient privilege.

Winkler learned the body was found two days after Monfils went missing and that it had a rope and weight attached. He states he wasn't part of the initial police team sent to the mill to investigate but went the following morning. He was looking for trace evidence—blood, hair, tissue, et cetera. When Kaplan asks Winkler about looking for evidence of an act of violence at the mill, including near the bubbler, he implies that Winkler had found none. But Winkler states this is incorrect. When Kaplan asks Winkler to clarify his answer and disclose what evidence he is referring to, Winkler states matter-of-factly that a body had been found. Kaplan rephrases his prior comment, this time excluding the body as the kind of evidence he was alluding to, and reiterates that there was no evidence found anywhere in the mill. Winkler says this is correct. Winkler doesn't recall if luminol was used with a blacklight to search for blood. Winkler believes there was a connection between the 911 call and Monfils' death.

The autopsy is discussed. Winkler doesn't recall the names of the police officers present at the autopsy. He is asked if he was aware that Dr. Young didn't believe the death was a suicide. An objection by the prosecution is sustained.

There are repeated objections regarding police detail sheets (i.e., reports and other exhibits) that Kaplan produces and presents to Winkler. These documents were part of the initial investigation but were signed by other officers. DA Lasee argues that Winkler couldn't speak for those other officers and that the defense should call them (the officers) to the stand. Kaplan contends Winkler was the lead detective of a major case and should be well-versed in the contents of these documents. Kaplan presses that Dr. Young had influenced Winkler's opinion that there had been a beating and that this theory guided his investigation, even though there was no eyewitness or physical evidence to support it. None of the presented documents are admitted as evidence, but they are placed in the record under an "offer of proof." Kaplan asks Winkler if the bubbler theory was developed before talking with Brian Kellner. He says "yes."

Kaplan states that the police could never match a blunt object to the skull fracture on Tom's head. Winkler says this is correct. Kaplan presents a list of nine suspects generated in December 1992. Winkler verifies the list and that six of the men on it were later charged. The name David Weiner is on the list, and Kaplan states that Weiner was never charged. Winkler says that is correct. Exhibit is admitted.

Kaplan states that David Weiner was interviewed on numerous occasions. Winkler says yes. Winkler also says that he believes Weiner took a leave of absence from the mill. When asked if he had testified that Weiner was an important witness, Winkler says he does not recall. Discussion ensues about Dale Basten and Mike Johnson carrying something heavy. An objection by DA Lasee is overruled.

Kaplan brings up Tom Monfils' height and weight and the distance between where he was allegedly beaten and the location of the vat. He asks if Winkler believes Weiner saw Basten and Johnson carrying the body to the vat. Winkler says yes. Kaplan discusses the logistics of carrying Monfils' body and expresses the added difficulty of having a rope and heavy weight attached.

When asked if he is interested in who tied the knots, Winkler says "yes." Kaplan suggests that if Monfils had tied the knots, it would lead them to believe that he had committed suicide. Winkler says "no." He also states that he assumed a beating had taken place. Kaplan presses that Winkler never found anyone who said they saw a beating, and Winkler says this is correct. No eyewitnesses? "No." Winkler states he presumed that there were witnesses and that the mill workers were lying or covering up for fellow mill workers. Winkler states that the knots were sent to the crime lab. When asked if Winkler was told the knots should be sent to the coast guard or navy, he says he doesn't know. Kaplan produces an exhibit, a detail sheet from December 1992 that states that the knots should be checked by the coast guard or the navy. When Kaplan asks Winkler if the knots were checked by either branch of service, Winkler says he doesn't know and that he never took steps to have them checked. Winkler says he obtained knots that Basten had tied but doesn't remember if they were the same type as on the body. He states that he didn't compare them. Winkler didn't find out if Monfils could have tied the knots, and Winkler states that he doesn't know the type of knot on the rope and weight.

Winkler states he knew Monfils had a skull fracture but that it had to have come from something other than contact with the rotating vat impeller blades. Steve produces autopsy photos of Monfils' skull and of the blade edge impressions. Winkler doesn't recall them. He also doesn't recall that a dentist made a plaster cast of the skull showing the fracture. He doesn't recall the width of the skull fracture or the width of the impeller blade. [Note: As the evidence shows, the dimensions and shape of the skull fracture matched those of the blade edges, confirming the likelihood that the fracture was caused by having contact with the rotating blades and not a beating as the State alleges.] Winkler says no object was found to match the skull fracture wound. Kaplan asks if anyone educated Dr. Young on the shape of the blades. Winkler says he doesn't recall. Kaplan presses whether any expert had determined what matched the blade. Winkler says he doesn't recall. Kaplan expresses his lack of understanding of Winkler's inability to remember many of the details of the case, despite having recent conversations with reporters and filmmakers about the case.

Detail sheets are discussed. Kaplan asks Winkler if detail sheets needed to be accurate. Winkler says yes. Winkler states he determined what went into them and that no one else confirmed their contents for accuracy. Winkler states that they were critical pieces of information used by the police and prosecutors in criminal cases. Winkler typed up witness interviews on his own typewriter. When asked if Winkler recalls visiting Steve Stein at Stein's home, he says "no." Winkler is asked if he conducted surveillance. He replies "yes." Were reports written up? Winkler can't say. When asked if he had access to tape recorders, he says "yes." Were tape recorders ever used during interviews? Winkler says "no, by choice." Kaplan asks if Winkler conducted about two hundred interviews during the Monfils investigation. Winkler says it was closer to five hundred. Winkler is asked if he did reports for each interview. Winkler says "no." He states that it wasn't always necessary. When asked to describe when it wasn't necessary, Winkler says it was when the content didn't pertain to the case or if the person didn't have any information. Kaplan asks if any interrogations got heated. Winkler says "no." When asked whether anyone who stated Winkler had gotten angry was lying, Winkler says "yes." Kaplan asks if there was a reward for any arrests and convictions. Winkler says "yes." When asked if it was $75,000, Winkler states he doesn't know. Winkler is asked if he had told people there was a reward. He replies "yes" but adds that no one said they saw anything.

The Reid Method of Interrogation is discussed. Winkler states that he was trained in this method. Kaplan asks how many hours were usually spent to question a witness. Winkler says two to four. Kaplan asks if the method allowed Winkler to lie to the subject. Winkler says "yes." Could you coerce a witness into giving false statements? Winkler says "no" but added that if witnesses didn't tell him what he wanted, he would do more of an interrogation. When asked if the method allowed him to threaten subjects by saying they would lose their jobs or have their kids taken away if they didn't tell him something, Winkler says "no." Kaplan asks if Winkler had interrogated Dale Basten for twelve hours. Winkler says "yes."

Winkler says he was authorized by Oconto County to conduct the investigation. When asked if Verna Irish and Brian Kellner lived there, he says he doesn't recall but that it is possible. Winkler says he doesn't recall if they (Verna and Brian) had children but that he was aware they were going through a divorce. When asked if he was aware that child custody was an issue, he says he wasn't. Winkler says he met with Brian Kellner to get information on many suspects. When asked if he documented every interview with Kellner, he says "yes." When asked if Winkler was aware that someone claiming to be from child welfare visited the Kellner children, he says he had no knowledge of that. When asked if Winkler remembers Kellner asking him to leave his kids out of it, Winkler says he does not.

Kaplan presents a nine-page detail sheet regarding a 2.75-hour interview from 1994 between Winkler and Brian Kellner. Winkler asks to read the entire document. Afterward, Kaplan asks if Winkler noticed in the detail sheet that the Fox Den reenactment incident was not referenced. Winkler says "yes." Kaplan presents an exhibit of the statement Kellner signed, and Winkler verifies he had prepared it. Kaplan notes minor changes made with Kellner's initials—three on one page, one on another—but that no substantive changes were made on the document. When asked if Kellner resisted signing the final statement, Winkler says he did not.

Winkler is asked if people at the mill told him about Monfils' obsessions with death and drowning. Winkler denies ever hearing this. Winkler is asked if he ever heard Susan Monfils say it was possible that her husband committed suicide. He says he did not. When asked if he ever obtained Monfils' medical records, he says he does not know. Winkler says Monfils' death was ruled a homicide and that was how it was investigated. Winkler also states that even if Monfils had tied the knots, this wouldn't have determined it was a suicide.

Kaplan asks Winkler if the DA ever made comments to him about a deal for Weiner after Weiner's arrest. Winkler says "no." Kaplan asks if Winkler recalls Weiner stating he wouldn't cooperate in the Monfils case without a deal. Winkler says he does not. When shown a news article containing Weiner's statement, Winkler says he still doesn't recall him saying this. Winkler says he doesn't recall visiting Weiner at Oshkosh Correctional to obtain writing samples. Kaplan then produces a letter from Weiner's lawyer referencing the visit and Winkler's own detail sheet documenting it. When Kaplan asks if Winkler told Weiner during the visit that Weiner could improve his position if he cooperated, Winkler says he hadn't. Discussion ensues about a series of letters from an attorney representing Weiner regarding a deal, including a possible reduced sentence for his testimony. Winkler denies any knowledge of them or that Weiner's lawyers contacted the DA's office before the Monfils trial. In fact, Winkler denies having any knowledge of Weiner's murder conviction for killing his brother in 1993, even though he was still working at the police department when Weiner was convicted.

Kaplan asks about a psychological disability claim Winkler filed with the department shortly after the Monfils Six had been sentenced. DA Lasee objects. Kaplan argues it goes to the credibility of a lead detective in a homicide case. It is decided that five specific documents in question will be entered under seal and that both sides will have a chance to argue for or against their relevance at a later time.

DA Lasee asks Winkler about his work history. Winkler states that he was employed by the GBPD in 1975. He says he rose to the rank of detective sergeant and worked on the Monfils case for three years. Winkler states that it was stressful being subjected to the conditions at the mill and that he was under constant scrutiny by the men there. He says he received a death threat. He also says that people claimed Monfils got what he had coming. There was a great deal of speculation within the community, and suicide was brought up often. The DA asks if Winkler had ever promised to give Weiner a deal for his testimony. He says he had no authority to make deals.

Kaplan establishes that Winkler had an office at the mill, that mill management made it clear that job retention was based on the workers' willingness to "cooperate with police," and that the office was available to perform interviews. Winkler also clarifies that he and other officers brought witnesses to the police station to talk.

Closing Comments:

Judge Bayorgeon commends Steve Kaplan on his "diligent" and "amazing" job during the entire hearing, before he admonishes him for insinuating that a "public servant" (the then DA and now Judge Zakowski) had lied when he denied there had been any deal with Weiner for his testimony. Bayorgeon states that he had examined all of the documentation and could not find anything to suggest a deal was made or that the DA had lied about it. He indicates that those are serious allegations to be making. He adds that specific letters presented at this hearing in regard to such a deal do not support the claim of a deal. He also says that it was a twenty-eight-day trial with eighty-one witnesses and that the jury was instructed to consider all witness testimony.

Judge Bayorgeon gives each side time to argue the merits of the sealed documents in writing and to submit briefs on the merits of the motion for post-conviction relief.

The hearing is concluded.

A cloud of doom lingered as we slowly filed out of the courtroom on that last day. In contrast, hastening past us toward the exit, tightly clutching his briefcase as though he was late for his next appointment, was the current DA, David Lasee. It reminded me of the similar manner in which his father, Larry Lasee, who incidentally had been the assistant DA during the Monfils case, had exited the courtroom following Mario Victoria Vasquez's exoneration hearing. As I watched, I supposed his unwillingness to undermine his father's position on the original outcome of this case took precedence over allowing the truth to guide his conscience. One bit of information worth mentioning is something I learned after the proceedings had concluded. Amanda Kellner, the witness from day two, had been so visibly shaken prior to testifying that she had wept uncontrollably in the hall while awaiting her turn. The one person who had comforted her during that frantic moment was none other than Cal Monfils, Tom Monfils' younger brother.

What we had witnessed during the 2015 hearing set the tone for future attempts to gain ground on Keith's behalf. On Wednesday, January 13, 2016, the motion for a new trial was denied. Immediately following, a similar appeal was filed in the Wisconsin Court of Appeals.

On Wednesday, December 28, 2016, that appeal was denied. The next step, a petition to the Wisconsin Supreme Court on April 10, 2017, was similarly denied. Later that year, the Seventh Circuit Court of Appeals denied Keith's request to file his second habeas corpus petition based on procedural grounds that limit the number of federal habeas petitions a defendant can file when seeking to overturn a state court conviction.

Although our legal team had followed the rule of law and had presented considerable facts supportive of the suicide theory, this postconviction phase had ultimately failed. It was indicative of why our courts have also failed the many innocent people who dare to file petitions in an effort to gain their own deserved freedom.

However, in many respects, we were not exactly hurled back to square one. While we had done our absolute best, and as justice continued to elude us in the months and years that followed, we remained steadfast in our refusal to succumb to absolute defeat. We would never give up hope completely. And we were certainly not about to allow this chapter to dictate the ending of an ardent journey. We would regroup and carry on with the same tenacity and shrewdness as before. A newly completed project of mine was about to take center stage and exacerbate an already contentious situation. At least I hoped it would.

Chapter 38
A NEW AVENUE OF
AWARENESS

I was deeply troubled that the arbitrators of truth and justice in Brown County were not interested in the obvious and unequivocal truths in this case and that they remained indifferent to abandoning a pitifully flawed theory.

Having admitted privately to what we all collectively knew on that final day of the 2015 hearing, that the courts in Wisconsin were uninterested in the truth, I clung desperately to that defiance as I poured every ounce of energy into my latest and most gratifying achievement.

In June 2017, two years after the evidentiary hearing and a mere two months after the final ruling by the Wisconsin Supreme Court, my book, *Reclaiming Lives: Pursuing Justice For Six Innocent Men*, was published. A sequel of sorts to *The Monfils Conspiracy*, this four-and-a-half-year effort had its own focus, to highlight the extensive growth of support over the past eight years and to highlight the findings of our legal team as presented to the court during the 2015 hearing. Equally important, the book humanizes the six men and describes the courage and commitment of their loved ones. I purposefully used a non-aggressive tone to tell their compelling story of hope, possibilities, and personal tragedies in order to touch hearts and hopefully inspire change in this specific case. An equally important goal was to offer this story as an example for those who otherwise feel powerless to initiate any kind of change for themselves or for others.

The first priority in my marketing strategy was to have copies of this book sent to the guys in prison. It was important to me that they view it as an accurate picture of the facts and as a satisfactory tribute to them. I was both relieved and elated to learn of their unanimous and overwhelming enthusiasm.

I immediately ordered copies for potential book events as I formulated a promotional campaign. I set up an author Facebook page, *Reclaiming Lives*, and joined related Facebook groups. One group of interest was *Blind Injustice*, which addresses the many facets of wrongful convictions and is run by Mark Godsey, Executive Director of the Ohio Innocence Project. Godsey was also in the process of publishing his own book, *Blind Injustice: A Former Prosecutor Exposes the Psychology and Politics of Wrongful Convictions,* and had begun monitoring the stats on Amazon for rankings of books in that genre. One day, to my delight, he shared with me his findings that my book was ranked the number one new release in the criminal-procedure-law category.

Although my book didn't remain in that spot for very long, decent reviews began to appear. Additional feedback from friends, acquaintances, and fellow writers was positive. While writing the book, I joined Women of Words (WOW), a local writing group comprised of many outstanding Minnesota authors. The sound advice from many within this group was helpful. Many of them explained to me that while it is exciting to have finally published, that process is the easy part. The real work comes with promoting and marketing your product and understanding who your target audience is. As daunting and humbling as this all sounded, I definitely felt that I had the last part of that equation figured out.

This rendition of a unique and memorable story was now officially documented. I felt confident that this new tool could make a major impact. But I was nervous about taking the next obvious step—bringing this publication on the road to Green Bay. Deciding not to dwell on this, I busied myself with researching and reaching out to possible venues in the area. Surprisingly, I was invited to local coffee shops, to bookstores, and, eventually, to participate in two large book fests in Wisconsin. UntitledTown, an annual book fest located in the heart of Green Bay, and the Southeast Wisconsin Festival of Books, located in the heart of the state—both of which allowed me to broaden my exposure to this tragedy. I also later learned through an article in the Green Bay *Press-Gazette* that the Central Library in Downtown Green Bay had ordered copies that were available at their branch. In the article was this generous review of my book:

> *Tom Monfils died at his job at the James River Paper Mill in Green Bay in 1992. Was he murdered by six of his coworkers or did he commit suicide? At the resulting trial, those six men were convicted of first-degree intentional homicide and sentenced to life in prison, but Treppa argues they were wrongfully convicted. In subsequent years, two of the men have been released, but the other four are still serving their sentences while they petition the court for release. This self-published title follows Treppa, a social justice advocate, from when she heard about this story and details her attempts and efforts to get these men exonerated. She works closely with the authors of* The Monfils Conspiracy *and, although that title would add background to this book, it's not necessary to read it first. Treppa's enthusiasm and passion is evident, and readers not familiar with this case will become captivated.*

The attention the book received was unexpected and refreshing. Each new platform became an important avenue to give presentations, distribute books, and lead educational discussions about the latest developments. Attendance at these events lagged at first but slowly increased as the ongoing legal battle on Keith's behalf captured the attention of the local media. Four years later, I continue to sell books and receive invites to various venues in Green Bay. I am grateful to the local media that I believe have contributed to a favorable shift in attitude regarding this case in more recent years.

I learned about applying for book awards and how they can help expedite exposure to additional retailers and readers. I entered into three national award programs for independent and self-published books. My book was a winner in all of them in the true-crime category.

These were the American Book Fest - Best Book Awards (2017), the Indie Excellence Book Awards (2019), and the Beverly Hills Book Awards (2019). My book did not win an award in a fourth contest, the Midwest Independent Publishers Association (MIPA), which is a local awards program. But I did receive invaluable critical feedback from their judges.

Promoting this book heavily in the Green Bay area became a key factor in keeping this story from fading back into obscurity. It was encouraging to see its message resonating with folks in the community, many of whom I've met over time at various book events. But while new avenues of communication opened up, the most important question remained; will this book actually help to free the remaining five men? Then, as though unseen forces had appeared to deliver answers to that nagging question, significant new developments again began to occur. However, the next major victory would be overshadowed with extreme sorrow and a wretched reminder of the vulnerable nature of the many individuals affected by this highly complex undertaking.

Chapter 39
"COMPASSIONATE RELEASE"

In September 2017, at age seventy-six, Dale Basten was offered a "compassionate release" due to his failing health. The parole commission cited his "advancing, maturing age" and "apparent cognitive decline" for the move. "It is clear from this encounter that you [Dale] have little or no orientation as to your surroundings," the commission's written decision stated.

This release option was presented to Dale's family provided they find suitable housing for him, such as a nursing home or assisted-living facility. It took months for them to find a place that would readily accept Dale. During their search, as a last-minute and temporary measure by the DOC, Dale was transferred to a maximum-security prison that was better equipped with the necessary medical amenities required for his level of care. Fortunately, he was housed in a section of the prison separate from the general population.

When the day of Dale's release arrived, there was no fanfare. No media presence. No acknowledgment of the absurdity of this outrageous and unlawful prison term. To try and make up for this deficiency, the focus of our 2017 Walk for Truth and Justice later in the fall was to commemorate Dale's life. His brother, Lee, delivered an emotional and deeply personal speech that evening. He shared fond memories and thoughtful opinions about his younger brother's conviction while proudly displaying a poster he had made in his honor. On it was a photo of Dale that had been taken prior to his incarceration. Underneath the photo read our yearly rallying call to action: "WHAT DO WE WANT? TRUTH AND JUSTICE!" We asked Lee to recite the annual prayer in front of St. Willebrord's Church. Our hearts wept for him, for Dale, and for the entire Basten family as Lee struggled to contain his grief. This rally will be remembered by all who attended as the most somber. The following year, a decision was made to cancel the Walk when tragedy again besieged the Basten family. Nine months after Dale had left prison, he had passed away. The following obituary was published in the Green Bay *Press-Gazette* on August 4 and 5 of 2018:

Dale Martin Basten started a new and better life on Saturday, June 23, 2018. Dale was born in Green Bay on May 11, 1941, to two of the most wonderful parents you could ever ask for, the late Harold F. Basten and Ethel M. (Larschied) Basten.

As a young man, he had more fun than one should have. In his mid-years, Dale enjoyed his cottage, his projects, and playing his guitar. Old country tunes were his favorite, and he knew the words to many songs. But most of all, he loved his daughters, "Red Rabbit" and "Blond Bunny." Dale wrote saying to them, "I will love you to the end of the earth."

His later years were hell on earth. He went away in 1995, never again to feel the warm morning sun or share in the events in the lives of his loved ones. This existence ended mercifully by actively dying in hospice care.

Dale is survived by his two daughters; brother, Lee (Susan) Basten, and numerous caring nieces, cousins, and friends.

Funeral Services were held at Resurrection Catholic Church with Bishop Robert Morneau officiating. Burial was at Allouez Catholic Cemetery. Blaney Funeral Home is assisting the family. To send online condolences, please go to www.BlaneyFuneralHome.com.

The family wishes to thank the doctors, nurses, and caregivers at St. Elizabeth Hospital, the team members of hospice, and all of the caregivers at Atrium Acute Care. These are all truly wonderful people.

Your prayers and kind thoughts are appreciated. For those interested in "Truth and Justice," go online to Wisconsin Innocence Project and please consider a donation for their work.

For those interested in Dale's case and the ongoing detention and misery of four good men, please read The Monfils Conspiracy *written by Dennis Gullickson and John Gaie, and* Reclaiming Lives *written by Joan Treppa. These writers, family, and friends of these men and Mike Piaskowski (convicted but exonerated) must be acknowledged as true champions of "Truth and Justice."*

Two days after Dale's passing, on June 25, an article written by reporter Paul Srubas appeared in the Green Bay *Press-Gazette.* Srubas, who had covered this case from the beginning, had reached out to a number of us asking if we'd like to submit comments for his article. My perspective was brief but potent: "The passing of Dale Basten is as tragic as the life he was forced to live. I place blame on Brown County and the State of Wisconsin for inadvertently instigating another death as a result of this injustice!"

In 2020, I reached out to Lee to let him know that I was working on this second edition. "I'm dedicating a chapter to Dale and the circumstances of his final days," I said. "I don't wish to be overly intrusive, but in order to be entirely accurate, I would like clarification on a few details." Lee gladly responded with this harrowing message:

Susan and I picked up Dale from prison on September 5, 2017. He passed away on June 23, 2018. From visiting him before being released, I knew he wasn't doing well, and I think they were good with letting him go because of his condition. As I recall, he really could no longer carry on a conversation, and I don't think he knew what was happening or where he was going. Once at the nursing home, he would now and then try to walk away, but for the most part, he would just lie in bed or sit in the common area of the dementia wing.

[His daughters] I think were with him when he passed, but I was not. I had previously consented to hospice care, and as the time drew near, I was alerted, so I told the girls. He looked rough, and he may not have been able to open his eyes. Even if he did, I don't think he would have known them. A sad ending. He was proud of his daughters. I put on his cemetery plaque, Father of [daughters' names].

Regardless of the dire circumstances of his life, regardless of the manner of his death, in his final days, Dale Basten was loved deeply by a family who will never escape the grief and despair of this entire experience. But gratifying to them is the serenity that in death, their loved one, Dale Basten, is now at peace and has gallantly and permanently preserved his absolute innocence.

Chapter 40
SIGNS OF PROGRESS

The Walk in 2017 ultimately became our last after having collectively decided to suspend all public rallies until further notice. We felt that this was in the best interest of the men who were still behind bars and an act of solidarity on our part in light of the potential for more releases.

While Mike and I were out one evening early in November 2018, three messages were left on our home phone. They were from Michael Hirn, who was currently at McNaughton Correctional Center, a minimum-security prison in Tomahawk, Wisconsin. Regrettably, by the time we arrived home, it was too late for him to reach out a fourth time. Being that these were collect calls, Michael had been unable to state the nature of his call. Sleep escaped me that night as I tried to guess the most likely reason. "Maybe he was actually going to be paroled after all," I thought.

Michael had alluded to this possibility in a few of his recent letters. I was skeptical, though, because of the repeated parole denials since 2010. Certainly, Dale had been released, but that was a different situation altogether.

The next morning, I emailed Tom, a mutual friend. He and Michael spoke on the phone often, so he would know what was up. Sure enough, Tom confirmed my suspicions. "Mike was calling to let you know he's been granted parole," he wrote. "He wanted to tell you himself. He could be released sometime in December."

Mike and I were delighted to receive another call the following evening.

"This is a collect call from . . . 'Michael Hirn.' To accept charges . . . press one."

While eagerly waiting for the automated system to connect us, part of me wished that we didn't know what Michael wanted to tell us. I felt that we had somehow robbed him of the surprise element of this extraordinary news. But trying to imagine how he must be feeling was exhilarating. Still, a voice deep within warned me to remain cautious about the likelihood of his release. The general assumption is that being granted parole requires admitting guilt for the given crime and showing remorse. All of the guys were clear on this point: none of them would lie in order to be paroled. And admitting to something they did not do would be a lie. Therefore, showing remorse for something they had not done was out of the question. Whether or not the parole commission could overlook this non-admission of guilt was anyone's guess.

The connection to our caller came through.

"Hello, Joan and Mike," the familiar voice said.

During our brief conversation, Michael reiterated what Tom had said and reassured us that he was going to be released the week before Christmas. He thought it might happen on Wednesday, December 19. After our conversation, it started to sink in that this *might* actually happen.

Michael and his family wanted his discharge to be private. They wanted to be left alone, to relish in this realization without the intrusion from the media—or from those with less savory opinions. But that idea was squashed when word traveled fast of Michael's impending release. I learned that it had reached the Green Bay media through a text I received from a local reporter looking for a comment. At first, there was speculation about a specific timeframe. It was finally decided that this was most likely going to happen on Tuesday, December 18, 2018, at 8:00 a.m. Mike and I discussed travel plans. We were not about to miss one of the most extraordinary events of this journey!

Mike and I booked a room at a motel near the prison that Monday evening. Clare made plans to join us. The following morning, I was scheduled to do an interview with Steve Hopper, photojournalist from

WBAY Action 2 News out of Green Bay. Shortly after 7 a.m., we spotted Steve parked outside of the prison gates. A close friend, Deb, was waiting there also. After the interview, to escape the frigid air, we piled back into our vehicles . . . and waited.

Soon, a man in a gray pickup pulled up and parked on the opposite side of the road from us. He glanced in our direction with a pained look. He looked to be on the verge of tears. As he climbed out of his vehicle and walked toward us, I was fairly certain that it was Marlene and Terry's son, and Michael's cousin, Randy. He and I had communicated through emails prior to that day, and Randy had assured me that he would be there for Michael's big moment. "Are you Joan?" he asked as he approached me. "Yes," I said. His robust hug spoke to his appreciation of my support.

Everyone gathered around to meet Randy and to help ease his anxiety about his current dilemma. "My elderly parents are the only ones up there waiting for Michael to come out," he said as he pointed to the prison entrance. "This is extremely emotional for them, and I feel I should be there to help." He then got back into his vehicle and drove up to the visitor lot inside the gate near the main entrance. He signaled for us to follow. We parked in the slot next to him. As I opened my door, Randy's distressed voice could be heard. "They are in their eighties," he pleaded with the corrections officer. "Why can't I go up there?" Unfortunately, all of us, including Randy, were directed to go back to where we had been parked before.

Finally, at approximately 7:45 a.m., we caught sight of Terry and Marlene's bright red pickup coming down the driveway toward us. The truck stopped just short of passing through the gates. Michael Hirn, looking taller and slimmer than we remembered, exited the passenger side of the vehicle and walked with dignity as he took his final steps on foot toward freedom. He was leaving the McNaughton Correctional Center and prison life for good.

Michael had taken the mandatory steps over the years to achieve parole. I felt it necessary to point this out when asked to submit a comment for a Green Bay *Press-Gazette* article that was published days before his scheduled release:

"People must understand that this [parole] was not simply handed to him," said Treppa, who met all six men as part of the research for a book of her own, Reclaiming Lives: Pursuing Justice For Six Innocent Men. *"He earned it through hard work, diligence, patience, and a positive attitude. I believe that, in moving forward, being angry over something he cannot change will never define who this man is."*

With nothing but the utmost respect for someone who many of us feel is destined to become an effective spokesperson for the other men, I believe Michael's sheer determination, understanding of the dynamics of this case, and ability to curb his anger and diplomatically express his point of view will create new avenues of exoneration for all of the men.

Mark Saxenmeyer and his videographer, Joe Pollock, had arrived and were all set up on the side of the road next to Steve Hopper, ready to record this historic event. Waiting for an opportunity to actually speak with Michael, they filmed and snapped photos, capturing poignant moments as they unfolded. The crew witnessed hugs, tears, smiles, and sighs of relief as we all gathered to congratulate a free man on this remarkable day.

What makes Michael's release particularly extraordinary, aside from its realization—is its delay. In 2004, nine years after the trial, and right before the original trial judge, James T. Bayorgeon, retired, he wrote an open letter to the parole commission on behalf of each of the six men, with this directive:

"Each of these individuals is presently serving time in the Wisconsin State Prison as a result of a sentence which I imposed. I customarily receive notices of parole hearings. I am now retiring and will not be on the bench when these individuals will be up for parole. Therefore, I would like to place on the record, at this time, my thoughts with respect to their parole . . .

The most unique aspect of this case was the fact that these individuals, other than the unique offense, were hard-working, stable members of the community. They were not criminals but got caught up in a situation which quickly got out of control.

I cannot speak for their conduct during their term of incarceration. However, from my point of view, of all that has transpired in this case, it would seem to me that favorable consideration for early parole would be appropriate. I set parole eligibility dates which I felt would provide adequate punishment for the offense, and absent other facts of which I am unaware, have seen nothing that would be gained by further confinement.

I would appreciate it if you would make notation in the respective records of these individuals with respect to this correspondence."

— Judge James T. Bayorgeon

What compels a judge to write such a letter on behalf of six "union thugs" and "murderers" who were, and still are, verbally slaughtered within their own communities? While some may have felt encouraged by this unprecedented recommendation, it came as no surprise to others that this directive was largely ignored when each of the men reached their respective eligible parole dates. Given the fact that Hirn's first bid for parole in 2010 was denied and that all successive bids for parole for him and the other men were repeatedly denied, it appeared that this directive had no impact at all on the decisions of the parole commission. But with Hirn's unexpected release, I wondered why the constraint of the commission had finally loosened.

While Michael was being interviewed on the day of his release, I reminisced with Marlene and Terry about the prison visit where Mike and I had met them. "Now you can finally have your photo taken with your nephew," I said excitedly to Marlene. "Yes!" she said as the smile on her face echoed a thousand unspoken hopes and dreams. Similar to our original visit, which now felt like ages ago, Marlene reiterated her gratitude for our support. This time, there was newfound joy in her heart as the weight of this new realization began to sink in.

Chapter 41
IMMINENT RELEASE TIMES TWO!

On March 4, 2019, as I sat at my desk putting the final touches on a writing project, my mobile phone pinged, alerting me to a Facebook notification. It was from Joan Van Houten. Staring back at me in bold letters was this forwarded message from her: "**Joan, Big Mike got his parole . . .**"

Joan and I had been told recently by her stepfather that his release from prison was imminent. We were confident that this would happen because of Hirn's unprecedented release. However, twice, a date had been set. And twice, as the day approached, the date had been postponed. A third date was scheduled. To our relief, July 3, 2019, became the day in which Michael Johnson would take his first breath of freedom in twenty-three years.

At the time, Johnson was located at the Sanger B. Powers Correctional Center in Oneida, Wisconsin—a minimum-security facility a few short miles west of the Green Bay city limits. Due to its close proximity to Green Bay, I suspected that a number of local reporters might show up. My assumptions were confirmed when I was contacted by a few of them asking if I was going to be there.

I had discussed media presence with the family beforehand to gauge their reaction to this unavoidable attention. As with Hirn's family, they resisted but understood the heightened attention over this high-profile case. They understood that the probability of bringing their loved one home without public scrutiny was highly unlikely.

And while we as outsiders easily characterize these releases as positive and celebratory for these folks, we neglect to realize the negative impact of the past two-and-a-half decades. We cannot fathom how these events can induce amplified recollection of the somewhat faded but ever-present horrors of this nightmare. So, to the media, I urged caution. To the family members, I offered to bridge the gap between them and the media.

My husband, Mike, and I were the first to arrive at the facility at 8:00 a.m. The window for Johnson's release was between 9:00 – 10:30 a.m., which gave us time to take photos, catch up with family members, and speak with reporters before Johnson's release.

We were forewarned about the high volume of traffic on the main road in front of the building, so Mike and I parked on a side street. Soon, a vehicle turned the corner and headed in our direction. It was Mark Saxenmeyer and Joe Pollock. They wanted to capture footage to include in their documentary, just as they had done for Hirn.

A vehicle with the WBAY Action 2 News logo arrived shortly after Mark and Joe. It was parked on the shoulder of the main highway. As we moved to pull in front of it, my cell phone rang. Kim Johnson was on the line. She was her usual talkative self. But on this day, her voice was full of both excitement and anxiety. "I'm with my sister, and we will be there soon," Kim said. I warned her that reporters had begun to arrive and assured her of my preparedness to speak with them on behalf of the family. Relief resonated in Kim's voice before we hung up.

By then, reporters from multiple local news outlets, as well as from *The Post-Crescent* newspaper in Appleton, had pulled up and begun setting up. As I stepped out of the car, they gathered around to introduce themselves. With cameras and microphones in hand, all attention was aimed in my direction. The respectful and patient manner of the reporters afforded me an unusual sense of calm, which helped during what became my first-ever press conference.

I felt the media's inclination to listen to a side of the story that had gotten lost in the shuffle years ago. Their coverage adequately reflected the difficulties of these families to gain acceptance from a community inundated with lies and misguided truths, a community that was decidedly reluctant to exhibit compassion as a result.

After answering questions, I spotted what appeared to be family members who had gathered in the parking lot directly in front of the correctional center's entrance. Reporters, who were confined to the street and unable to follow, looked on as Mike and I walked over to greet them. The only person I recognized was Kim's sister, Bonnie. We had gotten to know each other over the years while attending monthly FAF meetings and courthouse rallies. We hugged. Bonnie thanked us for being there and for our ongoing support. "This momentous occasion is because of *many* people who truly cared," I offered. I then asked if she'd seen Kim yet. "Kim is already inside. She brought street clothes for Michael to change into," she explained.

Kim soon exited the front door and walked toward us. She was barely recognizable in a large floppy hat and dark sunglasses. A reserved smile appeared on her face as I approached her. As we embraced, Kim held on tight in quiet desperation. I did my best to reassure her that all would be fine.

It was a delight to meet many new family members—siblings, children, grandchildren, and in-laws—and to participate in another major milestone in this ongoing saga. In that moment, an appropriate description came to mind that was reiterated time and again by dear friend and former colleague, Johnny Johnson—that this entire case is representative of nothing more than "blatant malfeasance" unnecessarily forced upon innocent lives.

Our attention turned toward the building's entrance as Michael Johnson appeared touting a white cap, button-down shirt, and dark pants. In front of him was a flatbed cart similar to those used in hardware stores. On it were numerous cardboard boxes filled with his belongings from the past twenty-three years. Images of a *FedEx deliveryman* came to mind as he expertly maneuvered the cart toward us.

Michael stood in awe at the sizable group standing before him. He took a deep breath and closed his eyes. He uttered thanks for the gift of freedom and for this display of support. In the next instant, the somewhat restrained crowd felt more at ease, engaging in hugs, spirited laughter, and shameless tears. This man was loved. There was no doubt in my mind that he would be in great hands while navigating this new reality.

As I've mentioned, Johnson's conviction was largely due to the trial testimony of David Weiner. This statement from Johnson sums up a personal coming-to-terms with his fate while illustrating a strong faith in the possibilities that only God has the power to control:

> *As a Christian man, I recognize the trials and tribulations I must face and endure in this world (2 Tim. 3:12). I realize that as I continue to profess my innocence, I will never be allowed to leave prison. Already this prison system has sought to withdraw my medium-security classification and send me to a maximum-security institution because I continue to claim I am falsely accused and unjustly convicted of a crime I did not commit or have any knowledge about. I wait patiently for my Lord to rescue me (Luke 18:7 and Rom. 8:28). I know I didn't harm Tom Monfils. God knows I didn't harm Tom Monfils. I can't understand why David Weiner pointed a finger at me like that!*
> — Excerpt from *The Monfils Conspiracy: The Conviction of Six Innocent Men*

The horrific circumstances that led to Johnson's conviction back in 1995 seemed to fade into oblivion as the sight of him casually making the rounds in the bright sunshine warmed our hearts. Having witnessed a similar sight a few months earlier when Hirn had been released in no way diminished the impact of this experience.

Johnson invited Mike and me to join the family at a nearby restaurant for breakfast. "We'll catch up with you when we're finished here," I said. Mike and I then walked back down the driveway, hand in hand, toward the street where the press once again gathered for a final statement. I did my best to respect the family's privacy as I conveyed the unwillingness of the family to make any statements at that time. Soon, a caravan of vehicles carrying the Johnson clan drove away. And as the car Michael was in turned the corner, each of the reporters and photojournalists turned in unison to catch a glimpse—and a quick photo. When asked about what Johnson's first words were, I shared the happiness he felt of now being free. I remained vague in identifying those who were present and the things we had discussed. I instead explained their need for privacy and adequate time to get used to this new reality and the new challenges they will face in the coming days and months. "They're excited that he's getting out, but it's also terrifying because they haven't lived with this person for twenty-five years," I had said. "And it's like . . . they're going to have to get to know each other all over again. There are traumas that have happened within the families and in prison that they're going to have to work through. This is very traumatic."

One vital concern I had brought up to Michael and this group of supporters was the necessity to eventually talk with the media. "You must take the initiative at some point to inform them of your truths," I urged. "Otherwise, they will continue to use the same narrative as in the past because they will have nothing new to report on. You will know when the time is right to do so," I assured them.

On March 4, 2020, Michael agreed to an exclusive interview with WBAY Action 2 News Reporter Sarah Thomsen. In it, he reiterates some of what I had communicated to the media on the day of his release. "There's a whole lot of things going through your mind. I didn't know. I hadn't been in my wife's apartment yet. I hadn't even driven her car yet, so there's a whole lot of things I had to experience yet, and it's been a real adventure, a good adventure, and it's not over yet," says Johnson to Thomsen. During the interview, Michael reads an excerpt from my book.

Afterward, Thomsen asks him, "I sense a little bit of anger still in your voice. Is there anger?"

Johnson replies, "Nope. I believe in God's will, and I don't think there's anything I could have done to change anything. I mean, I did what I was supposed to. I hired a lawyer, and we went to court. The rest is history. I had no control over the rest of it."

When Mike and I arrived at The Bay View Family Restaurant, we spotted Mark and Joe, who had decided to wait for us before going inside. Having been granted permission to capture additional footage in this more relaxed setting, they wanted us to make formal introductions first. Inside, the group had gathered in the far corner around a long row of tables that had been pushed together. After the introductions, Mark and Joe captured an amazing display of affection and camaraderie.

We felt honored to be part of this special occasion. Seeing this family together cracking jokes, sharing personal stories, and discussing everyday topics seemed, well . . . so normal. It was gratifying to witness their newfound ability to become familiar with what *is* normal for the majority of us.

Ironically, when Mike and I returned home from Green Bay a few days later, a final letter from Michael Johnson, written prior to his release, was waiting for us in our mailbox. The first sentence was absolutely surreal: "Dear Joan, July 3rd at 9:00-10:30, I walk out of prison a free man."

And as though this latest experience wasn't exciting enough, on July 2, a day prior to Johnson's release and before Mike and I had left to go to Wisconsin, we received great news about another one of our guys. I came across a Facebook post from Kayce Moore Sell, Rey Moore's daughter, which read: **"Today's the day! See you after work, Dad!"**

I had assumed that this meant Kayce was going to *visit* her dad. During a visit Clare and I had had with Rey during the summer of 2018, he had told us he was being considered for parole in eighteen months, which would have placed his release around the Christmas holiday in 2019. But there had been talk after that from Gina, another longtime friend of Rey's, of a possible release date of July 2, 2019. However, as the July date neared, a setback occurred regarding Rey's housing arrangements and needed to be resolved before he could be released. As far as we knew, those arrangements were still unresolved.

I reached out to Kayce and asked her to give her dad my best. She announced then that her dad was "free." She explained that he had been paroled that morning, on July 2, and said that this last-minute development was a surprise, even to the immediate family.

I was elated and a little sad. Due to the confusion, we had missed being there for Rey's momentous day. I hoped to talk with him soon to properly congratulate him. Rey called us after we had returned home from Green Bay. It was uncanny to see his name on the phone's caller ID and to hear his familiar and especially cheerful voice on the line. One of the first things he said to me was, "You had something to do with my release. You know that, right?" After a very frank and enlightening conversation with Rey, I knew for certain that the publication of both books about this case was never "a complete and utter waste of time." Not by any stretch of the imagination.

The unfortunate downside to all of this is that, with the exception of Michael Piaskowski, who was exonerated, the other four are classified as parolees and therefore still considered convicted felons. That's problematic because of the restrictions placed on them for the rest of their lives. The many restrictions placed on parolees in general are an immediate challenge, especially for these men who live in a relatively small community. Being in contact with each other is different for each of the guys, which presents a unique problem for all of them. Stipulations of their parole were decided not on the overall guidelines set by the parole commission, but by their assigned parole officers (POs). Some of the men are allowed to have contact with their codefendants. Some are not. Some are allowed to *only* have contact with Mike Pie because he was exonerated. One of the men is unable to have contact with any of his codefendants, including Mike Pie. Hence, my opinion about our overall criminal justice system: that the only consistency is the inconsistency. But this and all issues associated with being paroled can be remedied. The men still have the option of pursuing exoneration. So, the final conclusion to their story is yet to be determined.

Many years of letter writing have been replaced with phone calls, texts, and emails from the guys. It's amusing to listen to their struggles as they learn new technology and comment on how much has changed in two-and-a-half decades. I say *amusing* because of my own limited technical abilities.

I feel privileged to share the experiences I've had on this journey for justice over the past decade, including the good, the bad, and everything in between. I now have the option to schedule book events with the released men. But because of the stipulations of contact with each other, this poses its own set of problems. Having events with more than one of them will take planning but can be achieved when and if they are given permission beforehand by their POs.

It's exhilarating to bear witness as the men share their own personal impressions and experiences with audiences. Through letters, I used to tell them about the support they had gained over the years. Now they have the ability to see this firsthand, which has helped them to feel more comfortable about their interaction with the community. In talking with folks at our events, they hear the frustrations and the humanity in the voices of those who knew that this was wrong but felt powerless to act.

For these men, life took a bit of a detour. But circumstances have allowed them to regain the freedom to decide what their futures hold. Their willingness to leave the past behind and embrace new beginnings, well . . . that is nothing short of inspiring.

Chapter 42
VIRTUAL PANEL DISCUSSION

Following the flood of releases, the guys were motivated to participate in book events. Not surprisingly, their presence attracted decent attendance and remarkably engaged and supportive audiences. Two successful events, one with Michael Hirn and the other with Michael Johnson, both held in early 2020, encouraged creative feedback from both, while prompting a great new idea from one of them. While driving home to Minneapolis from Green Bay following the event with Michael Hirn, he called to share an idea that he was feeling especially excited about. "We should do a panel discussion and get all of us together to discuss the case," he declared excitedly.

My reaction carried the same enthusiasm. "I like that idea. Let's go for it! I will look into this."

Following our conversation, I was struck by how energized and empowered both men had become since their release. These special moments forced me to pause and reevaluate the many strides and victories we had achieved. They had all mattered, and this was proof. Our options seemed plentiful, and time looked to be on our side—that is, until COVID-19 hit and life as we all knew it came to a screeching halt.

As the pandemic slowly put the brakes on events everywhere, I hoped it would not be an obstacle for very long. We were too fired up by this time about additional prospects now being offered to us to let the momentum fade. But months into a new reality of "sheltering in place," it seemed unlikely that we would be engaging in book events or discussions of any kind in the near or distant future.

With excess time on my hands, I decided to refocus my attention on something I'd been considering for a while; a book revision or second edition of *Reclaiming Lives* to include all of the latest developments. And Hirn's idea of a panel discussion gave me an idea for one of the chapters. This chapter is the result of an important and meaningful collaboration with each of the guys. The best part is that it was inclusive to Keith as well, even with him being in prison. The second-best part is the honest and heartfelt recollection of what each of the men experienced as this nightmare unfolded in the 1990s. This chapter provides insight into their world as told from their perspectives. I cannot adequately express my appreciation for their willingness to demonstrate their humanity and vulnerabilities through the sharing of this information. I sincerely hope my readers will find value in learning about who they are as individuals.

Lastly, in retrospect, our mission never did come to a complete halt. It was merely redirected—and in the same vein as this journey has unfolded from the very beginning.

Discussion:

Joan: I will be moderating today's discussion. Joining me are guests exoneree Michael Piaskowski, Keith Kutska, Michael Hirn, Reynold Moore, and Michael Johnson. Welcome to all of you. Before we begin, I'd like to briefly mention someone who is unfortunately absent from this panel. Our thoughts are with Dale Basten, who sadly passed away in 2018. Our hearts go out to his family as well.

During our discussion, to create less confusion, I will address each of you by your last name. I'd like to start out by asking each one of you to share some detail that differentiates you from the other five men as it relates to this case. We know all of you were accused and convicted of taking part in the alleged confrontation, the disposal of Tom Monfils body, and of collectively covering it up. Tell us something that you alone were accused of that none of the others were. We'll start with you, Mr. Kutska.

Kutska: I'd have to reference an embellished version of an actual occurrence by former Detective Randy Winkler. He claims mill worker

Brian Kellner told him, sometime after Monfils' death, that he [Kellner] was working with me on repairs to his truck, and I accidentally dropped a wrench on his head, calling the resulting injury a "Monfils lump." To be perfectly clear, Brian Kellner did work on his truck in my shop, but I never helped him, nor did I drop a wrench on his head or call it a "Monfils lump." This fiction is just another example of Randy Winkler spoon-feeding perjury into Brian Kellner's mouth.

Joan: Mr. Moore, please tell us what you experienced.

Moore: Former Detective Randy Winkler claims that I nearly confessed in exchange for a deal with prosecutors but withdrew when former District Attorney John Zakowski refused the deal. First of all, when Randy Winkler lies, he speaks his native language. Now, Winkler did write something on a piece of paper and asked me if that's what happened. But when I said "no," he insisted that this was my confession, which is a lie! As far as a deal is concerned, one was offered to all of us. I didn't know what happened to Monfils, so I felt I was in no position to accept any deals. Incidentally, that piece of paper that had my so-called confession on it was never given to DA Zakowski!

Joan: Johnson, what accusation was made against you?

Johnson: Former Detective Randy Winkler claims that I used to park outside of his house and watch him and his family, which made him feel threatened to the point of his family having to move. How can I defend myself against something I know I didn't do but cannot prove? On the other hand, the facts about his credibility as an effective or believable investigator speak for themselves. What's wrong with what Winkler claims? He was the law and the authority. If you were him, what would you have done? There's no record of him solving anything because nothing happened.

Joan: Mr. Piaskowski, you've been exonerated. Therefore, you can say anything you want regarding this case without consequences. Please, enlighten us about your experience.

Piaskowski: Every time he is asked about what evidence convicted me specifically, former District Attorney John Zakowski responds that I was the one who went and got the rope and the weight. Nowhere in the entire twenty-eight-day trial was there any evidence or testimony that I had anything to do with these pieces of evidence. The reason for that is simple. I had nothing to do with them at any time. The only time my name and the weight and rope get mentioned together is in Zakowski's summation at the very end of the trial, a statement based on pure conjecture and speculation. Adding pretend drama to certain words like he has, in the Madison documentary—and I've seen him do so in other interviews—is just another example of how Zakowski handles a subject when he has nothing of substance to offer.

Joan: Mr. Hirn, what was your experience?

Hirn: Former Detective Randy Winkler has said that I once told him and another investigator, "I want to tell you what happened, but I'm afraid for my kid." Winkler also said, "It sounded real incriminating, but at the same time, we weren't sure at the time if he was a witness or a guilty party . . . you can take it different ways." First of all, I'd never say "my kid." It's a pet peeve of mine because it's so impersonal. I'd say "my son," but not "my kid." And second, I never made that statement, as I had no information that would incriminate anyone and no reason to fear for my son.

Joan: Okay, thank you. My next question is a follow-up to something Mr. Moore mentioned moments ago about all of you being offered a plea deal. Is this true? And please elaborate on your specific circumstances.

Johnson: I'd like to respond first. Technically, I was never offered any plea deal. Before they arrested me, they were trying to get me to say I was being threatened, which was their assumption of why I wasn't telling them what they wanted to hear. What they did offer was witness protection with lots of sugar on it. All lies, of course, but that's what they were good at.

Hirn: A plea deal was offered to me through my attorney. The police always said "the first one on the bus gets the best ride." The plea deal was through the DA's office. The terms were full immunity from prosecution for cooperation in solving the crime, witness protection, relocation, and a new life for my testimony. Like with Moore, the deal was declined because I didn't have knowledge of anyone committing a crime, so I didn't have pertinent information to get immunity from the prosecution.

Kutska: Very early on into the investigation, my trial attorney, Royce Finne, asked me to come to his office. Once there, he questioned me about what, if anything, I knew concerning the disappearance of Tom Monfils. After repeating what I had already told the police and him, he told me that if I knew anything concerning foul play, now was the time to tell him because immunity was on the table. I reiterated I did not know of anyone hurting Tom Monfils in any way and that from what I knew, I could only conclude he had committed suicide.

Piaskowski: In a roundabout way, I was offered a deal, but not by the police . . . at least not directly by the police—but I'm sure it was just a part of their overall plan to get someone to tell them what they wanted to hear. I don't recall the exact wording, but here's the gist of it: a plea deal was offered to me via Susan Monfils' civil suit attorney, Bruce Bachhuber, sometime in 1993-4. Bachhuber, Tim Pedretti, and I were in Pedretti's office on Washington St. in Green Bay. Bachhuber was referencing things like 'if anyone was afraid to speak up, witness protection programs, how helping the police would be a great benefit to their situation, how certain people were less culpable, how safe their family could be if they were to transfer to one of JR's other paper mills out west where JR had several mills, how he had checked into it and that he could make it happen without a loss of pay or seniority or vacation time or moving expenses—blah, blah, blah.' I remember cutting him off and telling him I wasn't afraid of anyone and that I didn't have any reason to be afraid. And I wasn't interested in any deals.

Joan: That none of you were interested in what the authorities were offering is remarkable given that your very lives were at stake. This brings me to a more recent statement made by the former DA Zakowski, who is still adamant about your absolute guilt. "If you've been lying, if you've been saying, I didn't do it for all these years . . . why would you do it [confess] now? When you've been telling your family that all of these years, and now you're getting out anyway, it's not a surprise." How do you respond to these remarks?

Moore: The only thing I have to say about this is, one day John Zakowski will stand before the throne of eternal judgment and will have to give an account. He thinks he is God because he thinks he cannot be wrong.

Piaskowski: Zakowski is just blowing smoke to cover up for sending six innocent men to prison when he talks like that. Like you pointed out, Joan, I was exonerated. The federal court recognized my innocence, and I was vindicated. I don't have to deny anything about any kind of a crime to anyone anymore . . . including my family. And I definitely don't have to admit to a crime I didn't commit—or admit to a crime that might not have even happened, just to pad John Zakowski's ego. I don't have to worry about this case at all anymore. I sleep well at night. It's Zakowski's reputation and legacy that's on the line here, certainly not mine. He is the *professional* that has to worry about what the public thinks, just so he can keep his job . . . and his ego.

Kutska: My response to John Zakowski's statement as to why I continue to stand by my innocence is very simple. I did not physically harm Tom Monfils in any way, nor did I encourage or have any knowledge of anyone harming him. Furthermore, the facts from the complete record of this case do not support these convictions; rather, they reveal that these convictions rest squarely on perjured testimony in which Mr. Zakowski fails to acknowledge. It is Mr. Zakowski who fears the truth.

Johnson: I and my codefendants were model prisoners with a letter from the presiding judge telling the parole board that if we behaved ourselves, not to prolong our imprisonment. There were no letters in our files with negative indicators (i.e., no one was saying throw away the key or keep them locked up.) Yet, for eight years, my imprisonment was extended for no reason. If I would have played their game, eight years would have been added to my life as a free man. Innocent men do not play games. Again, the facts in this case speak for themselves. By the way, I did not know ahead of time that I was getting released. They played their game right up to the end of my imprisonment.

Hirn: My response is simple. Who has more to lose at this point? I served almost twenty-four years for a crime I have no knowledge of or participated in. If I came forward at this point, I would probably lose some friends and their support, but that's it. Now let's put the shoe on the other foot. If Zakowski came forward and said he wrongly convicted us, what would happen? He currently serves as a judge for the Green Bay community, the same community he lied to for all these years by saying we were guilty when, in fact, he wrongfully convicted us. The ripple effect would be huge on this community and would be career suicide for John Zakowski. So who really has more to lose by not telling the truth in this case? We didn't know we were going to get out, but there was always the hope that one day we would.

Joan: Such interesting perspectives from all of you. Okay, let's go back to when you first learned about Tom Monfils' death. Did you believe he had been murdered or, instead, had committed suicide? What facts, circumstances, and assumptions led you to that initial belief or conclusion? Who'd like to go first?

Hirn: When I first learned of Tom's death, I definitely believed it was a suicide. I just thought nobody I worked with was capable of killing anyone because the mill was like one big family. As the investigation dragged on, I continued to believe it was a suicide because of all of the stories that came out about Tom and his dealings with his time in the coast guard. As the investigation wore on, it was more and more apparent that things weren't what they were made out to be. Investigators were lying to us and other employees at the mill. It was odd that no solid leads ever came about, and the investigators were using the tactics they did to create activity in the investigation. They put rumblings in the air to see what would come about. Even on the day I was arrested, I figured it was just another ploy to get us to talk and that we'd be released. I wondered at times if someone did kill Tom, but that never really seemed likely to me based on me being a witness, knowing I had no knowledge nor participation in any harm to Tom. I even had one investigator get in my face and tell me that Tom was brutally beaten and killed by my coworkers when I had stated to him that I believed Tom killed himself.

Moore: When I first heard about it, I didn't have any idea what happened. Then I heard about the weight, and I thought murder. But after a while, I started to hear stories, and I thought it could be suicide.

Johnson: The thought of murder never entered my mind. They had anybody who wanted to searching for him after he disappeared. All anyone figured was that they would find him hanging somewhere after having committed suicide. And there was never any anger from people when we all learned what had happened, only concern.

Kutska: When I first learned of Tom Monfils death, I, like everyone else, believed he committed suicide. I based this belief on my understanding that he disappeared from his work area shortly after I played the tape for him, noting that his last entry into the machine's logbook revealed a distinct apprehension in his penmanship. Furthermore, there was nothing to my knowledge that suggested foul play.

Piaskowski: Joan, the simple answer to your question is suicide. However, please allow me to elaborate further because I feel a more complete answer needs to go on the record. Mine goes more like this: I learned about Tom's death in a phone call from Randy Lepak on Sunday evening 11-22-1993, the day after Tom had gone missing. By this time, we had already been searching for Tom for about thirty-six hours. By the time I heard about his death, I had already been stopped by the police on the I-43 bridge while driving home from work Sunday evening and had been interviewed at the police station by Detective Van Haute. At about 9:30 – 10:00 p.m. or so, shortly after I had gotten home from the Van Haute interview, Lepak called me and said, "They found him" or "They found Monfils." When Lepak said that, I had an immediate sense of relief and responded, "Wow, where the hell was he?" (I figured that they must have heard from Tom or that Tom had finally shown up somewhere). But when Lepak answered, "In the tissue chest," my sense of relief quickly turned to confusion and dread. "What?!" I said, "OMG!" To me, the words themselves, "In the Tissue Chest," and the solemn way Lepak said them could only mean one thing. I don't recall exactly what Lepak said next, but it was at that point that I firmly believed that Tom had taken his own life. I definitely had no thoughts of any kind of homicide at all. The thought of a homicide didn't occur to me until after David Wiener entered the picture. Before learning of Tom's death, the fact that Tom couldn't be found, especially after being missing for so long, likely caused many to consider, early on in the search for him, that he might not be alive. But I don't believe any normal thinking person seriously thought that if he was indeed dead, his death was the result of a murder. Heck, the mill certainly wasn't an evil place to work. In fact, quite the opposite. The James River Mill family was family-orientated and a great place to have a career. Contrary to a couple of ridiculous rumors, there weren't real thefts or drug rings there. Sure, there was the occasional violation of the scrap-pass policy, or the making of a "government project" on company time with company materials [theft], or the sale of a lid of marijuana [drug dealing]. But none of it could be called excessive or widespread. And in the bigger picture, the city of Green Bay has always had a very low crime rate and was a very safe community to live in, especially back in 1993. There was absolutely no reason at all for anyone to jump to that kind of a conclusion about murder . . . ever.

When Tom first went missing, common sense was used while looking for him. Clearly, we were looking for an *alive* Tom Monfils. We were doing things like checking the obvious places: the operating floor around all of the paper machines, in the basements, in the break rooms, the mill lobby, eventually expanding to second-floor converting, third-floor napkins, the shipping department, the pulp mill, up on the roof, et cetera. You name it. Even the "brownstone" office building and the temporary office trailers, the parking lots and outbuildings were checked. Every and any place you could think of. But as more time went on and Tom still wasn't found, that same common sense told us that we had better start looking closer and harder, that we may have overlooked something; like the victim of a suicide—*not* a homicide! By late Saturday night or early Sunday morning, more and more people had to be thinking if Tom is still in the mill (and all things seemed to point to the fact that he was), that we might just be looking for a body. But even at this point, I can't believe anyone thought we were looking for a homicide victim. The search continued nonstop, this time more thoroughly—every possible place we could think of, all the nooks and crannies and unthought-of places from the prior searches, up in the ceiling rafters, in the many normally empty and locked places around the mill, and then some. Everything feasible was checked and double-checked. On Sunday afternoon, I remember Bob Thut, the paper mill superintendent, coming to us in the #7 Control Room and giving us a small speech about not giving up the hope of finding Tom alive. Thut told us the story about Rollie Lambert, one of the construction shop supervisors from years ago that went missing one time. Rollie wandered off and couldn't be found. It was discovered later that he'd had a stroke. They had an all-out search, but Rollie wasn't found until the next day—dazed, confused, and disoriented, but still alive. He was discovered in a small cubby-hole area, huddled on the floor in a fetal position behind a pile of sand in the basement under the #2 Paper Machine, where the construction shop workers made up their mortar and concrete for mill projects. Thut's "pep talk" really seemed to help. Even after the police came and started helping with the search, people, including the cops, continued to look in areas that indicated suicide. Nothing was said about a possible homicide. By the end of the day on Sunday, most everyone seemed to be concerned with the reality that Tom might be dead, that he may have taken his own life. Not that someone killed him.

Kutska: I'd like to add some thoughts on what I believe is the root cause of what went wrong in this case. The injustice is very simple to understand for anyone reviewing the facts with a clear, unbiased lens of objectivity. When I acquired the tape from the Green Bay Police Department and then Tom Monfils committed suicide, it made the police look foolish. Simply put, it hurt their pride. In response, they targeted me and set off on a course that would lead to my conviction, along with the convictions of five other innocent men, who stood in the way of what the police wanted the truth to be. The rule of law and the facts were obstacles easily trampled upon in their reptilian quest to repair their tarnished image.

Joan: We appreciate your thoughts on that important point, Keith. To my panelists, this discussion has been eye-opening for us outsiders who were not there that day and who can only base our judgments on what we've heard. Mike Pie, thank you as well for the detailed commentary of that crucial day. It certainly has given us a sense of how chaotic and emotionally charged the atmosphere was.

As we near the end of our discussion, I'd like to lighten the tone a bit for this final question. Mike Pie, you've been enjoying freedom for the longest amount of time. For the rest of you, this transition back to freedom has been relatively recent. However brief the time has been, please describe for us a few of the most significant moments of your personal lives since your release.

Johnson: Enjoying all of the wonderful provisions of our heavenly Father at every turn in my life.

Moore: Without a doubt, holding my grandkids. Being able to go to church and experiencing the fellowship. Being able to go to my sister's funeral. And being able to eat healthy foods.

Piaskowski: As a "free man," I would have to say being able to exercise all the rights and liberties of a United States citizen again, and to be able to say "Thank you!" in person to everyone for all the wonderful faith and support over the years. As a father, being able to attend my daughter's wedding and walk her down the aisle. As a son and a grandson, I would have to say the ability to pay proper respects at the graves of my father and my grandmother, both of whom I lost while I was incarcerated. As a friend, I would have to say . . . well, just being able to be a true friend to others. Finally, as an unlisted coauthor along with Denis Gullickson and John Gaie, I would have to say the completion of our book, *The Monfils Conspiracy: The Conviction of Six Innocent Men*.

Hirn: It's been amazing reconnecting with old friends who have supported me throughout all of the years I was incarcerated—and making new friends as well. I've done some traveling and was able to attend some sporting events too. I've been able to do a lot of the things I loved to do before, like hunting, fishing, and water skiing. Life is amazing, and I'm going to enjoy each day because it is a gift. I can't take for granted the things I so desired while I was incarcerated because I can do them again after all these years. Life is good, and I'm blessed by all of the people I have in my life that love and support me!

Joan: In closing, I'd like to mention the most recent and particularly sad development in this case. On March 24, 2021, the parole commission denied Keith's request for parole. However, they scheduled his next hearing for January 2022. The commission also specified certain conditions Keith must satisfy before it will consider granting his release. All things considered, the recent hearing can be viewed in a positive light. Keith, know that we all share in your sorrow and wish nothing but the best for you and your family as you navigate these final steps closer to freedom. Lastly, I'd like to extend my appreciation to all of you for sharing your individual perspectives and valuable insight into this hopelessly complicated case. This concludes our discussion, which I hope will shed light on the realities of how being pressured into quickly closing a case can cause oversights, incomplete evidence gathering, and, yes, abuse of power tactics to achieve a conviction. Thank you as well to those in attendance for their interest and impartiality.

FINAL THOUGHTS

My heart ached for Keith and for his family, who were once again burdened with the demoralizing letdown of him being denied parole. Nonetheless, for Keith's sake especially, I will remain hopeful of the possibility that his parole will be granted in the near future.

Looking back to when I first combed through old Green Bay *Press-Gazette* newspaper articles covering this case from the beginning, I found the stories fascinating and thought-provoking. It felt strange to have the actual print in my hands but quite disturbing to read the same rhetoric that is rampant today. Vicious attacks from some locals back then regarding the guilty verdicts read:

> *Justice has finally been served. Tom Monfils can rest in peace. May the six defendants rot in Hell. I think we all know the man was murdered. If only one or two of these men actually committed the crime, the fact that the rest obviously withheld information that would have con-victed them makes them just as guilty. I think that justice was served.*

One person with a differing viewpoint cited the O.J. Simpson verdict, which had been reached less than a month prior to the verdicts in the Monfils case:

On a mountain of evidence, O.J. Simpson walks. On circumstantial and hearsay evidence, where their main witnesses were one guy who was in prison and another guy who's all pissed up in a bar, they can convict innocent people.

Although our mission to achieve full exonerations for all of the men is not yet realized, I'm encouraged by the momentum gained through the increasing number of exonerations on record today—a number that is fast approaching three thousand. According to the National Registry of Exonerations, there are, on average, three exonerations a week across the country. This is especially evident in recent years, with exonerations totaling 87 in 2013 and as many as 161 in 2016. As those numbers climb, so does my hope that the names of these additional five men will eventually be added.

Johnny states, "It is my belief that we have the best system in the world because of our ability to go back and fix what is broken." His belief is legitimized each time another exoneration occurs. While we don't know for sure how many innocents have been wrongfully convicted, estimates range from 3-10 percent. But we do know that if a single person is wrongfully convicted, that's one too many. I'm grateful for programs like *60 Minutes* and *48 Hours* that lend constructive airtime to this topic. The many documentaries and movies being made and the many books that are and have been written all contribute to that knowledge as well. In the meantime, we, as a society, can no longer look away or claim ignorance as our awareness is heightened through these types of projects. I often hear complaints from the public about their biased slants. I'm certain that the same will be said about this book. But in defense of my book and related programming, I ask where the concerns over bias were when the individuals portrayed in them were unlawfully mischaracterized and misrepresented in the first place.

Legal battles of this nature become financial nightmares for those unable to find pro bono assistance. Many innocent people with already-drained bank accounts from which money went into the coffers of ineffective lawyers remain in prison because, in reality, it is only a select few who have the good fortune of being represented by an Innocence Project or pro bono lawyer.

How do the six men and their families feel about the overwhelming support on their behalf? The short answer is appreciative and grateful that others listened and heard their truths. As a result, they no longer feel forgotten or bereft of hope. To them, no matter the final outcome, they will always remember being given a rare opportunity that they know many others will never receive.

What is the solution to the widespread occurrence of wrongful convictions? For those who cannot offer their time but who want to help in some way, please consider a monetary donation to organizations that specifically take cases of innocence. Among them are the highly visible and trusted Innocence Project affiliates across the country that rely heavily (but not solely) on the use of DNA technology. Dating back to the late 1980s, this scientific tool may in some cases correctly identify actual perpetrators while proving the innocence of someone wrongly accused. Chances are that you'll find an Innocence Project in your area or in your state. They rightly claim responsibility for the many exonerations we hear about and represent a direct pathway to freedom. Often, they are the only lifeline for innocent victims. Direct dollars can make a huge impact in the lives of many.

Start a conversation about a case you've heard about, a documentary or movie you've watched, or a book you've read. A great talking point is something that is often overlooked. When an innocent person goes to prison for another person's crime, that other person is no longer under the radar and is free to commit additional crimes. This does happen, and it creates a false sense of security for us all. Unfortunately, it is impossible to determine how often this occurs because of the many wrongful conviction cases that are never revisited despite obvious or ill-achieved conclusions.

Submitting reviews on Amazon or other retailers for this book and those with similar stories is extremely helpful in broadening readership.

For the record, I'd like to mention a small matter of concern. On occasion, people have asked me to get involved in their cases. I am not equipped with the legal knowledge necessary, nor do I claim to be an expert on the subject. I'm simply an advocate. All I can provide is a blueprint of my process and the knowledge I've gained about wrongful convictions. Through my writings, I've simply voiced my opposition to a case I read about and acted upon, doing what little I could. Anyone can do this. If you find yourself in a situation with a loved one in prison for a crime he or she did not commit, act immediately. The best place to start is to research the case. Collect data and any legal documents you can find, many of which are public record at the courthouse and the police department. Be aware that there are costs involved when collecting some of this information. Raise awareness by writing to your state legislators—repeatedly. Get others involved. Pool your talents. Make noise in a constructive way, and never settle for less than what you deem as appropriate. Own it! You'll be met with a lot of grief, but like my friend Byron Lichstein says, "Persistence is key." It will take time, but the results will be worth the effort. I guarantee you will also see yourself and the world in a whole new light.

My personal experience of having stayed involved in this mission for the past twelve years has conjured every available emotion within my being. Those emotions have empowered me to remain vigilant in speaking out about the issues I care about. They have emboldened me to continue to educate others on important aspects of our criminal justice system. And they have cautioned me to *see* what is happening around me rather than allowing me to make improper assumptions based simply on opinions or beliefs. My eyes have been opened to the idea that nothing is ever completely as it seems and that there are always two sides to every story. I feel extremely fortunate to have had this experience, to have walked alongside these folks, and to have done something worthwhile for others.

One wish I have is for the simplicity of this book to help others who may not otherwise understand the enormity of this critical issue. Whether we want to admit it or not, it does affect all of us, either directly or indirectly. I also implore everyone to realize how extremely difficult it is to undo an injustice such as this one and to understand that if we get it right the first time, we can avoid having to correct any and all of them.

Therefore, I urge my readers to become engaged. Speak up about whatever moves you *before* it is too late. There are plenty of causes that desperately need a helping hand. I invite you to challenge yourself as I have. Leave some sort of imprint no matter how small. Imagine your legacy as having the potential to help even one person, to inspire loved ones, and to educate generations of knowledge seekers. You *can* make a difference. So, go on. Be brave. Be bold. You will never look back.

ACKNOWLEDGMENTS

A s an outsider, I've done my best to speak out about the difficulties faced by the individuals described in this book. I've searched deep within to accurately describe their pain, their heartache, and the hopelessness that accompanies an injustice such as this. With that said, I'd like to acknowledge the many others who've helped in the completion of this project, and the unique way in which they've become part of the movement to create a necessary awareness about wrongful convictions.

My deepest love and respect go to my sister, Clare Martinson, for her mentorship for as long as I can remember and for bridging the connection to my involvement in this mission. I'd also like to thank her daughter, my niece, Jordan Teague, for lending her continued support and technical expertise at book events as well as valuable feedback on the contents of this second edition.

Authors, friends, and colleagues John Gaie and Denis Gullickson deserve high recognition for combining forces to publish *The Monfils Conspiracy* and for being the example of what can be accomplished with a little determination. Exoneree Michael Piaskowski is to be commended for his unyielding courage and commitment to helping them with crucial details for this book and for inspiring me to stay in this fight.

Retired crime scene expert Johnny Johnson afforded me invaluable assistance to fuel this mission. I thank him for his service to mankind, to those he has aided in the past, and to countless others he will encounter in the future. I especially thank him for being the best friend a "housewife" could ever have.

Attorney Steve Kaplan became our shining light when he picked up a burdensome torch and took all of us on a wild ride through the complexities of the judicial system. I thank him for his tenacity in proving that truth and justice do go hand in hand. I am indebted to Steve as well for his patience and due diligence in critiquing the transcripts for both editions.

I thank my incredibly caring husband, Mike, and my talented son, artist and writer Jared Manninen, for their support and ability to recognize the importance of my mission, for their patience during my pursuit of it, and for their thoughtful feedback and encouragement to finish both editions. I acknowledge Jared also for his assistance with technical support and for the many hours he devoted to helping me transform my words into a comprehensible message.

Appreciation also goes to Erik Stewart (1974-2021) for his support and proactive actions in regard to my first televised interview. Sadly, Erik died much too soon in a terrible crash on a Nevada Highway. We thought of him as an important part of our family. He will be deeply missed.

Special thanks to Ann Aubitz and the folks at Kirk House Publishers for their superb expertise and invaluable assistance in publishing this second edition.

I warmly applaud my former bosses and coworkers at Gentle Transitions who support my mission and who offered valuable feedback and reassurances, especially during times of doubt.

I respectfully recognize the priceless financial and legal assistance from Fredrikson & Byron, PA and the numerous pro bono lawyers from Wisconsin who eventually joined the team. My gratitude also goes out to the staff and interns at both the Great North Innocence Project and the Wisconsin Innocence Project for generously providing legal assistance.

I thank all those not listed here who helped me to remain motivated during the completion of this project and who helped me to work through the daunting steps of publishing both editions of this important book.

My heartfelt gratitude goes to the many family members and close friends of the six men for welcoming me with open arms and showing me and the world that love and a promise to never give up hope surpasses all obstacles.

To the many exonerees I've met on this arduous journey, I offer my deepest appreciation for entrusting me with your horrific but inspiring stories of overwhelming grief and pain and for the infinite wisdom you've gained through resilience, courage, and an ability to find inner peace. You have unlocked important doors, allowing an understanding of your truths to reach hundreds upon thousands, all of whom have benefited from your positive energy.

Lastly, my sincerest gratitude goes toward five future exonerees: Keith Kutska, Michael Hirn, Reynold Moore, Michael Johnson, and Dale Basten. Thank you for your friendship, audacity, and the inner strength to stay true to yourselves. I truly admire your spirit and strong commitment to never sacrifice integrity for freedom. You've taught us all what it means to have a meaningful life, about the power of love, and of the necessity of hope. You have stirred many hearts.

CONNECTING WITH JOAN

Reclaiming Lives explains the importance of taking a stand and why we must fight for the things that matter to us. It lends proof that we as individuals have the power to, at the very least, create an atmosphere of change. In this instance, change occurred within our judicial system when a significant number of ordinary citizens used their collective voices to question the status quo. No matter the topic or the cause, taking appropriate actions can and will discourage those things that should never have become acceptable in the first place.

To follow Joan's journey, to book a speaking engagement, or to inquire about an appearance for your book club, contact her through her website at joantreppa.com or connect with her through Facebook or Twitter. She's available for groups, large or small.

RESOURCES

<u>Innocence and Pro Bono Organizations:</u>

Great North Innocence Project:
https://www.greatnorthinnocenceproject.org/

Fredrikson & Byron, PA:
http://www.fredlaw.com

Wisconsin Innocence Project:
https://law.wisc.edu/fjr/clinicals/ip/

Jeffrey Deskovic Foundation:
https://www.deskovicfoundation.org/

<u>Appeals:</u>

Rey Moore (2012):
https://www.wicourts.gov/ca/opinion/DisplayDocu-ment.pdf?content=pdf&seqNo=77188

State of Wisconsin v. Keith Kutska (full transcript):
https://monfilscase.com/wp-content/uploads/2017/02/10-30-14_Keith_Kutska_Motion_for_Retrial-1.pdf

Exonerees:

Mike "Pie" Piaskowski:
https://www.law.umich.edu/special/exoneration/Pages/casedetail.aspx?caseid=4057

Mario Victoria Vasquez:
https://www.law.umich.edu/special/exoneration/Pages/casedetail.aspx?caseid=4637

Audrey Edmunds:
http://www.law.umich.edu/special/exoneration/Pages/casedetail.aspx?caseid=3201

Fred Saecker:
http://www.innocenceproject.org/cases/fredric-saecker/

Koua Fong Lee:
https://www.greatnorthinnocenceproject.org/koua-fong-lee-1

Mike Hansen:
https://www.greatnorthinnocenceproject.org/michael-hansen-1

Damon Thibodeaux:
http://www.innocenceproject.org/cases/damon-thibodeaux

West Memphis Three (Damien Echols):
http://www.westmemphisthreefacts.com

Steven Avery:
http://www.law.umich.edu/special/exoneration/Pages/casedetail.aspx?caseid=3003

Jeffrey Deskovic:
https://www.law.umich.edu/special/exoneration/Pages/casedetail.aspx?caseid=3171

Documentaries:

The Syndrome:
http://www.thesyndromefilm.com/

Guilty Until Proven Innocent:
http://www.thereporters.org/project/righting-wrongful-convictions/

Beyond Human Nature:
https://www.beyondhumannature.com/

Conviction:
https://www.amazon.com/Conviction-Jeffrey-Deskovic/dp/B08F9CN2XG

Interviews:

"Seville Disobedience":
https://www.youtube.com/watch?v=G9lsvolNxzY

"Walking without 'Treppa-dation":
https://joantreppa.com/2014/12/06/walking-without-treppa-dation/

Suzanne Wigginton blog radio interview:
https://www.blogtalkradio.com/suzannewigginton/2014/06/19/follow-your-passions-find-your-purpose-with-joan-treppa

Charlotte View blog radio interview:
http://www.blogtalkradio.com/charlotteview/2015/03/09/charlotte-view-joan-treppa-the-erin-brockovich-of-the-wrongfully-convicted-1

Alex Okoroji blog radio interview:
http://www.blogtalkradio.com/thenakedtalk/2015/02/25/a-voice-for-the-hopeless-w-joan-treppa

Alex Okoroji (second interview):
http://www.blogtalkradio.com/thenakedtalk/2016/01/06/raising-that-voice-of-innocence-w-guest--joan-treppa

News Articles:

October 29, 1995 *Desert News* (Monfils case):
https://www.deseret.com/1995/10/29/19201408/6-mill-workers-guilty-of-killing-informant

Blaine Life:
http://abcnewspapers.com/2013/09/17/blaine-residents-host-car-show-exonerated/

The Reporters Inc:
http://www.thereporters.org/article/how-i-became-a-citizen-advocate/

Miscellaneous:

The Monfils Conspiracy book:
 https://www.amazon.com/Monfils-Conspiracy-Conviction-Six-Innocent/dp/0595484735

Jared Manninen:
https://jaredmanninen.com/

Voice of Innocence Facebook page:
https://www.facebook.com/thevoiceofinnocence?pnref=story

Reclaiming Lives Facebook page:
https://www.facebook.com/reclaiminglives6/

National Registry of Exonerations:
http://www.law.umich.edu/special/exoneration/Pages/about.aspx

Center on Wrongful Convictions:
http://www.law.northwestern.edu/legalclinic/wrongfulconvictions/

National Institute on Corrections:
https://nicic.gov/

Amnesty International:
http://www.amnestyusa.org/our-work

False confessions and the Alford Plea:
http://scholarlycommons.law.northwestern.edu/cgi/viewcontent.cgi?article=1005&context=jclc

National Coalition to Abolish the Death Penalty:
http://www.ncadp.org/pages/innocence

Mothers Opposed to Bullying Foundation:
https://www.facebook.com/Mothers-Against-Bullying-81300682446/

Families Against Mandatory Minimums:
https://famm.org/our-work/compassionate-release/

Wisconsin Department of Justice:
https://www.doj.state.wi.us/

Wisconsin Department of Corrections:
http://doc.wi.gov/about/parole-commission

GALLERY

2009 book signing at The Reader's Loft in Green Bay with
John Gaie, Clare Martinson, exoneree, Michael Piaskowski,
Joan Treppa, and Denis Gullickson

Joan with exoneree Michael Piaskowski at
2013 GN-IP benefit for Innocence

Joan and Mike visiting Keith Kutska at Jackson Correctional
on February 21, 2015

Joan and Mike visiting Michael Hirn at Oakhill Correctional
on April 18, 2015

Joan and Mike visiting Reynold Moore at Oshkosh Correctional
on July 11, 2015

Joan and Mike visiting Dale Basten at Stanley Correctional
on December 12, 2015

Joan and Mike visiting Michael Johnson at Oakhill Correctional
on June 6, 2016

2012 GN-IP Benefit for Innocence with exonerees
Koua Fong Lee, Audrey Edmunds, Fred Saecker,
Damon Thibodeaux, and Michael Piaskowski

Joan with Damien Echols at the 2012 GN-IP
Benefit for Innocence

Joan with exoneree Audrey Edmunds at the
2012 GN-IP Benefit for Innocence

Exoneree Michael Hansen speaking at the 2015 'Hotrod
Breakout' Car Show

Mario Victoria Vasquez on February 15, 2015; the
day he was exonerated with his WIP legal team:
Cristina, Katie, Kyle, and Curtiss

Johnny Johnson and Steve Kaplan at
the 2013 GN-IP Benefit for Innocence

July 22, 2015; Inside the Brown County Courtroom for the last day of the 3-day Evidentiary Hearing for Keith Kutska

Six Innocent Men banner on display in front of the Brown
County Courthouse for the 2014 Walk for Truth and Justice

Lee Basten speaking at the 2017 Walk for Truth and Justice

Supporters at the 2015 Walk for Truth and Justice

December 18, 2018; Hirn's release date. (L-R) Mike T, Randy,
Aunt Marlene, Michael Hirn, Joan, and Uncle Terry

Rey and Clare celebrating Rey's July 2, 2019 release

July 3, 2019; Johnson's release date. Joan and Mike with Kim
and Michael Johnson

(L to R) Decedent, Tom Monfils, convicted men; Dale Basten, Michael Johnson, Michael Hirn, Reynold Moore, Keith Kutska and exoneree, Michael Piaskowski. Photo courtesy of Jordan Teague and taken during our Walk for Truth and Justice in 2015